HEALTH CARE ISSUES, COSTS AND ACCESS

SOCIAL SECURITY

MAJOR CONGRESSIONAL DECISIONS AND REFORM ISSUES

HEALTH CARE ISSUES, COSTS AND ACCESS

Additional books in this series can be found on Nova's website under the Series tab.

Additional e-books in this series can be found on Nova's website under the e-book tab.

HEALTH CARE ISSUES, COSTS AND ACCESS

SOCIAL SECURITY

MAJOR CONGRESSIONAL DECISIONS AND REFORM ISSUES

TREVOR L. GROVER
EDITOR

Copyright © 2014 by Nova Science Publishers, Inc.

All rights reserved. No part of this book may be reproduced, stored in a retrieval system or transmitted in any form or by any means: electronic, electrostatic, magnetic, tape, mechanical photocopying, recording or otherwise without the written permission of the Publisher.

For permission to use material from this book please contact us:
Telephone 631-231-7269; Fax 631-231-8175
Web Site: http://www.novapublishers.com

NOTICE TO THE READER

The Publisher has taken reasonable care in the preparation of this book, but makes no expressed or implied warranty of any kind and assumes no responsibility for any errors or omissions. No liability is assumed for incidental or consequential damages in connection with or arising out of information contained in this book. The Publisher shall not be liable for any special, consequential, or exemplary damages resulting, in whole or in part, from the readers' use of, or reliance upon, this material. Any parts of this book based on government reports are so indicated and copyright is claimed for those parts to the extent applicable to compilations of such works.

Independent verification should be sought for any data, advice or recommendations contained in this book. In addition, no responsibility is assumed by the publisher for any injury and/or damage to persons or property arising from any methods, products, instructions, ideas or otherwise contained in this publication.

This publication is designed to provide accurate and authoritative information with regard to the subject matter covered herein. It is sold with the clear understanding that the Publisher is not engaged in rendering legal or any other professional services. If legal or any other expert assistance is required, the services of a competent person should be sought. FROM A DECLARATION OF PARTICIPANTS JOINTLY ADOPTED BY A COMMITTEE OF THE AMERICAN BAR ASSOCIATION AND A COMMITTEE OF PUBLISHERS.

Additional color graphics may be available in the e-book version of this book.

Library of Congress Cataloging-in-Publication Data

ISBN: 978-1-60021-438-7

Published by Nova Science Publishers, Inc. † New York

CONTENTS

Preface		**vii**
Chapter 1	Social Security: Major Decisions in the House and Senate Since 1935 *Gary Sidor*	**1**
Chapter 2	Social Security Reform: Current Issues and Legislation *Dawn Nuschler*	**115**
Index		**167**

PREFACE

This book briefly summarizes discussions on individual major amendments. These summations do not characterize the complete range of motivations behind Social Security votes; rather, they record the arguments expressed at the time and, by so doing, attempt to give the reader the tone and context of the debate on major Social Security issues brought before the House and Senate chambers. This book also looks at Social Security program financing and the long-range projections for the Social Security trust funds as reported by the Social Security Board of Trustees; and the various objectives and proposals for reform.

Chapter 1 – Since its enactment in 1935, the Social Security Act has been amended numerous times. This report is not fully comprehensive. It briefly summarizes discussions on individual major amendments. These summations do not characterize the complete range of motivations behind Social Security votes; rather, they record the arguments expressed at the time and, by so doing, attempt to give the reader the tone and context of the debate on major Social Security issues brought before the House and Senate chambers.

This report is intended to respond to the many inquiries that the Congressional Research Service (CRS) gets for Social Security vote information, which range from requests for general information about legislative action over the years to requests for information about specific floor amendments. Thus, it is intended to be a reference document on the major statutory decisions made by Congress on the Social Security program.A detailed table of contents and a summary table of the legislation discussed are provided to aid the reader.

Chapter 2 – Social Security reform is an issue of ongoing interest to policy makers. In recent years, Social Security program changes have been discussed in the context of negotiations on legislation to increase the federal debt limit and reduce federal budget deficits. For example, in August 2011, the Budget Control Act of 2011 (P.L. 112-25) established a Joint Select Committee on Deficit Reduction tasked with recommending ways to reduce the deficit by at least $1.5 trillion over the fiscal year period 2012 to 2021. Social Security program changes were among the measures discussed by the Joint Committee. The Joint Committee, however, did not reach agreement on a legislative proposal by the statutory deadline. Looking ahead, Social Security program changes could again be considered as part of any future negotiations on broad deficit reduction legislation or as stand-alone Social Security legislation.

The spectrum of ideas for reform ranges from relatively minor changes to the pay-as-you-go social insurance system enacted in the 1930s to a redesigned, "modernized" program based on personal savings and investments modeled after IRAs and 401(k)s. Proponents of the fundamentally different approaches to reform cite varying policy objectives that go beyond simply restoring long-term financial stability to the Social Security system. They cite objectives that focus on improving the adequacy and equity of benefits, as well as those that reflect different philosophical views about the role of the Social Security program and the federal government in providing retirement income. However, the system's projected long-range financial outlook provides a backdrop for much of the Social Security reform debate in terms of the timing and degree of recommended program changes.

On May 31, 2013, the Social Security Board of Trustees released its latest projections showing that the trust funds will be exhausted in 2033 and an estimated 77% of scheduled annual benefits will be payable with incoming receipts at that time (under the intermediate projections). The primary reason is demographics. Between 2015 and 2035, the number of people aged 65 and older is projected to increase by about 65%, while the number of workers supporting the system (people aged 20-64) is projected to increase by about 6%. In addition, the trustees project that the system will run a cash flow deficit each year of the 75-year projection period. When current Social Security tax revenues are insufficient to pay benefits and administrative costs, federal securities held by the trust funds are redeemed and Treasury makes up the difference with other receipts. When there are no surplus governmental receipts, policy makers have three options: raise taxes or other income, reduce other spending, and/or borrow from the public.

Public opinion polls show that less than 50% of respondents are confident that Social Security can meet its long-term commitments. There is also a public perception that Social Security may not be as good a value for future retirees. These concerns, and a belief that the nation must increase national savings, have led to proposals to redesign the system. At the same time, others suggest that the system's financial outlook is not a "crisis" in need of immediate action. Supporters of the current program structure point out that the trust funds are projected to have a positive balance until 2033 and that the program continues to have public support and could be affected adversely by the risk associated with some of the reform ideas. They contend that only modest changes are needed to restore long-range solvency to the Social Security system.

In: Social Security
Editor: Trevor L. Grover

ISBN: 978-1-60021-438-7
© 2014 Nova Science Publishers, Inc.

Chapter 1

SOCIAL SECURITY: MAJOR DECISIONS IN THE HOUSE AND SENATE SINCE 1935[*]

Gary Sidor

SUMMARY

Since its enactment in 1935, the Social Security Act has been amended numerous times. This report is not fully comprehensive. It briefly summarizes discussions on individual major amendments. These summations do not characterize the complete range of motivations behind Social Security votes; rather, they record the arguments expressed at the time and, by so doing, attempt to give the reader the tone and context of the debate on major Social Security issues brought before the House and Senate chambers.

This report is intended to respond to the many inquiries that the Congressional Research Service (CRS) gets for Social Security vote information, which range from requests for general information about legislative action over the years to requests for information about specific floor amendments. Thus, it is intended to be a reference document on the major statutory decisions made by Congress on the Social Security program.A detailed table of contents and a summary table of the legislation discussed are provided to aid the reader.

---

[*] This is an edited, reformatted and augmented version of a Congressional Research Service publication, CRS Report for Congress RL30920, dated January 15, 2014.

INTRODUCTION

The Social Security Act of 1935 established a federal old-age pension financed with employee-employer payroll taxes for most workers in commerce and industry. Congress since then has changed the Social Security program many times.

Table 1. Social Security Laws, 1935-2012

Year	Title	Public Law	Bill Number
1935	Social Security Act	P.L. 74-271[a]	H.R. 7260
1939	Social Security Amendments of 1939	P.L. 76-379[a]	H.R. 6635
1942	Revenue Act of 1942	P.L. 77-753[a]	H.R. 7378
1943	Joint Resolution Regarding Tariff Act	P.L. 78-211[a]	H.J.Res. 171
1943	Revenue Act of 1943	P.L. 78-235[a]	H.R. 3687
1944	Federal Insurance Contributions Act of 1945	P.L. 78-495[a]	H.R. 5564
1945	Revenue Act of 1945	P.L. 79-214[a]	H.R. 4309
1946	Social Security Amendments of 1946	P.L. 79-719[a]	H.R. 7037
1947	Social Security Amendments of 1947	P.L. 80-379[a]	H.R. 3818
1948	Exclusion of Certain Newspaper and Magazine Vendors from Social Security Coverage	P.L. 80-492[a]	H.R. 5052
1948	Maintain Status Quo Concept of Employee	P.L. 80-642[a]	H.J.Res 296
1950	Social Security Act Amendments of 1950	P.L. 81-734[a]	H.R. 6000
1952	Social Security Act Amendments of 1952	P.L. 82-590[a]	H.R. 7800
1954	Social Security Amendments of 1954	P.L. 83-761[a]	H.R. 9366
1956	Social Security Amendments of 1956	P.L. 84-880[a]	H.R. 7225
1958	Social Security Amendments of 1958	P.L. 85-840	H.R. 13549
1960	Social Security Amendments of 1960	P.L. 86-778	H.R. 12580
1961	Social Security Amendments of 1961	P.L. 87-64	H.R. 6027
1964	Proposed Social Security Amendments of 1964		H.R. 11865
1965	Social Security Amendments of 1965	P.L. 89-97	H.R. 6675
1966	Tax Adjustment Act of 1966	P.L. 89-368	H.R. 12752
1967	Social Security Amendments of 1967	P.L. 90-248	H.R. 12080
1969	Tax Reform Act of 1969	P.L. 91-172	H.R. 13270
1971	Public Debt Limit, Increase; Social Security Act, Amendments	P.L. 92-5	H.R. 4690

Social Security: Major Decisions in the House and Senate Since 1935   3

Year	Title	Public Law	Bill Number
1972	Public Debt Limit; Disaster Losses; Social Security Act, Amendments	P.L. 92-336	H.R. 15390
1972	Social Security Amendments of 1972	P.L. 92-603	H.R. 1
1973	Social Security Benefits, Increase	P.L. 93-233	H.R. 11333
1977	Social Security Amendments of 1977	P.L. 95-216	H.R. 9346
1980	Social Security Disability Amendments of 1980	P.L. 96-265	H.R. 3236
1980	Reallocation of OASl and Dl Taxes	P.L. 96-403	H.R. 7670
1980	Earnings Test Amendments	P.L. 96-473	H.R. 5295
1981	Omnibus Budget Reconciliation Act of 1981	P.L. 97-35	H.R. 3982
1981	Social Security Amendments of 1981	P.L. 97-123	H.R. 4331
1983	An Act Relating to Taxes on Virgin Islands Source Income and Social Security Disability Benefits	P.L. 97-455	H.R. 7093
1983	Social Security Amendments of 1983	P.L. 98-21	H.R. 1900
1984	Social Security Disability Benefits Reform Act of 1984	P.L. 98-460	H.R. 3755
1985	Public Debt Limit—Balanced Budget and Emergency Deficit Control Act of 1985	P.L. 99-177	H.J.Res. 372
1985	COLA Constraints in FY86 Budget Resolution		S.Con.Res. 32
1986	Omnibus Budget Reconciliation Act of 1986	P.L. 99-509	H.R. 5300
1987	Budget Reconciliation Act of 1987	P.L. 100-203	H.R. 3545
1988	Technical and Miscellaneous Act of 1988	P.L. 100-647	H.R. 4333
1989	Omnibus Budget Reconciliation Act of 1989	P.L. 101-239	H.R. 3299
1990	Omnibus Budget Reconciliation Act of 1990	P.L. 101-508	H.R. 5835
1993	Omnibus Budget Reconciliation Act of 1993	P.L. 103-66	H.R. 2264
1994	Social Security Administrative Reform Act of 1994	P.L. 103-296	H.R. 4277
1994	Social Security Domestic Reform Act of 1994	P.L. 103-387	H.R. 4278
1996	Senior Citizens Right to Work Act of 1996	P.L. 104-121	H.R. 3136
1999	Ticket to Work and Work Incentives Improvement Act of 1999	P.L. 106-170	H.R. 1180

Table 1. (Continued)

Year	Title	Public Law	Bill Number
2000	Senior Citizens Freedom to Work Act	P.L. 106-182	H.R. 5
2004	Social Security Protection Act of 2004	P.L. 108-203	H.R. 743
2010	Tax Relief, Unemployment Insurance Reauthorization, and Job Creation Act of 2010	P.L. 111-312	H.R. 4853
2011	Temporary Payroll Tax Cut Continuation Act of 2011	P.L. 112-78	H.R. 3765
2012	Middle Class Tax Relief and Job Creation Act of 2012	P.L. 112-96	H.R. 3630

a. The printed law does not show the ordinal number of the Congress that passed it. The number is given here for reference purposes.

Amendments to the original act have added survivors' and dependents' benefits; added disability, hospital, and medical insurance; expanded coverage to new groups of workers; lowered the minimum age for retirement benefits; increased payroll taxes; raised benefits; provided for automatic adjustment of benefits to reflect inflation; and made numerous other changes. This report reviews the major votes taken by the House and Senate in passing the original act and in amending it from 1936 to the present. Discussion centers on Old-Age, Survivors and Disability Insurance (OASDI) votes, although Medicare and other programs are brought up occasionally. Votes on programmatic proposals are included, but votes on funding and the appropriations process generally are not. The discussion of the votes is set forth in terms of House action, Senate action, and conference agreements, and it gives the party breakdown for most votes discussed (D = Democrat, R = Republican, I = Independent). The report looks not only at votes on final passage of bills and adoption of conference reports, but also at votes on amendments considered on the floor of the House and Senate and at votes for recommittal to committee just before passage. It generally does not examine votes that occurred at the committee level. The primary source of the vote information was the *Congressional Record*. The primary source of the information for the separation of the vote by political party was the *Congressional Quarterly*.

From the start the old-age benefits program aroused argument. Opponents said that the payroll or Social Security tax was likely to overburden industry, reduce the purchasing power of workers, and endanger the growth of private pension plans. In addition, some argued that huge reserves to be built up in the old-age reserve account would become a tempting source of funds that the government could borrow for current spending and, thus, would lead to an increase in the federal debt. Fear that the reserve account would be used to subsidize "New Deal" projects was one reason why some Members argued for current financing (pay-as-you-go) of old-age benefits. Some opponents maintained that the federal government did not have the constitutional power to create a national pension plan. Some questioned whether the system could be kept financially sound and whether adequate earnings records could be maintained for so many millions of workers. Still others said that the program was not generous enough. They protested that it gave only partial protection and minimal benefits and that it imposed a regressive "soak-the-poor" tax.

Proponents maintained that Social Security would provide protection against destitution and dependency in old age and that it would provide persons with an opportunity to care for themselves on a more adequate basis than could be obtained from state old-age assistance payments (welfare). Some regarded the proposal's self-financing method—payroll taxes on employers and employees—as a strength. As workers would be required to pay taxes on their wages in order to receive Social Security, they would acquire an earned right to benefits, and no income test would apply. Further, some said that because the system would be financed by earmarked payroll taxes, it would be relatively free from political and economic pressures that might impair its financial soundness and capacity to do the job intended.

CHAMBER VOTES

A. P.L. 271—74th Congress, Enactment of the Social Security Act

The Social Security Act became law on August 14, 1935, when President Roosevelt signed H.R. 7260. Title II of the act created a compulsory national old-age benefits program, covering nearly all workers in commerce and industry and providing monthly pensions at age 65 for insured workers. A benefit weighted toward lower-paid workers was to be based on cumulative wages and was to be payable beginning in 1942 to persons aged 65 and over who had paid Social Security taxes for at least five years. The benefit was to be withheld from an otherwise qualified person in any month in which he or she did any work. Under Title VIII of the act, a payroll tax of 1%, each, on employees and employers, payable on earnings up to $3,000 each year, was to be imposed as of January 1, 1937, on covered jobs and was scheduled to rise in steps to 3% by 1949.

Besides old-age benefits, the act provided for a system of federal-state unemployment compensation funded with employer payroll taxes, and for grants to states to help fund assistance payments to certain categories of needy persons (the aged, the blind, and children under 16 who had been deprived of parental support), child welfare services, and maternal and child health services.

When the act was debated in Congress, prominent Republicans in the House and Senate made attempts to delete the provisions creating the old-age pension system. They said they preferred to rely solely on the assistance (charity/welfare) approach to help the aged. They argued that the payroll tax/insurance mechanism of the old-age benefits provisions might be unconstitutional and that it would impose a heavy tax burden on businesses that would retard economic development. Members of the minority stated, in the Ways and Means Committee's report to the House, that the old-age benefits program (Title II) and the method by which the money was to be raised to pay for the program (Title VIII) established a "bureaucracy in the field of insurance in competition with private business." They contended further that the program would "destroy old-age retirement systems set up by private industries, which in most instances provide more liberal benefits than are contemplated under Title II."[1] Although some party members tried to remove the old-age benefits provisions, the majority of Republicans in both chambers nevertheless did vote for the final Social Security bill. During congressional debate, Democrats generally supported the proposed old-age benefits program.

1. House Action

Debate on the Social Security bill started in the House on April 11 and lasted until April 19, 1935. Approximately 50 amendments were offered, but none passed. According to Edwin Witte, a key player in the development of the Social Security Act, House leaders passed the word that they wanted all amendments defeated.[2]

Four particularly significant votes were Mr. Monaghan's amendment proposing a revised "Townsend plan" and Mr. Connery's amendment proposing the Lundeen plan, both of which (described below) called for a more generous social insurance system; Mr. Treadway's motion to recommit H.R. 7260 to delete the old-age benefits program and its related taxes; and the vote on final passage of the bill.

Social Security: Major Decisions in the House and Senate Since 1935   7

a. On April 18, 1935, Mr. Monaghan (D-MT) offered an amendment, introduced in its original form by Mr. Groarty (D-CA) and referred to as the Townsend plan, which required the federal government to pay a $200-a-month pension to everyone 60 years of age and older, to be financed by a 2% tax on "all financial" transactions (essentially a sales tax). (For more details on the Townsend plan see discussion of the 1939 amendments, beginning on page 9.) Mr. Monaghan's amendment, although less costly than the original Townsend plan, was rejected by a vote of 56 to 206.[3]

b. On April 18, 1935, Mr. Connery (D-MA) offered an amendment that contained the provisions of a bill sponsored by Mr. Lundeen (Farmer-Laborite-MN). The Lundeen bill, which was approved 7-6 by the House Labor Committee, called for the "establishment of a system of social insurance to compensate all workers and farmers, 18 years of age and over, in all industries, occupations, and professions, who are unemployed through no fault of their own ..."[4] Mr. Lundeen's plan offered higher benefits than the committee's bill, and tied benefits to the cost of living. Under the Lundeen proposal, a more generous social insurance program was to be extended to all workers and farmers unable to work because of illness, old age, maternity, industrial injury, or any other disability. This system was to be financed by taxes falling most heavily on persons with higher incomes (by levying additional taxation on inheritances, gifts, and individual and corporation incomes of $5,000 a year and over). There was a division vote of 52 in favor and 204 opposed. Mr. Connery asked for tellers. The Connery amendment was rejected by a 40-158 teller vote.[5]

c. On April 18, 1935, Mr. Treadway (R-MA), the ranking minority Member of the Ways and Means Committee, offered an amendment to strike Title II, the old-age benefit provisions, from the bill. Mr. Treadway was opposed to the old-age benefits provision and to the taxing provisions of Title VIII. He said that the financing arrangement was unconstitutional. He indicated that the tax would be particularly burdensome on industry, running up to 6% on payrolls. He said that "business and industry are already operating under very heavy burdens" and maintained that to add a payroll tax to their burden would probably cause more unemployment and more uncertainty.[6] Mr. Jenkins (R-OH), supporter of the Treadway amendment, stated that making each worker pay 3% of his money for old-age benefits, whether he wanted to or not, and requiring employers to do the same, was clearly unconstitutional. He said, "Why talk about wanting to relieve the Depression, why talk about charity, why talk about all these other things when you are placing a financial lash upon the backs of the people whose backs are breaking under a load of debts and taxes?" He described the old-age benefits system as "compulsion of the rankest kind."[7] The Treadway amendment was defeated by a 49-125 teller vote.[8]

d. On April 19, 1935, Mr. Treadway made a motion to recommit H.R. 7260, including instructions to the Ways and Means Committee to strike out the old-age and unemployment insurance provisions and to increase the federal contribution for the welfare program of old-age assistance, Title I of the bill.[9] Mr. Treadway stated that the old-age benefit and unemployment insurance provisions of the bill were not emergency measures and that they "would not become effective in time to help present economic conditions, but, on the contrary would be a definite drag on recovery." He was opposed to levying a tax against both the employer and the employee. During his remarks on April 12, 1935, Mr. Treadway stated that he would "vote most strenuously in opposition to the bill at each and every opportunity."[10] During hisApril 19, 1935, remarks, Mr. Treadway said he was disgusted "at the attitude of business in that it has not shown the proper interest in protecting itself by stating its case before Congress."[11] His motion to recommit was rejected by a vote of 149 (95-R, 45-D, 9-1) to 253 (1-R, 252-D).[12]

e. On April 19, 1935, the House passed the Social Security bill by a vote of 372 (77-R, 288-D, 7-I) to 33 (18-R, 13-D, 2-I).[13]

2. Senate Action

There were also four major votes in the Senate: Mr. Long's (D-LA) proposal to substitute taxes on wealth and property for the payroll tax; Mr. Clark's amendment to exempt from coverage employees in firms with private pensions; Mr. Hastings' motion to recommit; and the vote on final passage of the bill.

a. On June 17, 1935, Mr. Long offered an amendment to liberalize the proposed old-age assistance program (Title I of the bill) and delete the payroll tax provisions (Title VIII and IX). In place of the payroll tax, Mr. Long recommended that states levy a tax on wealth or property. Mr. Long's amendment was rejected by voice vote.[14]

Social Security: Major Decisions in the House and Senate Since 1935   9

b. On June 19, 1935, Mr. Clark (D-MO) offered an amendment to exempt from coverage under the old-age benefits system employees in firms with private old-age pension systems. This idea came from an official of a Philadelphia insurance brokerage firm that specialized in group annuity contracts. Proponents of the amendment stated that employees would benefit from more liberal private annuities which would be in true proportion to earnings and service; joint annuities to protect spouses; earlier retirement for disability; and other reasons. Supporters of the amendment also maintained that the government would benefit because the reserves of private annuity plans would increase investment and create more income to tax. The Administration (being opposed to the amendment) argued that the amendment did not provide true retirement income guarantees because private pension programs could be cancelled, or the firm sponsoring them could go out of business. Critics also maintained that the amendment discouraged the employment of older men. The Ways and Means Committee rejected the proposal and so did the Finance Committee (by a narrow margin), but when Senator Clark offered it as an amendment on the Senate floor, it was passed by a vote of 51 (16-R, 35-D) to 35 (3-R, 30-D, 2-I).[15]

c. On June 19, 1935, Mr. Hastings (R-DE) made a motion to strike out the old-age benefits provisions from the bill. Mr. Hastings stated that those provisions were an effort to write into law a forced annuity system for a certain group of people. He maintained that the reserve account to take care of people in the future was not a contract and the American public could not depend upon it. He stated that the accumulation of huge sums of money for persons who had not yet reached retirement age would be subjected to many demands and most likely could not be preserved intact. He also said "let us not deceive that youth by making him believe that here is an annuity whereby he is contributing 50% and his employer is contributing 50%, and that it goes to his credit, when as a matter of fact, part of it is taken from him in order that we may take care of the older people of today."[16] Mr. Hastings' amendment was rejected by a vote of 15 (12-R, 3-D) to 63 (7-R, 54-D, 2-I).[17]

d. On June 19, 1935, Mr. George (D-GA) offered an amendment to encourage formation of industrial pensions as a substitute for Titles II and VIII. Under the amendment, employers were to operate and manage their own plans. The amendment called for a uniform schedule of benefits nationwide and provided for disability and survivor benefits along with old-age and unemployment benefits. The amendment was defeated by voice vote.[18]

e. The Senate passed the bill on June 19, 1935, by a vote of 77 (15-R, 60-D, 2-1) to 6 (5-R, 1-D).[19]

3. Conference Action

The conferees settled all differences except on the Clark amendments related to employees under private pension plans. The conference committee reported the bill without the Clark amendments, but with an understanding that the chairmen of the Ways and Means and Finance Committees would appoint a special joint committee to study whether to exempt industrial employers with private pension plans from coverage under Social Security and to report to the next Congress.[20]

a. On July 17, 1935, the House rejected Mr. Treadway's motion to accept the Clark amendment by a vote of 78 to 268;[21] then agreed by a vote of 269 to 65 to a motion by Mr. Doughton (D-NC) that the House insist that the Senate drop the Clark amendment.[22]

b. On July 17, 1935, the Senate agreed, by voice vote, to Mr. Harrison's motion to insist on keeping the Clark amendment and ask for a further conference.[23]

c. On August 8, 1935, the conference report cleared the House by a voice vote.[24]

d. On August 9, 1935, the Senate conferees agreed to delete the Clark amendment;[25] the Senate then agreed to the conference report by a voice vote.[26]

B. P.L. 379—76th Congress, Social Security Amendments of 1939

H.R. 6635, the Social Security Amendments of 1939, was signed into law on August 10, 1939, by President Roosevelt. Congress expressly provided in the 1935 Act that the Social Security Board (a three-member panel appointed by the President with advice and consent of the Senate) study and make recommendations on the most effective methods of providing economic security through social insurance. An advisory council appointed by the Senate Special Committee on Social Security and the Social Security Board was created in May 1937 to work with the Social Security Board to study amending Titles II and VII of the Social Security Act. Some members of the advisory council represented employees, some represented employers, and others represented the general public. Both the Social Security Board and the advisory council made recommendations on how the old-age benefits program should be changed, and many of their recommendations were the same. The President sent the Social Security Board's recommendations to Congress on January 16, 1939. The 1939 amendments incorporated most of the Board's recommendations.

The 1939 amendments extended benefits to dependents and survivors of workers covered by Social Security. Dependents included an aged wife, a child under 16 (under 18 if attending school), a widowed mother caring for an eligible child, an aged widow, and a dependent aged parent if there were no eligible widow or child. Widows would receive 75% of the primary insurance amount (PIA)[27] of the worker, and all other dependents would receive 50% of the PIA.

The starting date for monthly benefits was accelerated to January 1, 1940, instead of January 1, 1942. Also, benefits were based on average monthly wages rather than on cumulative wages. In addition, Congress repealed the tax rate increase to 1.5%, scheduled to go into effect in 1940, replacing it with an increase to 2% in 1943-45. The amendments also modified qualifying provisions, including the definition of insured status, for consistency with other changes in the act.[28] Further, people receiving OASI benefits were permitted to earn up to $14.99 monthly: dollar-for-dollar deductions were to be made for any month in which the recipient earned $15 or more in covered employment. The system now was called old-age and survivors insurance (OASI). Congress also changed the old-age reserve account to a trust fund, managed by a board of trustees.

1. House Action

On June 2, 1939, following public hearings on the proposed amendments and six weeks of executive sessions, the Committee on Ways and Means reported to the House H.R. 6635, embodying its recommendations for amendments to the Social Security Act. The day before, the House had debated and voted on the Townsend old-age pension bill. The Townsend plan, embodied in H.R. 6466 introduced by Mr. McGroarty (D-CA) in January 1935, was offered as a substitute for H.R. 6635.[29] The Townsend plan would have provided a monthly pension of $200 to every citizen 60 years of age or older who had not been convicted of a felony. To receive the pension, a person could not earn wages and was required to spend the entire pension within 30 days. The plan would have been financed by a 2% tax on every commercial and financial transaction; the President would have been given discretionary power to raise the tax to 3% or to lower it to 1%. During a 1935 Ways and Means Committee hearing, Mr. Townsend stated that his plan was only incidentally a pension plan. He said the principal objectives of the proposal were to solve the unemployment problem and to restore prosperity by giving people purchasing power. He cited Census Bureau data that 4 million people over the age of 60 held jobs in 1930. He reiterated that in order to be eligible for the proposed pension of $200 a month, those elderly people would have to give up their jobs, which he said meant that 4 million jobs would become available to middle-aged and younger people. In addition, he said that requiring 8 million elderly persons to buy $200 worth of goods and services each month would increase demand and result in more jobs.[30]

Mr. Sabath (D-IL) said he thought it was "decidedly out of place to bring the Townsend bill to the floor." He said that the bill "had no chance of passing in the first place; neither was it feasible nor possible of operation."[31] Others branded the bill as "crackpot," and in general objected because they thought that the Social Security program was a better means of caring for the aged, asserting that any liberalization of pensions should be done within the framework of the Social Security Act.

Mr. Witte, in his book on the development of the Social Security Act, said:

> The members of the House of Representatives at all times took the Townsend movement much more seriously than did the senators. The thousands of letters that the members received in support of this plan worried them greatly. With the exception of probably not than a half dozen members, all felt that the Townsend plan was utterly impossible; at the same time they hesitated to vote against it.[32]

The House rejected H.R. 6466, the Townsend plan bill, on June 1, 1939, by a vote of 97 (55-R, 40-D, 2-I) to 302 (107-R, 194-D, 1-I).[33]

A *New York Times* editorial reported that "the psychological effect of the presentation of the Townsend bill was to make these liberalized benefits (referring to the provisions in H.R. 6635) seem small. Most of those who voted against the Townsend plan will be eager to vote for these liberalized benefits to show that their hearts are in the right place. The result is that the real cost of the new Social Security scale of benefits is not likely to receive very serious attention."[34]

Social Security: Major Decisions in the House and Senate Since 1935   13

The House took up H.R. 6635 on June 6, 1939. The bill had the general support of the Ways and Means Committee. The minority stated in the committee's report to the House that "while the bill in no sense represents a complete or satisfactory solution of the problem of Social Security, it at least makes certain improvements in the present law (some of which we have ourselves heretofore suggested) which we believe justify us in supporting it despite its defects."[35]

a. On June 9, 1939, Mr. Havenner (D-CA) offered an amendment, endorsed by the American Federation of Labor, to extend Social Security coverage to workers employed in college clubs or fraternities or sororities; employees in nonprofit religious, charitable, or educational institutions; student nurses; and some agricultural workers. The amendment was rejected by voice vote.[36]

b. On June 9, 1939, Mr. Kean (R-NJ) offered an amendment that required that the money derived from the Social Security payroll tax be invested in one-year marketable U.S. government bonds rather than in special nonmarketable Treasury obligations. Mr. Kean remarked that the adoption of the amendment would "prevent the present practice of using old-age taxes for current expenses." The amendment was rejected by voice vote.[37]

c. On June 9, 1939, Mr. Carlson (R-KS) offered an amendment to exclude non-citizens from coverage under Social Security. Mr. Carlson was opposed to putting foreigners under the U.S. old-age insurance provisions. Opponents of the amendment argued that exemption of such people would give employers of aliens a competitive advantage over vessels owned and manned by Americans. Mr. Carlson's amendment was rejected 24 to 59 by a division vote.[38]

d. On June 10, 1939, Mr. Carlson moved to recommit H.R. 6635 to the Committee on Ways and Means. The motion was rejected by voice vote.[39]

e. On June 10, 1939, the House passed H.R. 6635 by a vote of 364 (142-R, 222-D) to 2 (2-R).[40]

2. Senate Action

On July 13, 1939, Mr. Downey (D-CA), in the course of his statement on how "unworkable, unjust, and unfair" the Social Security Act was, moved that the bill be recommitted to the Finance Committee for more study of the whole pension and savings field. Mr. Downey stated that under H.R. 6635 covered workers in 1942 would receive only one-half as much in old-age benefits as those receiving government subsidies (old-age assistance benefits/cash relief). Under H.R. 6635, the average monthly Social Security benefit was projected at between $19 and $20 for 80% of workers in 1942, whereas the maximum old-age assistance benefit was $40. The motion was rejected by a vote of 18 (12-R, 5-D, 1-I) to 47 (4-R, 41-D, 2-I).[41]

a. On July 13, 1939, Mr. Reynolds (D-NC) offered an amendment to prohibit non-U.S. citizens from being eligible for Social Security coverage or benefits. Mr. Harrison (D-MS) offered additional language to Mr. Reynolds' amendment that allowed benefit payments to aliens if they lived within 50 miles of the United States. The amendment as modified was agreed to by voice vote.[42]

b. The Senate passed H.R. 6635 on July 13, 1939, by a vote of 57 (8-R, 45-D, 4-I) to 8 (6-R, 2-D).[43]

3. Conference Action

The conference report was approved by the House on August 4, 1939, by voice vote,[44] and by the Senate on August 5, 1939, by a vote of 59 (14-R, 42-D, 3-I) to 4 (4-D).[45]

C. Payroll Tax Freeze, 1942-1947

Between 1942 and 1947, the Social Security payroll tax rate increase was postponed seven times. It was not until 1950 that the 1% Social Security tax rate was allowed to rise to 1.5%.

1. The Revenue Act of 1942, P.L. 753 (H.R. 7378, 77th Congress) was signed by President Roosevelt on October 21, 1942. It provided that for calendar year 1943, the payroll tax rate for old-age and survivors benefits would be frozen at the existing rate of 1% for employees and employers, each, instead of being increased to 2% on each as otherwise would have been required.

2. P.L. 211, (H.J.Res. 171, 78th Congress), a joint resolution regarding the Tariff Act, signed by President Roosevelt on December 22, 1943, froze the payroll tax at the 1% rate until March 1, 1944. The purpose of the resolution was to give Congress time to consider the scheduled payroll tax increase before it went into effect.

3. The Revenue Act of 1943, P.L. 235 (H.R. 3687, 78th Congress), was vetoed by President Roosevelt on February 22, 1944; the veto was overridden by the House on February 24, 1944, and by the Senate on February 25, 1944. The bill deferred the scheduled payroll tax increase (from 1 to 2%) until 1945.

   P.L. 235 also contained an amendment by Senator Murray (D-MT) that authorized the use of general revenues if payroll taxes were insufficient to meet Social Security benefit obligations. Senator Murray stated that the amendment merely stated in law what had been implied in the Senate Committee report. Senator Vandenberg (R-MI) replied that the amendment "has no immediate application, it has no immediate menace, it contemplates and anticipates no immediate appropriation; but as the statement of a principle, I agree with the amendment completely."[46] The amendment passed by voice vote.[47] The "Murray-Vandenberg" general revenue provision was repealed in 1950, when the tax rate was increased.

4. The Federal Insurance Contributions Act (FICA) of 1945, P.L. 495 (H.R. 5564, 78th Congress), signed by President Roosevelt on December 16, 1944, froze the payroll tax rate at 1% until 1946 and scheduled the payroll tax rate to rise to 2.5% for the years 1946 through 1948, and to 3% thereafter.

5. The Revenue Act of 1945, P.L. 214 (H.R. 4309, 79th Congress), signed by President Truman on November 8, 1945, deferred the tax rate increase until 1947.

6. The Social Security Amendments of 1946, P.L. 719 (H.R. 7037, 79th Congress), signed by President Truman on August 10, 1946, deferred the tax rate increase until 1948.

7. The Social Security Amendments of 1947, P.L. 379 (H.R. 3818, 80th Congress), signed by President Truman on August 6, 1947, continued the freeze on the tax rate increase until 1950 and provided that it would rise to 1.5% for 1950-51 and to 2% thereafter.

Members who favored these payroll tax freezes argued that the Social Security reserves were adequate and that benefit payments in the immediate future could be met with the current payroll tax rate. In a 1942 letter to the Senate Finance Committee, President Roosevelt said that "a failure to allow the scheduled increase in rates to take place under the present favorable circumstances would cause a real and justifiable fear that adequate funds will not be accumulated to meet the heavy obligations of the future and that the claims for benefits accruing under the present law may be jeopardized." He also stated that "expanded Social Security, together with other fiscal measures, would set up a bulwark of economic security for the people now and after the war and at the same time would provide anti-inflationary sources for financing the war."[48] Members who were opposed to the freeze argued that the scheduled payroll tax increase was important for the long-term soundness of the OASI trust fund and that postponing the tax increase would mean higher payroll tax rates in the future and perhaps government subsidies to meet obligations. Some proponents of the freeze maintained that the Administration wanted the tax increase to retire the public debt accumulated by wartime expenditures.

Although Senator Vandenberg (R-MI) was the main spokesman for postponing the payroll tax increases, the legislative effort to defer tax increases was bipartisan. "Without regard to party or ideology, elected representatives of the people were not willing to argue for increases in an earmarked tax if a current need for them could not be demonstrated," one scholar observed.[49]

D. P.L. 492—80th Congress, 1948 Provision for Exclusion of Certain Newspaper and Magazine Vendors from Social Security Coverage (H.R. 5052) and P.L. 642—80th Congress, 1948 Provision to Maintain Status Quo Concept of Employee

Two pieces of 1948 legislation, H.R. 5052 and H.J.Res. 296, settled the argument of who was considered an employee for purposes of Social Security coverage. The term "employee" was not defined in the Social Security Act or in the Internal Revenue Code. However, in 1936 the Social Security Board and the Treasury Department issued regulations that to a certain extent explained the meaning of the terms "employee" and "employer." In defining "employer," both sets of regulations emphasized the concept of "control"—the right to give instructions, but other significant factors such as the right to discharge, the furnishing of tools and a place to work were also mentioned in the regulations. During the next few years, the Social Security Board and the Treasury Department issued numerous rulings to clarify the boundaries of the employee-employer relationship and a number of court cases established generally applicable precedents. The common-law meaning of the term employee, however, was very unclear in cases of outside salesmen.[50]

On December 31, 1946, the U.S. district court, in the case of *Hearst Publications, Inc. v. The United States*, ruled that newspaper vendors should be considered employees rather than independent contractors. H.R. 5052, introduced in 1948, proposed to treat newspaper and magazine vendors as independent contractors rather than employees and thereby to exclude them from Social Security coverage. In addition, in 1948 Congress addressed the broader issue of who was to be considered an employee by passing H.J.Res. 296, a resolution to maintain the status quo of treating newspaper vendors as independent contractors, by stating that Congress, not the courts nor the Social Security Administration (SSA), should determine national policy regarding Social Security coverage. It was reported that H.J.Res. 296 was primarily introduced to prevent the release of new federal regulations defining the meaning of the term "employee" along the lines interpreted by the Supreme Court in three cases decided in June 1947.[51] H.J.Res. 296 excluded from Social Security coverage (and unemployment insurance) any person who was not considered an employee under the common-law rules. In effect, H.J.Res. 296 said that independent contractors (e.g., door-to-door salesmen, insurance salesmen, and pieceworkers) were not to be considered employees. H.R. 5052 and H.J.Res. 296 were vetoed by President Truman. Congress overrode both vetoes.

In his veto of H.R. 5052, President Truman asserted that the nation's security and welfare demanded that Social Security be expanded to cover the groups excluded from the program: "Any step in the opposite direction can only serve to undermine the program and destroy the confidence of our people in the permanence of its protection against the hazards of old age, premature death, and unemployment."[52] The action taken on H.R. 5052 illustrated the controversial issues involved in determining who should be covered under Social Security.

1. House Action

On March 4, 1948, Mr. Gearhart (R-CA) asked unanimous consent for immediate consideration of H.R. 5052. Mr. Gearhart stated that "until the rendition of the federal court decisions I have referred to were rendered the status of the newspaper and magazine vendors was considered by everyone, and as this Congress clearly intended, to be that of independent contractors since they bought their periodicals at a low price and sold them at a higher price, deriving their livelihood from the profit in the operation." Under the court decisions[53] "these vendors were arbitrarily declared to be employees and therefore subject to the payroll taxes though the money they receive is not wages, as generally understood, but profits derived from an independent business operation of their own." Under the court decisions, newspaper and magazine vendors were in essence "employees" of all of the newspaper and magazine companies with which they had an arrangement. H.R. 5052 excluded newspaper and magazine vendors from coverage under the Social Security Act. Mr. Gearhart stated in his remarks that "when newspaper vendors are covered into the Social Security system—and I believe they will be by act of Congress before this session ends—they will be brought in as the independent contractors which they are, as the self-employed ..." H.R. 5052 was passed in the House on March 4, 1948, by unanimous consent.[54]

    c. On February 27, 1948, H.J.Res. 296 was passed by a vote of 275 to 52.[55]

2. Senate Action

On March 23, 1948, the Senate passed by unanimous consent H.R. 5052 in form identical to that passed by the House.[56]

    a. On June 4, 1948, H.J.Res. 296 was passed, after public assistance amendments increasing federal assistance to states were added, by a vote of 74 to 6.[57]

    b. Although there was no conference on H.J.Res. 296, the House concurred in the Senate amendments on June 4, 1948, by voice vote.[58]

3. Veto

    a. On April 6, 1948, in the veto message on H.R. 5052, President Truman stated that some vendors work under arrangements "which make them bona fide employees of the publishers, and, consequently, are entitled to the benefits of the Social Security Act." President Truman further stated that "It is said that news vendors affected by this bill could more appropriately be covered by the Social Security laws as independent contractors when and if coverage is extended to the self-employed. Whether that is true or not, surely they should continue to receive the benefits to which they are now entitled until the broader coverage is provided. It would be most inequitable to extinguish their present rights pending a determination as to whether it is more appropriate for them to be covered on some other basis."[59]

    b. On June 14, 1948, President Truman vetoed H.J.Res. 296, saying that "If our Social Security program is to endure, it must be protected against these piecemeal attacks. Coverage must be permanently expanded and no employer or special group of employers should be permitted to reverse that trend by efforts to avoid the burden which

Social Security: Major Decisions in the House and Senate Since 1935   19

millions of other employers have carried without serious inconvenience or complaint."[60]

4. Veto override

a. The House overrode President Truman's veto of H.R. 5052 and passed the bill on April 14, 1948, by a vote of 308 (207-R, 101-D) to 28 (2-R, 24-D. 2-I).[61] On April 20, 1948, the Senate overrode the President's veto and passed H.R. 5052 by a vote of 77 (48-R, 29-D) to 7 (7-D).[62]

b. On June 14, 1948, President Truman's veto of H.J.Res. 296 was overridden in the House by a vote of 298 to 75;[63] and in the Senate by a vote of 65 (37-R, 28-D) to 12 (2-R, 10-D).[64]

E. P.L. 734—81st Congress, Social Security Act Amendments of 1950

H.R. 6000, the Social Security Act Amendments of 1950, was signed by President Truman on August 28, 1950. H.R. 6000 broadened the Social Security Act to cover roughly 10 million additional persons, including regularly employed farm and domestic workers; self-employed people other than doctors, lawyers, engineers, and certain other professional groups; certain federal employees not covered by government pension plans; and workers in Puerto Rico and the Virgin Islands. On a voluntary group basis, coverage was offered to employees of state and local governments not under public employee retirement systems and to employees of nonprofit organizations. Dependent husbands, widowers, and, under certain circumstances children of insured women were also made eligible for benefits (before, such benefits were not generally available to children of women workers).

In addition, Congress raised benefits by about 77%; raised the wage base from $3,000 to $3,600; raised employer and employee taxes gradually from 1.5% to an ultimate rate of 3.25% each in 1970 and years thereafter; set the OASI tax rate for the self-employed at 75% of the combined employer-employee rate; eased requirements for eligibility for benefits by making 1950 the starting date for most people in determining the quarters of coverage needed; permitted recipients to have higher earnings ($50 a month) without losing any OASI benefits (those aged 75 and over could now earn any amount without losing OASI benefits); and gave free wage credits of $160 for each month in which military service was performed between September 16, 1940, and July 24, 1947.[65]

1. House Action

On August 22, 1949, the Committee on Ways and Means reported H.R. 6000. H.R. 6000 did not include President Truman's recommendations for health insurance or his request to lower the OASI eligibility age to 60 for women, but it did include disability protection for both Social Security and public assistance recipients. It also extended coverage to farm and domestic workers.

All 10 Republicans on the committee (including 7 who voted to send H.R. 6000 to the floor) filed a minority report stating that OASI coverage and benefits should be limited so as to provide only a "basic floor" of economic protection. The minority report opposed the disability insurance provision, saying that aid to the disabled should be limited to charity aid provided under the proposed public assistance program for the permanently and totally disabled.[66]

The Committee on Rules at first refused to send H.R. 6000 to the floor, but, after much debate, a closed rule barring floor amendments was granted. A number of Members opposed the rule because they said it foreclosed their right to improve the bill through floor amendments.

a. On October 4, 1949, Mr. Sabath (D-IL) offered a resolution for four days of debate, with only the Committee on Ways and Means having the right to offer amendments, and with only a motion to recommit being in order. Those favoring the resolution stated that the Ways and Means Committee had devoted six months to considering the bill, had heard testimony from 250 witnesses and thus knew best how to improve the program. Those opposing the closed rule said the bill was very controversial and that the whole House should settle difficult questions of policy. They said the closed rule negated the importance of other House Members and usurped their rights.

The House agreed to the resolution for a closed rule by a vote of 189 (12-R, 176-D, 1-I) to 135 (123-R, 12-D) on October 4, 1949.[67]

b. On October 5, 1949, Mr. Mason (R-IL) moved to recommit H.R. 6000, and offered H.R. 6297 (a bill that carried out the minority view on H.R. 6000) as its substitute. H.R. 6297, introduced by Mr. Kean (R-NJ) on October 3, 1949, held the wage base to $3,000; recommended greater coverage for domestic workers so that those who were less regularly employed would be included; exempted teachers, firemen, and policemen with their own pension systems from coverage; confined disability payments to the public assistance program; and recommended that Congress establish an independent Social Security system in Puerto Rico, the Virgin Islands, and other possessions rather than include them in the existing OASI program. The motion to recommit was defeated by a vote of 113 (112-R, 1-D) to 232 (29-R, 202-D, 1-I).[68]

c. Immediately following the rejection of the motion, H.R. 6000 was passed in the House by a vote of 333 (R-130, D-202, 1-I) to 14 (R-12, D-2).[69]

2. Senate Action

Since Congress adjourned shortly after the House action, the Senate did not consider H.R. 6000 until 1950. The Senate Finance Committee held extensive hearings and adopted many amendments to H.R. 6000. The committee stated that the chief purpose of the bill was to strengthen the OAS1 system so that OASI would be the primary method of offering "basic security to retired persons and survivors,"[70] with public assistance (particularly old-age assistance) playing strictly a supplementary and secondary role. The Finance Committee version of the bill did not include the disability insurance provision passed by the House nor the provision providing federal grants to states for needy persons who were permanently and totally disabled, nor President Truman's health insurance proposal. The bill was reported to the Senate on May 17, 1950, and debate began on June 12, 1950.

a. On June 14, 1950, following a Senate Republican Policy Committee meeting, Mr. Millikin (R-CO) and Mr. Taft (R-OH) indicated that Republicans would support H.R. 6000 but favored a study to determine whether the OASI and old-age assistance programs eventually should be united in a universal pay-as-you-go system. Under this proposal, all elderly persons in the United States would become eligible for subsistence-level pensions at age 65, with pension amounts the same for all (rather than varied to reflect earnings during the work career), and financed from current revenues rather than a trust fund.[71]

b. An amendment offered by Mr. Myers (D-PA) to add a disability insurance program to OASI was rejected by a voice vote.[72]

c. On June 20, 1950, another amendment offered by Mr. Myers to boost the OASI wage base from $3,000 to $4,200, closer to what President Truman had requested (instead of $3,600 specified in the George amendment—see below), was rejected 36 (9-R, 27-D) to 45 (27-R, 18-D).[73]

d. On June 20, 1950, Mr. Long (D-LA) introduced an amendment to provide federal grants to States for needy disabled persons. The amendment was rejected by a vote of 41 (4-R, 37-D) to 42 (33-R, 9-D).[74]

e. On June 20, 1950, Mr. George's (D-GA) amendment to increase the basic wage base from $3,000 to $3,600 was agreed to by voice vote.[75]

f. On June 20, 1950, by a voice vote, the Senate adopted S.Res. 300, authorizing a study of a universal pay-as-you-go old-age pension system.[76]

g. The Senate passed H.R. 6000 on June 20 by a vote of 81 (35-R, 47-D) to 2 (2-R).[77]

3. Conference Action

Conferees dropped the disability insurance proposal, but retained the public assistance program for the permanently and totally disabled (the so-called charity approach). The conference report was submitted to the House on August 1, 1950.

a. On August 16, 1950, Mr. Byrnes (R-WI) moved to recommit the conference report on H.R. 6000. He stated that his main reason for doing so was to prevent any attempt to remove from the bill a Senate floor amendment by Mr. Knowland (R-CA) to reduce federal control over state administration of unemployment insurance. Mr. Doughton (D-NC) moved the previous question on the motion to recommit.[78] The motion on the previous question was passed by a vote of 188 (120-R, 68-D) to 186 (20-R, 165-D, 1-I). The motion to recommit the conference report was rejected.

b. The conference report passed the House on August 16, 1950, 374 (140-R, 234-D) to 1 (1-R);[79] and the Senate on August 17, 1950, by voice vote.[80]

F. P.L. 590—82nd Congress, Social Security Act Amendments of 1952

H.R. 7800, the Social Security Amendments of 1952, was signed into law on July 18, 1952, by President Truman. The amendments increased OASI benefits for both present and future recipients (by an average of 15% for those on the rolls), permitted recipients to earn $75 a month (instead of $50) without losing OASI benefits, extended wage credits of $160 for each month in which active military or naval service was performed during the period from July 24, 1947, through December 1953, and provided for a disability "freeze," which in principle preserved the Social Security benefits of qualified workers who became permanently and totally disabled before retirement by averaging the person's wages only over his or her working years. (See following conference action section for more details.)

1. House Action

In the House, debate centered largely on a so-called "disability freeze" proposed by the Committee on Ways and Means. Under the provision, if a person became permanently and totally disabled, the period of disability was to be excluded in computing the number of quarters of coverage he or she needed to be eligible for benefits, and in computing the average earnings on which the benefits would be based. The provision, in effect, preserved benefit rights while a person was disabled. Medical examinations by doctors and public institutions would be designated and paid for by the Federal Security Agency (FSA). The American Medical Association (AMA) claimed that this arrangement would lead to socialized medicine. Mr. Reed (R-NY), the minority leader of the Ways and Means Committee, was the primary spokesman for Members who endorsed the AMA position.

a. On May 19, 1952, when H.R. 7800 was brought to the floor under suspension of the rules procedure—requiring a two-thirds vote for passage and barring amendments—the majority of Republicans voted against it because of the disability provision, and it was rejected by a vote of 151 (52-R, 98-D, 1-I) to 141 (99-R, 42-D), failing to win a two-thirds vote.[81]

b. On June 16, 1952, Democratic leaders brought H.R. 7800 to the floor under suspension of the rules. An amended version of the revised bill empowered the FSA to make disability determinations, but omitted the language specifying how the FSA administrator should do so. Mr.

Reed said "... let no person on this floor be deceived. You have the same old H.R. 7800 here before you. While the socialized medicine advocates pretend to remove the specific instructions to the Administrator, they now give him more powers under general provisions of the law than he had before. You have socialized medicine here stronger in this bill than was H.R. 7800, heretofore defeated."[82] Mr. Reed later contended that because of the approaching election many Members chose to go on record in favor of the other OASI provisions and so voted for the amended version of H.R. 7800. The bill was approved 361 (165-R, 195-D, 1-I) to 22 (20-R, 2-D) on June 17, 1952.[83]

2. Senate Action

When the bill came to the Senate Finance Committee, it dropped the disability freeze provision. The Finance Committee said there was inadequate time to study the issue properly.

- a. The committee amendment, offered by Mr. George (D-GA), to drop the disability freeze provision, was passed by voice vote on June 26, 1952.[84]
- b. H.R. 7800 (without the disability freeze provision) was passed in the Senate by a voice vote on June 26, 1952.[85]

3. Conference Action

The conferees retained the disability freeze provision, in principle. The compromise terminated the freeze provision on June 30, 1953; at the same time, it did not allow an application to be accepted before July 1, 1953. Thus, the disability freeze provision was made inoperative unless Congress, in subsequent legislation, were to take action to remove the bar. The stated intent in making the provision inoperative was to permit "the working out of tentative agreements with the States for possible administration of these provisions."[86] In addition, the conferees gave responsibility for determining whether an applicant was disabled to appropriate state agencies (public assistance, vocational rehabilitation, or workmen's compensation), instead of the FSA. The Federal Security Administrator would be able to overturn a ruling by the State agencies that a person was disabled, but would not be able to reverse a ruling by the State agencies that a person was not disabled.

a. The conference report was agreed to July 5, 1952, by voice votes in both chambers.[87]

G. P.L. 761—83d Congress, Social Security Amendments of 1954

H.R. 9366, the Social Security Amendments of 1954, was signed by President Eisenhower on September 1, 1954. In his 1953 State of the Union Message, the President recommended that "OASI should promptly be expanded to cover millions of citizens who have been left out of the Social Security system." The Social Security Amendments of 1954 extended *mandatory* coverage to, among others, some self-employed farmers, self-employed engineers, architects, accountants, and funeral directors, all federal employees not covered by government pension plans, farm and domestic service workers not covered by the 1950 amendments, and *voluntary* coverage to ministers and certain state and local government employees already covered by staff retirement systems. The bill also raised the wage base for the OASI tax to $4,200; raised the tax rate to 3.5%, each, for employers and employees beginning in 1970, and to 4.0%, each, beginning in 1975, with the tax rate for the self-employed continuing at 1.5 times the employee rate (or 75% of the combined employee-employer rate). OASI benefits for recipients were raised by roughly 15%, with the maximum individual benefit rising from $85 to $98.50 a month, and a revised benefit formula was provided for future retirees that increased benefits by roughly 27%, with the maximum benefit rising from $85 a month to $108.50. The bill also put the disability freeze into effect (see discussion of House action on the 1952 amendments, beginning on page 20), with disability determinations to be made by the appropriate State agencies, permitted a recipient to earn up to $1,200 a year without deductions, eliminated the earnings test for people age 72 and over, and dropped the five years of lowest earnings from average monthly wage determinations for benefit computation purposes.

1. House Action

On June 1, 1954, Mr. Smith (D-VA) and other farm area Democrats objected to bringing H.R. 9366 to the floor under a closed rule because coverage of farmers was included in the bill. Mr. Smith stated, "I object to the feature of this bill that prohibits you from offering any amendment. I think that requires a little discussion and a little understanding. We all agree that on an ordinary tax bill it is not feasible or practical to write it on the floor of the

House, and therefore we have adopted the theory that we have closed rules on tax bills ... all we asked for in the Rules Committee was that the individual members of this House be given an opportunity to offer amendments to designate what classifications of persons should be included."[88] On June 1, 1954, by a vote of 270 (171-R, 98-D, 1-I) to 76 (5-R, 71-D),[89] debate of the closed rule was cut off, and the closed rule was then adopted by voice vote.

a. The House bill also included provisions extending mandatory coverage to all self-employed professionals but doctors (dentists and other medical professionals would have been covered under the House bill).[90]

b. The House passed H.R. 9366 on June 1, 1954, by a vote of 356 (181-R, 174-D, 1-I) to 8 (2-R, 6-D).[91]

2. Senate Action

H.R. 9366 as reported by the Finance Committee included the coverage of farm and domestic service workers, ministers, employees of state and local governments covered by a retirement system, and a small number of professionals. It also increased the earnings test threshold to $1,200 a year, reduced to 72 the age at the earnings test no longer applied, and increased the lump-sum death benefit from $255 to $325.50. During the Senate debate on H.R. 9366, nine amendments were adopted, six were rejected, and six were presented and then withdrawn.[92]

a. Among the amendments adopted on the floor by the Senate was a provision by Mr. Long (D-LA) to require the Department of Health, Education, and Welfare to study the feasibility and costs of providing increased minimum benefits of $55, $60, and $75 a month under the Social Security program. On August 13, 1954, Mr. Long's amendment was agreed to by voice vote.[93]

b. Among the amendments defeated were the Johnston (D-SC) amendment to reduce the Social Security eligibility age to 60; the Stennis (D-MS) amendments that would have left the coverage of farm workers unchanged; and the Humphrey (D-MN) amendment to increase the widow's benefit to 100% of the primary insurance amount. On August 13, 1954, Mr. Johnston's amendment was rejected by voice vote.[94] On August 13, 1954, the Stennis amendments were rejected en bloc by voice vote.[95] On August 13, 1954, Mr. Humphrey's amendment was rejected on a division vote.[96]

Social Security: Major Decisions in the House and Senate Since 1935   27

c. Among the amendments that were presented and then withdrawn was an amendment by Mr. Lehman (D-NY) to extend Social Security coverage, increase benefits, add permanent and total disability and temporary disability Social Security benefits, and to make other changes.[97]

d. On August 13, 1954, the Senate passed H.R. 9366, by voice vote.[98]

3. Conference Action

The conferees, among other things, accepted a provision mandatorily covering self-employed farmers, accountants, architects, engineers, and funeral directors, but excluding lawyers, doctors, dentists, or other medical professionals, and extended coverage to federal employees not covered by staff retirement systems.

a. Both chambers agreed to the conference report without amendments by voice vote on August 20, 1954, the last day of the session.[99]

H. P.L. 880—84th Congress, Social Security Amendments of 1956

H.R. 7225, the Social Security Amendments of 1956, was signed by President Eisenhower on August 1, 1956. The amendments provided benefits, after a six-month waiting period, for permanently and totally disabled workers aged 50 to 64 who were fully insured and had at least 5 years of coverage in the 10-year period before becoming disabled; to a dependent child 18 and older of a deceased or retired insured worker if the child became disabled before age 18; to women workers and wives at the age of 62, instead of 65, with actuarially reduced benefits; reduced from 65 to 62 the age at which benefits were payable to widows or parents, with no reduction; extended coverage to lawyers, dentists, veterinarians, optometrists, and all other self-employed professionals except doctors;[100] increased the tax rate by 0.25% on employer and employee each (0.375% for self-employed people) to finance disability benefits (thereby raising the aggregate tax rate ultimately to 4.25%); and created a separate disability insurance (DI) trust fund. The Social Security program now consisted of old-age, survivors, and disability insurance (OASDI).

1. House Action

Major House Ways and Means Committee provisions provided benefits to disabled persons age 50 and older and reduced the age at which women could first receive OASI benefits to 62. Although some Members maintained that not enough time was spent in working out the details of these two controversial provisions, H.R. 7225 was brought to the floor under suspension of the rules, which barred floor amendments and required a two-thirds vote for passage. H.R. 7225 was passed by the House on July 18, 1955, by a vote of 372 (169-R, 203-D) to 31 (23-R, 8-D).[101]

2. Senate Action

At Senate Finance Committee hearings on the House-passed bill, the Secretary of Health, Education, and Welfare, Mr. Folsom, stated that the Administration was opposed to reducing the retirement age to 62 for women and providing disability benefits. According to *Congress and the Nation*, Mr. Folsom said that OASI had stayed actuarially sound without excessive taxes because it had been restricted to one purpose with "predictable costs": providing income for the aged.[102] Spokesmen for the AFL-CIO and several other groups maintained that union experience with welfare plans and federal studies dating back to 1937 showed that disability insurance was both administratively and financially sound.

a. On June 5, 1956, the Senate Finance Committee reported H.R. 7225 after eliminating the Disability Insurance program and the tax increase to pay for it, and limiting retirement benefits at age 62 to widows only.

b. On July 17, 1956, Mr. George (D-GA) offered an amendment reinstating the Disability Insurance program and the tax increase to finance it. The amendment provided for a separate disability insurance trust fund (instead of operating the new program out of the OASI fund). The amendment was passed by a vote of 47 (6-R, 41-D) to 45 (38-R, 7-D).[103]

c. Also, on July 17, 1956, the Senate agreed to Mr. Kerr's (D-OK) amendment to permit women to receive benefits at age 62 at actuarially reduced rates. The amendment passed by a vote of 86 (40-R, 46-D) to 7 (5-R, 2-D).[104]

d. On July 17, 1956, the Senate passed H.R. 7225 by a vote of 90 (45-R, 45-D) to 0.[105]

Social Security: Major Decisions in the House and Senate Since 1935   29

3. Conference Action

The House on July 26, 1956,[106] and the Senate on July 27, 1956,[107] cleared the conference report on H.R. 7225 without amendments by voice votes.

I. P.L. 85-840, Social Security Amendments of 1958

H.R. 13549, the Social Security Amendments of 1958, was signed by President Eisenhower on August 28, 1958. The amendments raised recipients' benefits an average of 7%, with benefits ranging from $33 to $127 per month for future recipients; increased maximum family benefits from $200 to $254; raised the wage base from $4,200 to $4,800 a year; increased the tax rate by 0.25% on employers and employees each and 0.375% for the self-employed; provided benefits to dependents of workers receiving disability benefits; and permitted the aged dependent parents of an insured deceased worker to receive survivors' benefits even if the worker's widow or dependent widower or child were alive and also eligible for benefits.

1. House Action

Most of the controversy over H.R. 13549 pertained to public assistance programs. There was relatively little controversy over the proposed OASDI provisions. During debate on H.R. 13549, Mr. Reed (R-NY) stated that the bill would strengthen the actuarial soundness of the Social Security program.[108]

    a. On July 31, 1958, the House passed H.R. 13549 by a vote of 374 to 2.[109]

2. Senate Action

On August 15, 1958, Mr. Yarborough (D-TX) offered an amendment to increase benefits by 10%, rather than 7%, as proposed in H.R. 13549. Mr. Yarborough stated that in many states old-age public assistance payments were higher than the "Social Security payments the people have earned by putting their money into the Social Security fund."[110]

    a. Proponents of the amendment mentioned that a 10% increase would alleviate erosion of benefits due to inflation. Opponents of the amendment argued that many persons getting Social Security also received income from other sources. Some opponents of the amendment maintained that it would jeopardize the enactment of the bill. Mr. Yarborough's amendment was rejected by a vote of 32 (6-R, 26-D) to 53 (33-R, 20-D).[111]

b. On August 16, 1958, Mr. Kennedy (D-MA) offered an amendment to increase Social Security benefits by 8% (rather than 7%). The Kennedy-Case amendment was rejected by voice vote.[112]

c. On August 16, 1958, Mr. Morse (D-OR) offered an amendment to increase Social Security benefits by 25%, to provide health insurance, and to make other changes. Mr. Morse's amendment was rejected by voice vote.[113]

d. On August 16, 1958, Mr. Humphrey (D-MN) offered an amendment to provide health insurance (Mr. Morse's amendment was based in part on this Humphrey amendment). Mr. Humphrey withdrew his amendment.[114]

e. On August 16, 1958, Mr. Kennedy offered an amendment for himself and Mr. Smathers (D-NJ) to eliminate the dollar ceiling of $255 on the lump-sum death benefit and restore the 3-to-1 ratio between the death benefit and the regular monthly benefit. The amendment was rejected by voice vote.[115]

f. On August 16, 1958, Mr. Revercomb (R-WV) offered an amendment to provide full Social Security retirement benefits at age 62, for both men and women. Mr. Revercomb's amendment was rejected by voice vote.[116]

g. The Senate passed H.R. 13549 on August 16, 1958, by a vote of 79 (37-R, 42-D) to 0.[117]

3. House Concurrence

On August 19, 1958, the House by a voice vote agreed to the Senate amendments.[118]

J. P.L. 86-778, Social Security Amendments of 1960

H.R. 12580, the Social Security Amendments of 1960, was signed by President Eisenhower on September 13, 1960. Health care for the aged was the primary issue in 1960. At the crux of the debate was the question of whether the federal government should assume major responsibility for the health care of the nation's elderly people, and, if so, whether medical assistance should be provided through the Social Security system or through the public assistance programs (charity approach).

The 1960 amendments provided more federal funds for old-age assistance (OAA) programs so that states could choose to improve or establish medical care services to OAA recipients. In addition, the legislation known as "Kerr-Mills" established a new voluntary program (under jurisdiction of the OAA program) of medical assistance for the aged, under which states received federal funds to help pay for medical care for persons aged 65 and older who were not recipients of OAA but whose income and resources were insufficient to meet their medical expenses.

The 1960 amendments also contained a number of OASDI provisions. The amendments made disability benefits available to workers under age 50; established a new earnings test whereby each dollar of yearly earnings between $1,200 and $1,500 would cause only a 50-cent reduction in benefits with a dollar-for-dollar reduction for earnings above $1,500; liberalized requirements for fully insured status so that to be eligible for benefits a person needed only one quarter of covered work for every three calendar quarters (rather than 1 for every 2 quarters, as under the old law) elapsing after 1950 and before retirement, disability, or death; and raised the survivor benefit of each child to 75% of the parent's PIA.

1. House Action

H.R. 12580 as reported by the Ways and Means Committee contained two medical care provisions for elderly people. The first provision provided the states with additional funding to improve or to establish medical care programs for old-age assistance recipients. The second provision established a new federal-state program (under a new title of the Social Security Act) designed to assist aged persons who were not eligible for public assistance but who were unable to pay their medical bills.

The Ways and Means Committee rejected H.R. 4700, introduced by Mr. Forand (D-RI), which would have provided insurance against the cost of hospital, nursing home, and surgical services for OASDI recipients, by a vote of 17 to 8.[119]

Proponents of H.R. 12580 said that it provided medical assistance for every aged person in any state that implemented a medical assistance program. Mr. Thompson (D-NJ), a supporter of the Forand bill stated that, under H.R. 12580, people would be "denied the opportunity of contributing to their old-age health insurance coverage while employed and would be forced to rely upon charity after their working days were over."[120] He contended further that "even this charity ... is contingent upon the action of the separate states."[121]

32 Gary Sidor

a. The House passed H.R. 12580 on June 23, 1960, by a vote of 381 (137-R, 244-D) to 23 (7-R, 16-D).[122]

2. Senate Action

The Senate deleted the bill's new title, and instead adopted an amendment by Mr. Kerr (D-OK) and Mr. Frear (D-DE) that amended Title I of the Social Security Act to provide medical services for medically needy aged persons.

a. On August 20, 1960, Mr. Javits (R-NY) offered an amendment to provide federal matching grants to states to enable them to give health care to needy persons aged 65 or older. (This proposal was more generous than the provisions—also based on the public assistance, i.e., charity approach—already in the report by the Finance Committee.) On August 23, 1960, Mr. Javits' amendment was rejected by a vote of 28 (28-R) to 67 (5-R, 62-D).[123]

b. Also on August 20, 1960, Mr. Anderson (D-NM) offered an amendment to use Social Security as well as the public assistance program for the aged to provide health care to the elderly. On August 23, 1960, Mr. Anderson's amendment was rejected by a vote of 44 (1-R, 43-D) to 51 (32-R, 19-D).[124]

c. On August 23, 1960, the Senate passed by voice vote Mr. Byrd's (D-WV) amendment to permit men to retire at age 62 with actuarially reduced benefits. (The amendment was later dropped in conference.)[125]

d. The Senate passed H.R. 12580 on August 23, 1960, by a vote of 91 (31-R, 60-D) to 2 (1-R, 1-D).[126]

3. Conference Action

The conferees agreed to the medical care provisions in the Senate-passed bill (i.e., no new title for a program for aged persons not eligible for OAA benefits). The medical provisions became known as the Kerr-Mills program, named for Senator Robert Kerr (D-OK) and House Ways and Means Committee Chairman Wilbur Mills (D-AR).

a. The House agreed to the conference report on August 26, 1960, by a vote of 369 (132-R, 237-D) to 17 (8-R, 9-D).[127]

b. The Senate agreed to the conference report on August 29, 1960, by a vote of 74 (31-R, 43-D) to 11 (1-R, 10-D).[128]

K. P.L. 87-64, Social Security Amendments of 1961

H.R. 6027, the Social Security Amendments of 1961, was signed into law on June 30, 1961, by President Kennedy. In general, the amendments made many of the changes in the Social Security program recommended by President Kennedy in his February 2, 1961, message to Congress, in which he outlined a program to restore momentum to the national economy.[129] The amendments raised the minimum benefit to $40 per month; permitted men to retire at age 62, instead of 65, with actuarially reduced benefits; liberalized the insured status requirement so that, subject to the 6-quarter minimum and the 40-quarter maximum, an individual was fully insured if he had one quarter of coverage for every calendar year that elapsed between January 1, 1951, or age 21, whichever was later, and the year before he died, became disabled, or reached retirement age; increased benefits to a surviving aged widow, widower, or dependent parent of an insured deceased worker from 75 to 82.5% of the benefit the worker would have been entitled to if alive; changed the earnings test so that an aged recipient had no benefits withheld for the first $1,200 a year of earnings, $1 withheld for each $2 earned between $1,200 and $1,700, and a dollar-for-dollar reduction of earnings above $1,700; and raised the employer and employee tax rates by 0.125% and the self-employed tax rate by 0.1875%.[130]

1. House Action

In the House, the principal point of dissension was the provision in H.R. 6027 that lowered the eligibility age for men from 65 to 62. Several Republicans opposed the provision on the basis that it would likely start a trend toward "compulsory retirement" at age 62. Speaking for himself and most of the minority committee members, Mr. Curtis (R-MO) stated, "The reason [we are] against the age 62 [provision] is this: our older people are having a hard enough time now to stay in the labor market. This provides further incentive to drive them out."[131]

a. On April 20, 1961, Mr. Curtis made a motion to recommit H.R. 6027[132] and substitute a measure that cut out the provisions for lowering the first eligibility age for men, increased benefits for widows, and raised the minimum benefit from $33 to $40. The motion was rejected by voice vote.[133] Note that the provisions raising the minimum benefit and increasing benefits for widows were already in H.R. 6027 as reported out of committee.

b. The House passed H.R. 6027 on April 20, 1961, by a vote of 400 (149-R, 251-D) to 14 (14-R).[134]

2. Senate Action

In the Senate, debate focused on Mr. Cotton's (R-NH) amendment made on June 26, 1961, to increase the earnings test limit to $1,800 a year.[135] Mr. Kerr (D-OK) said that Mr. Cotton's amendment failed to provide increased OASDI taxes to pay for the additional $427 million-$615 million that would be paid out each year under the proposed amendment.[136] Mr. Kerr stated that "an amendment which would result in the impairment of the fiscal integrity of the fund should not be pressed."[137]

a. Mr. Hartke (D-IN) offered a substitute amendment that provided a slightly less generous new earnings test limit ($1,700). The substitute amendment was passed June 26, 1961, by a vote of 59 (3-R, 56-D) to 30 (30-R).[138] Provisions to finance this change were agreed to by unanimous-consent.[139]
b. On June 26, 1961, Mr. Hartke's amendment to broaden the definition of disability was rejected by voice vote.[140]
c. The Senate passed H.R. 6027 90 (33-R, 57-D) to 0 on June 26, 1961.[141]

3. Conference Action

Both chambers cleared the conference report by voice votes June 29, 1961.[142]

L. Proposed Social Security Amendments of 1964

H.R. 11865, the *proposed* Social Security Amendments of 1964, was passed by both the House and the Senate but the conference committee could not reach agreement, adjourning on October 3, 1964, without making any recommendations.

The proposed Social Security Amendments of 1964 as passed by the House contained a 5% across-the-board Social Security benefit increase; extended the child's benefit to age 22 if he or she were in school; allowed widows to retire at age 60, with actuarially reduced benefits; provided limited benefits to persons aged 72 and over who had some Social Security coverage but not enough to meet the minimum requirements of existing law; and

Social Security: Major Decisions in the House and Senate Since 1935   35

extended Social Security coverage to groups of persons who previously had been excluded. The House-passed bill contained no provision relating to hospital insurance for the aged.

The proposed Social Security Amendments of 1964 as passed by the Senate contained a hospital insurance program, the so-called King-Anderson bill; increased benefits: raised the earnings base; liberalized the earnings test; changed the eligibility requirements for the blind; and permitted religious groups to reject Social Security coverage if they had religious objections to social insurance).

1. House Action

H.R. 11865, the proposed Social Security Amendments of 1964, was reported out of the Ways and Means Committee on July 7, 1964. The bill was debated under a rule that permitted only committee amendments. No amendments were offered.

a.   On July 29, 1964, the House passed H.R. 11865 by a vote of 388 to 8.[143]

2. Senate Action

The Finance Committee approved H.R. 11865 on August 21, 1964. The committee rejected several amendments that would have created a hospital insurance program for the aged through the Social Security program.

a.   On August 31, 1964, Mr. Gore (D-TN) offered an amendment to Mr. Long's (D-LA) amendment[144] to increase the proposed across-the-board benefit increase to 7% (instead of the proposed 5% increase) and liberalized the earnings test.[145] Mr. Gore's amendment included the 1963 King (D-CA)-Anderson (D-NM) bill (H.R. 3920/S. 880), that would have provided hospital insurance benefits for the aged under the Social Security program.

b.   On September 2, 1964, the Gore amendment passed by a vote of 49 to 44.[146]

c.   On September 3, 1964, the Senate passed H.R. 11865 by a vote of 60 to 28.[147]

3. Conference Action

The conference committee on H.R. 11865 could not reach agreement. The conferees from the Senate voted 4 to 3 to insist on including the hospital

36 Gary Sidor

insurance provisions; the conferees from the House, by a 3 to 2 vote, refused to accept such provisions.[148] The conference committee adjourned on October 2, 1964.

M. P.L. 89-97, Social Security Amendments of 1965

H.R. 6675, the Social Security Amendments of 1965, was signed into law on July 30, 1965, by President Johnson. Although a federally operated health insurance program covering the entire nation was considered by the Roosevelt Administration in 1935, it was not explicitly endorsed until January 1945, when President Roosevelt's budget message called for an "extended Social Security including medical care." Such a plan was submitted to Congress by President Truman in November 1945, but neither chamber acted on the proposal, in large part due to strong opposition by the AMA. The controversy surrounding the establishment of a federal health insurance program for the aged was finally ended by the 1965 amendments (H.R. 6675),[149] which established a basic two-part health insurance program called Medicare (Title XVIII of the Social Security Act). The costs of hospitalization and related care would be met in part by a compulsory program of Hospital Insurance (HI, part A), financed by a separate payroll tax. The program would serve recipients of the Social Security and railroad retirement programs, age 65 and older. A voluntary Supplementary Medical Insurance (SMI) plan (Part B) would help pay doctor bills and related services, for all persons age 65 and older, financed through monthly premiums paid by the recipient and a matching federal payment from general revenues.

The amendments also provided a 7% across-the-board increase in OASDI benefits, extended compulsory self-employment coverage to doctors, made child's benefits available through age 21 if the child attended school full time (under prior law, they were available only through age 17), permitted widows to receive actuarially reduced benefits at age 60 rather than age 62, provided benefits to divorced wives and widows under certain conditions, increased the earnings test amount to $1,500 with $1 withheld for every $2 earned up to $2,700, and provided that an insured worker would be eligible for disability benefits if his or her disability was expected to end in death or to last for 12 consecutive months, instead of indefinitely. The 1965 amendments also increased the payroll tax rate and the taxable wage base. In addition, P.L. 89-97 reduced the number of quarters of work necessary for persons age 72 or over to have insured status (from 6 quarters to 3 quarters for a worker and

Social Security: Major Decisions in the House and Senate Since 1935   37

from 6 quarters to 3 quarters for a wife who reached age 72 in or before 1966, to 4 quarters for a wife who turned 72 in 1967, and to 5 quarters for a wife who attained age 72 in 1968).

Further, a new federal-state medical assistance program established under Title XIX of the Social Security Act replaced the Kerr-Mills law (medical assistance for the aged that was enacted in 1960). The program was to be administered by the states, with federal matching funds. The new Medicaid program was available to all people receiving assistance under the public assistance titles (Title I, Title IV, Title X, and Title XIV) and to people who were able to provide for their own maintenance but whose income and resources were insufficient to meet their medical costs.

1. House Action

A federal hospital insurance program, or "Medicare," had been passed only once by the Senate, in 1964, and then by a narrow margin. It had never been approved by the Ways and Means Committee and thus had not been put to a House vote. The 1964 congressional elections, however, brought 42 new Northern Democrats into the House, almost all of them Medicare supporters.[150]

The Ways and Means Committee began holding executive sessions on H.R. 1, a bill to establish a social insurance program for hospital and related care for the aged, on January 27, 1965. The committee reported H.R. 6675 March 29, 1965, with all 17 Democrats favoring the bill and all 8 Republicans opposing it.

House floor debate centered on the Medicare proposal. Supporters said it was long overdue. Critics opposed its compulsory nature, argued that it would be financed by a "regressive" payroll tax, and said it would endanger the Social Security cash benefit program. Republican spokesmen instead wanted a voluntary health plan (as opposed to a mandatory social insurance approach) with a Medicaid-like program underpinning it to provide medical assistance for the needy aged.

a. On April 8, 1965, the House rejected Mr. Byrnes' (R-WI) motion to recommit H.R. 6675 to the Ways and Means Committee with instructions to substitute the text of H.R. 7057, a bill that Mr. Byrnes had introduced a week earlier. H.R. 7057 was not offered as an amendment because the rule did not permit such action. H.R. 7057 provided for all hospitalization, nursing home, medical and surgical care to be financed through a voluntary system with payment split between the patient and general revenues, rather than from a tax on the payrolls of employers. The motion to recommit was rejected by a vote of 191 (128-R, 63-D) to 236 (10-R, 226-D).[151]

b. On April 8, 1965, the House passed H.R. 6675 by a vote of 313 (65-R, 248-D) to 115 (73-R, 42-D).[152]

2. Senate Action

On June 30, 1965, the Finance Committee reported its version of H.R. 6675. The committee approved the bill by a vote of 12 (2-R, 10-D) to 5 (4-R, 1-D).

a. On July 7 and 8, 1965, three moves to expand H.R. 6675 were rejected. Mr. Ribicoff's (D-CT) amendment to remove all time limits on length of hospital stays under Medicare was rejected by a vote of 39 (13-R, 26-D) to 43 (12-R, 31-D).[153] Mr. Miller's (R-IA) amendment to provide for an automatic 3% increase in Social Security pensions whenever a 3% increase occurred in the "retail" price index was rejected by a vote of 21 (15-R, 6-D) to 64 (9-R, 55-D).[154] Mr. Prouty's (R-VT) amendment to provide benefit increases ranging from 75% in the low-income brackets to 7% in the upper-income brackets was rejected by a vote of 12 (10-R, 2-D) to 79 (18-R, 61-D).[155] In addition, Mr. Curtis' (R-NE) amendment to provide that the Medicare patient pay a deductible based on ability to pay was rejected by a vote of 41 (25-R, 16-D) to 51 (4-R, 47-D).[156]

b. On July 7, 1965, Mr. Byrd's (D-WV) amendment to lower the age at which workers could receive Social Security benefits to 60 (rather than age 62, the existing minimum) was agreed to by voice vote.[157]

c. On July 8, 1965, Mr. Kennedy's (D-NY) amendment to prohibit federal payments to any hospital not meeting the standards required by the state or local government was passed by voice vote.[158]

d. On July 9, 1965, Mr. Hartke's (D-IN) amendment to liberalize the definition of blindness under the Social Security program, provide benefits to blind workers with at least 6 quarters of Social Security coverage, and permit blind workers to receive benefits regardless of other earnings was passed by a vote of 78 (28-R, 50-D) to 11 (11-D).[159]

e. On July 9, 1965, Mr. Hartke's amendment to eliminate the time limit on hospital care under the proposed program was agreed to by voice vote.[160]

f. On July 9, 1965, Mr. Smathers'(D-FL) amendment to raise payroll taxes to finance the benefits provided in floor amendments passed by a voice vote.[161]

g. On July 9, 1965, Mr. Curtis (R-NE) offered an amendment to strike Medicare, parts A and B, from the bill. The amendment was rejected by a vote of 26 (18-R, 8-D) to 64 (11-R, 53-D).[162] Mr. Curtis also reintroduced, in a slightly different form, his amendment to provide a deductible based on the Medicare patient's ability to pay. This amendment, too, was rejected by a vote of 40 to 52.[163] In addition, Mr. Curtis moved to recommit H.R. 6675 with instructions to strike out the portions related to Medicare and substitute a plan patterned after the health insurance program used by retired federal employees, but financed from current premiums. The motion to recommit H.R. 6675 was rejected by a vote of 26 (18-R, 8-D) to 63 (10-R, 53-D).[164]

h. H.R. 6675 was passed by the Senate on July 9, 1965, by a vote of 68 (13-R, 55-D) to 21 (14-R, 7-D).[165]

3. Conference Action

a. On July 27, 1965, the House adopted the conference report by a vote of 307 (70-R, 237-D) to 116 (68-R, 48-D).[166]

b. On July 28, 1965, the Senate adopted the conference report by a vote of 70 (13-R, 57-D) to 24 (17-R, 7-D).[167]

N. P.L. 89-368, Tax Adjustment Act of 1966

H.R. 12752, signed by President Johnson on March 15, 1966, raised income taxes to help pay for the Vietnam War. In addition, it extended OASI benefits of $35 per month to persons over age 71 who were not covered, but with the benefit reduced by the amount of payments received under government pension plans, veteran's or civil service pensions, teacher's retirement pension plans, or welfare programs.

1. House Action

a. The House passed H.R. 12752, the Tax Adjustment Act of 1966, by a vote of 246 (46-R, 200-D) to 146 (88-R, 58-D).[168] H.R. 12752, as passed by the House, did not contain any Social Security provisions.

2. Senate Action

During the floor debate on H.R. 12752, Mr. Prouty (R-VT) offered an amendment to extend a minimum Social Security payment of $44 a month to all persons age 70 or older who were not then eligible for benefits (an estimated 1.8 million persons at a cost of $760 million in FY1967).[169]

    a. On March 8, 1966, Mr. Long (D-LA) moved to table the Prouty amendment but his motion was rejected by a vote of 37 (1-R, 36-D) to 51 (30-R, 21-D).[170]

    b. On March 8, 1966, the Senate passed the Prouty amendment by a vote of 45 (21-R, 24-D) to 40 (9-R, 31-D);[171] and adopted by a vote of 44 (25-R, 19-D) to 43 (6-R, 37-D) a motion by Mr. Prouty to table Mr. Mansfield's (D-MT) motion to reconsider the vote on passage of the amendment.[172]

    c. On March 9, 1966, the Senate passed the Tax Adjustment Act of 1966 by a vote of 79 (24-R, 55-D) to 9 (4-R, 5-D).[173]

3. Conference Action

On March 10, 1966, the conferees included the Prouty amendment in the final version of H.R. 12752, but changed the monthly benefit to $35.

    a. On March 15, 1966, the House adopted the conference report on H.R. 12752 by a vote of 288 (68-R, 220-D) to 102 (59-R, 43-D).[174]

    b. On March 15, 1966, the Senate adopted the conference report on H.R. 12752 by a vote of 72 (23-R, 49-D) to 5 (4-R, I-D).[175]

O. P.L. 90-248, Social Security Amendments of 1967 (H.R. 12080)

H.R. 12080, the Social Security Amendments of 1967, was signed by President Johnson on January 2, 1968. The amendments provided a 13% across-the-board increase in benefits; raised the taxable wage base from $6,600 to $7,800; increased the payroll tax rate from 4.4% on employers and employees to 4.8% in 1969; raised the minimum benefit from $44 to $55 per month; raised the earnings test limit to $1,680 a year instead of $1,500 (recipient lost $1 for every $2 earned between $1,680 and $2,880, and lost dollar-for-dollar for earnings above $2,880); added benefits for disabled widows and widowers at age 50, with a stricter definition of disability;

Social Security: Major Decisions in the House and Senate Since 1935 41

liberalized the definition of blindness for disability payments; and clarified the definition of disability.

President Johnson had called for a 15% across-the-board increase in OASDI benefits and numerous other changes in the Social SecurityAct. The proposals were embodied in H.R. 5710, introduced in the House on February 20, 1967, by the Committee on Ways and Means chairman, Wilbur Mills (D-AR).

1. House Action

The Ways and Means Committee held hearings on the Administration's bill (H.R. 5710) in March and April, 1967. On August 7, 1967, it reported a new bill, H.R. 12080, that included most of the Administration's Social Security proposals, notably a provision that raised the earnings test limit from $1,500 to $1,680.[176]

a. On August 17, 1967, Mr. Utt (R-CA) moved to recommit H.R. 12080. Mr. Utt's motion was rejected by voice vote.[177]

b. On August 17, 1967, the House passed H.R. 12080 by a roll call vote of 416 (182-R, 234-D) to 3 (1-R, 2-D).[178] The bill was debated under a closed rule prohibiting floor amendments.

2. Senate Action

On November 14, 1967, the Senate Finance Committee reported a heavily-amended bill that contained several of the OASDI provisions as they had been recommended by the Administration rather than as they had been modified by the House. The Senate bill provided a 15% across-the-board Social Security increase, in contrast to the 12.5% increase in the House bill.

a. On November 17, 1967, Mr. Prouty (R-VT) offered an amendment to finance the higher benefits out of general revenues rather than Social Security taxes. The amendment was rejected by a vote of 6 (3-R, 3-D) to 62 (23-R, 39-D).[179]

b. On November 17, 1967, Mr. Metcalf (D-MT) offered an amendment to delete from H.R. 12080 a more stringent definition of disability. The Metcalf amendment was passed by a vote of 34 (6-R, 28-D) to 20 (16-R, 4-D).[180]

c. On November 21, 1967, Mr. Williams (R-DE) offered an amendment to implement the Finance Committee's recommended payroll tax increase in January 1968 (before the general election) rather than in

January 1969. The amendment was defeated by a vote of 27 (22-R, 5-D) to 49 (4-R, 45-D).[181]

d. On November 21, 1967, the Senate, by a vote of 22 (17-R, 5-D) to 58 (9-R, 49-D), rejected a Republican proposal offered by Mr. Curtis (R-NE) and Mr. Williams (R-DE) substituting the 12.5% OASDI benefit increase and financing plan contained in the House bill for the 15% benefit increase and financing plan recommended by the Finance Committee.[182]

e. On November 21, 1967, Mr. Bayh (D-IN) offered an amendment to raise the earnings test limit from $1,680 to $2,400. Mr. Bayh's amendment passed by a vote of 50 (14-R, 36-D) to 23 (10-R, 13-D).[183]

f. The Senate passed H.R. 12080 on November 22, 1967, by a 78 (23 R, 55-D) to 6 (4-R, 2-D) roll call vote.[184]

3. Conference Action

The conference report on H.R. 12080 was filed on December 11, 1967. All of the major Senate floor amendments were dropped from the bill. The conferees split the difference between many of the other provisions.

a. The House adopted the conference report on December 13, 1967, by a vote of 390 (167-R, 223-D) to 3 (1-R, 2-D).[185]

b. The Senate adopted the conference report on December 15, 1967, by a vote of 62 (26-R, 36-D) to 14 (3-R, 11-D).[186]

P. P.L. 91-172, The Tax Reform Act of 1969

H.R. 13270, the Tax ReformAct of 1969, was signed by President Nixon on December 30, 1969. The new law included a 15% increase in Social Security benefits beginning in January 1, 1970.

1. House Action

On August 7, 1969, the House passed H.R. 13270 by a vote of 395 (176-R, 219-D) to 30 (10-R, 20-D).[187] The bill did not contain any Social Security provisions.

2. Senate Action

On December 5, 1969, Mr. Long (D-LA) offered an amendment to raise basic Social Security benefits by 15% beginning in January 1970.

a. Mr. Long's amendment was passed by a vote of 73 (23-R, 50-D) to 14 (14-R).[188]

b. A Byrd (D-WV)-Mansfield (D-MT) amendment to increase the minimum benefit to $100 for single persons and to $150 for couples and to increase the taxable wage base from $7,800 to $12,000 beginning in 1973 was passed December 5, 1969, by a vote of 48 (8-R, 40-D) to 41 (28-R, 13-D).[189]

c. On December 5, 1969, Mr. Williams (R-DE) offered a substitute amendment to provide a 10%, rather than a 15%, benefit increase. The substitute amendment was rejected by a vote of 34 (33-R, 1-D) to 56 (5-R, 51-D).[190]

d. On December 11, 1969, the Senate passed H.R. 13270 by a vote of 69 (18-R, 51-D) to 22 (20-R, 2-D).[191]

3. Conference Action

The conferees agreed to increase Social Security benefits by 15%, effective January 1, 1970. The House had not included the increase in H.R. 13270 but had approved an identical provision in another bill, H.R. 15095. The conferees dropped the other provisions that were added on the Senate floor.

a. On December 22, 1969, the House adopted the conference report on the Tax Reform Act, H.R. 13270, by a vote of 381 (169-R, 212-D) to 2 (2-R).[192]

b. On December 22, 1969, the Senate adopted H.R. 13270 by a vote of 71 (25-R, 46-D) to 6 (6-R).[193]

Q. P.L. 92-5, Public Debt Limit Increase; Social Security Amendments

President Nixon signed H.R. 4690 on March 17, 1971. It provided a 10% across-the-board increase in OASDI benefits, retroactive to January 1, 1971; raised the minimum benefit from $64 to $70.40 per month; increased the taxable wage base from $7,800 to $9,000 effective January 1, 1972; increased the OASDI tax rates on employers and employees to 5.15% each beginning in

1976 (from 5% scheduled to take effect in 1973 under prior law); and provided a 5% increase in special benefits payable to individuals age 72 and older who were not insured for regular benefits, retroactive to January 1, 1971.

1. House Action

In 1970, a comprehensive Social Security bill (H.R. 17550) was passed by the House by a vote of 344 (166-R, 178-D) to 32 (32-D).[194] H.R. 17550 increased benefits by 5%, provided for automatic benefit increases with rises in the cost of living, and made other changes in the OASDI and Medicare programs.

2. Senate Action

In the Senate, H.R. 17550 became a conglomerate bill containing import quotas and welfare provisions as well. On December 29, 1970, the Senate separated Social Security changes from the rest of the bill. H.R. 17550, with provisions raising benefits 10%, providing a $100 minimum benefit, raising the taxable wage base from $7,800 to $9,000, and making changes in the Medicare and Medicaid programs, was passed by the Senate on December 29, 1970, by a vote of 81 (35-R, 46-D) to 0.[195] However, the House never agreed to a conference.[196]

Mr. Long (D-LA), chairman of the Finance Committee and floor manager of H.R. 4690, said that he had asked the House to take immediate action to raise Social Security benefits and as the House had not responded, he was offering a benefit increase as an amendment to H.R. 4690, a bill to increase the debt ceiling.[197]

a. On March 12, 1971, Mr. Long's amendment to provide a 10% increase in Social Security payments, a $100 minimum benefit, increases in earnings limitations, and other changes passed by a vote of 82 (38-R, 44-D) to 0.[198]
b. The Senate, on March 12, 1971, passed H.R. 4690, after approving several Social Security changes, including the benefit increase proposed by Mr. Long, by a vote of 80 (37-R, 43-D) to 0.[199]

3. Conference Action

Conferees accepted the Senate's 10% benefit increase but reduced the $100 minimum benefit to $70.40 and made several other modifications.

Social Security: Major Decisions in the House and Senate Since 1935   45

a. On March 16, 1971, the House adopted the conference report by a vote of 360 (150-R, 210-D) to 3 (3-R).[200]
b. On March 16, 1971, the Senate adopted the report by a vote of 76 (37-R, 39-D) to 0.[201]

R. P.L. 92-336, Public Debt Limit; Disaster losses; Social Security Act Amendments

President Nixon signed H.R. 15390, a bill to extend the limit on the public debt, on July 1, 1972. At the beginning of the year, the President included a number of Social Security proposals, along with a controversial welfare reform plan, in H.R. 1. Congress at midyear used a more promising vehicle to pass a separate 20% increase in Social Security benefits. The increase was added in the Senate to a House-passed bill that raised the debt limit (H.R. 15390). The bill also provided for future automatic increases in Social Security benefits when the consumer price index (CPI) rose by 3% or more. To finance the increase, the taxable wage base was raised from $9,000 to $10,800 in 1973 and to $12,000 in 1974, with automatic adjustment thereafter. The *Congressional Quarterly Almanac* reported that:

> Backers of the Social Security benefits package decided to attach it to the debt increase bill for two reasons: (1) President Nixon, who opposed a 20% increase as inflationary, would be unlikely to veto a bill that contained a debt limit increase, and (2) H.R. 1, the bill under which a benefit increase was then being considered, faced an uncertain future because of controversy over its welfare provisions.[202]

1. House Action
a. On June 22, 1971, the House had passed H.R. 1 (See P.L. 92-603, below) which included provision for a general benefit increase of 5%.
b. On February 23, 1972, Mr. Mills (D-AR), chairman of the Ways and Means Committee, introduced H.R. 13320, which provided for an immediate benefit increase of 20%.[203]
c. On June 27, 1972, the House passed H.R. 15390, providing only for an increase in the debt ceiling, by a vote of 211 to 168.[204]

2. Senate Action

    a. On June 29, 1972, Mr. Aiken (R-VT) offered an amendment to the Church amendment [See (c) below] to increase Social Security benefits by 30%. Following Mr. Long's (D-LA) motion, Mr. Aiken's amendment was tabled by a vote of 71 (31-R, 40-D) to 18 (8-R, 10-D).[205]

    b. On June 30, 1972, an amendment by Mr. Bennett (R-UT) to increase Social Security benefits by 10% instead of 20% was rejected by the Senate by a vote of 20 (17-R, 3-D) to 66 (21-R, 45-D).[206]

    c. On June 30, 1972, Mr. Church's (D-ID) amendment calling for a 20% benefit increase and the automatic adjustment of benefits and the taxable wage base in the future was adopted by the Senate by a vote of 82 (34-R, 48-D) to 4 (4-R).[207] The amendment made benefit increases automatic whenever the consumer price index rose more than 3% in any calendar year.

    d. On June 30, 1972, the Senate passed H.R. 15390 by a vote of 78 (36-R, 42-D) to 3 (1-R, 2-D). H.R. 15390 was then sent back to the House.[208]

3. House Response to Senate Amendment

The House sent the debt ceiling bill to the conference committee on June 30, 1972, without accepting the Senate-passed benefit increase. Immediate congressional action was necessary because the debt limit was to revert automatically to $400 billion (from the existing $450 billion) at midnight on June 30, 1972.

4. Conference Action

On June 30, 1972, the conferees informally accepted the Senate-passed version of H.R. 15390. Under House rules, however, House conferees could not agree to non-germane amendments added by the Senate. Thus, the conference report was reported back to the House in disagreement.[209]

    a. On June 30, 1972, Mr. Byrnes (R-WI) called the proposed 20% increase "irresponsible" and moved that the House concur with the Senate amendment but with the benefit increase limited to 10%. Mr. Byrnes' motion was rejected by a vote of 83 (63-R, 20-D) to 253 (73-R, 180-D).[210]

    b. On June 30, 1972, Mr. Mills'(D-AR) motion that the House concur with the Senate-passed amendment granting a 20% Social Security

Social Security: Major Decisions in the House and Senate Since 1935   47

benefit increase and annual automatic cost-of-living adjustments (COLAs) was accepted by a vote of 302 (108-R, 194-D) to 35 (28-R, 7-D).[211]

S. P.L. 92-603, Social Security Amendments of 1972

H.R. 1, the Social Security Amendments of 1972, was signed into law on October 30, 1972, by President Nixon. During 1969-72, Congress raised OASDI benefits 3 times. In 1969, benefits were raised by 15%; in 1971, by 10%, and by 20% in 1972 (P.L. 92-336). P.L. 92-336 also provided for future automatic benefit increases, called cost of living adjustments (COLAs), starting in January 1975, whenever the consumer price index rose more than 3% in a year. These benefit increases were amendments to bills dealing with other subjects. President Nixon had requested a number of other Social Security liberalizations in 1969, but those proposals were entangled with his controversial welfare reform plan. It was not until 1972, when H.R. 1 became P.L. 92-603, that the requested Social Security recommendations became law.[212]

The 1972 amendments (H.R. 1) increased benefits for widows and widowers; raised the earnings limit from $1,680 to $2,100 with automatic adjustment to average wages thereafter (earnings above $2,100 benefits were reduced dollar-for-dollar without limit); reduced the waiting period for disability benefits from six to five months; extended Medicare protection to disabled recipients who had received benefits for at least two years; and provided a special minimum benefit of up to $170 a month for those who had worked many years, but at low earnings. In addition, OASDHI tax rate-increases scheduled for the periods 1973-1977, 1978-1980, 1981-1985, 1986-1992, 1993-1997, 1998-2010, and 2011 and years thereafter, were further raised.[213]

H.R. 1 also contained the President's controversial Family Assistance Plan. The bill remained in the Senate for more than a year because of controversy over welfare reform. The Senate finally approved H.R. 1 with a provision for tests of rival welfare plans, but in conference all family welfare provisions were dropped. In addition, the final version of H.R. 1 contained provisions federalizing and consolidating adult public assistance programs for needy aged, blind, and disabled persons in a new "Supplemental Security Income" (SSI) program.

1. House Action

Most of the debate on H.R. 1 dealt with the family welfare provisions, with little debate on the OASDI and Medicare provisions.

a. H.R. 1 was passed by the House on June 22, 1971, by a vote of 288 (112-R, 176-D) to 132 (64-R, 68-D).[214]

2. Senate Action

a. On September 27, 1972, Mr. Mansfield (D-MT) offered an amendment to increase the earnings test limit from $1,680 to $3,000. Mr. Mansfield's amendment was agreed to by a vote of 76 (32-R, 44-D) to 5 (4-R, 1-D).[215]

b. On September 28, 1972, Mr. Percy's (R-IL) amendment to require the Secretary of the Department of Health, Education, and Welfare to review the Social Security earnings test, and report to Congress on the feasibility of eliminating it, was accepted by voice vote.[216]

c. On September 29, 1972, Mr. Long (D-LA) offered an amendment to provide a federal Supplemental Security Income (SSI) program for needy aged, blind, or disabled persons (in place of the existing State adult assistance programs). The amendment was passed by a vote of 75 (32-R, 43-D) to 0.[217]

d On September 29, 1972, the Finance Committee's amendment to guarantee every person who worked in employment covered under the Social Security program for at least 30 years a minimum monthly benefit of $200 ($300 for a couple) passed by a vote of 73 (30-R, 43-D) to 0.[218]

e. On September 30, 1972, Mr. Byrd's (D-WV) amendment to lower to 60 the age at which reduced Social Security benefits could be received and to 55 the age at which a woman could receive reduced widow's benefits was agreed to by a vote of 29 (10-R, 19-D) to 25 (12-R, 13-D).[219]

f. On September 27, 1972, Mr. Goldwater (R-AZ) offered an amendment to repeal the earnings limitation for all Social Security recipients age 65 and over. The amendment was rejected by voice vote.[220]

g. H.R. 1 passed the Senate on October 5, 1972, by a vote of 68 (33-R, 35-D) to 5 (1-R, 4-D).[221]

Social Security: Major Decisions in the House and Senate Since 1935   49

3. Conference Action

    a. On October 17, 1972, the House adopted the conference report on H.R. 1 by a vote of 305 (129-R, 176-D) to 1 (1-D).[222]

    b. On October 17, 1972, the Senate adopted the conference report on H.R. 1 by a vote of 61 (24-R, 37-D) to 0.[223]

T. P.L. 93-233, Social Security Benefits Increase

A two-step 11% benefit increase became law when President Nixon signed H.R. 11333 on December, 31, 1973. This increase was in lieu of a 5.9% increase scheduled by legislation, P.L. 93-66, that had been enacted in July 1973.[224] In passing H.R. 11333, congressional sentiment was that the earlier increase was inadequate to offset recent rapid increases in inflation.

P.L. 93-233 increased benefits by 7% in March 1974 and by another 4% in June 1974. To finance the increases, the Social Security taxable wage base was raised from $12,600 to $13,200 in January 1974. In addition, the automatic COLA mechanism was revised. Under P.L. 93-233, the COLA was to be based on the rise in the CPI from the first quarter of one year to the first quarter of the next year, rather than second quarter to second quarter, with benefit increases starting in June 1975 rather than in January. As a result, the increases would appear in checks received in July, creating only a three-month lag from the close of the measuring period (i.e., the first quarter) rather than the seven-month lag under the prior mechanism.

1. House Action

With a rule allowing only one floor amendment (pertaining to SSI), the House passed H.R. 11333 on November 15, 1973.[225]

The November 14-15 debate on H.R. 11333 was devoted to the need for a quick cost-of-living Social Security benefit increase and to questions about the fiscal soundness of the Social Security trust funds.[226] H.R. 11333 as reported by the Ways and Means Committee recommended a two-step 11% Social Security benefit increase in 1974, accelerated SSI benefit increases, and payroll tax increases.

    a. On November 15, 1973, the House passed H.R. 11333 by a vote of 391 (168-R, 223-D) to 20 (15-R, 5-D).[227]

2. Senate Action

The Senate Finance Committee approved a number of provisions affecting Social Security, including an initial 7% benefit increase effective upon enactment and a further 4% increase in June 1974. Rather than acting on H.R. 11333, the Senate attached its Social Security amendments to H.R. 3153, a Social Security bill passed by the House on April 2, 1973. (H.R. 3153 made a number of technical and conforming amendments to the Social SecurityAct that had been omitted in drafting the conference agreement on H.R. 1, which became P.L. 92-603.) The Senate debated H.R. 3153 for three days and adopted 38 amendments.

a. On November 29, 1973, Mr. Byrd (D-WV) introduced an amendment that reduced to 55 the age at which a woman could claim a Social Security widow's benefit. Under existing law, a widow could elect to retire at 60 with reduced benefits. Mr. Byrd said that his amendment would help widows between the ages of 55 and 60, who would be unlikely and perhaps unable to establish a new career, or to reactivate an old one. Terming the Byrd amendment "inequitable," Mr. Curtis (R-NE) objected that it would be unjust to reduce the eligibility age for widows "who have not worked under covered employment" while keeping the existing requirement at age 62 for "women who have had to work all their lives and will have to work until they are of retirement age." Mr. Byrd's amendment was adopted by a vote of 74 (28-R, 46-D) to 13 (9-R, 4-D).[228]

b. Mr. Byrd introduced a second amendment that increased the earnings test limit from $2,400 to $3,000 and lowered from 72 to 70 the age at which the earnings limit would no longer apply. The amendment was accepted November 29, 1973, by a vote of 83 (33-R, 50-D) to 1 (1-R).[229]

c. On November 29, 1973, Mr. Hartke's (D-IN) amendment making blind persons eligible for disability benefits after working 18 months in covered employment was adopted by voice vote. (Ordinarily a disabled person had to work in 20 out of the last 40 quarters to be eligible.)

d. On November 30, 1973, the Senate passed H.R. 3153 by a vote of 66 (24-R, 42-D) to 8 (6-R, 2-D).[230]

3. Conference Action

After the Senate passed H.R. 3153, it asked the House for a conference, but the House appointed conferees with only two days before the end of the session. The conferees did not act on H.R. 3153. Instead, they agreed to work on revisions to H.R. 11333, the House-passed Social Security bill, on which the Senate had never acted.[231]

As part of a compromise reached on December 20, the House conferees agreed to hold a further conference on H.R. 3153 in 1974 to consider additional Senate amendments, but the conference never took place.

The conference report on H.R. 11333 included a two-step 11% increase in benefits, effective March 1974 and June 1974, raised the wage base to $13,200 in 1974, and increased the initial federal SSI benefit level.

a. The Senate passed H.R. 11333 with the amendments agreed to in conference on December 21, 1973, by a vote of 64 to 0.[232]
b. The House, on December 21, 1973, concurred in passing the bill by a vote of 301 (123-R, 178-D) to 13 (10-R, 3-D).[233]

U. P.L. 95-216. The Social Security Amendments of 1977

H.R. 9346, the Social Security Amendments of 1977, was signed by President Carter on December 20, 1977. H.R. 9346 was passed to meet major Social Security financing problems that emerged in the mid-1970s. The *Congressional Quarterly Almanac* says that the main cause of the immediate financial problems was the "combination of rapid inflation and a recession, which together raised Social Security benefit costs and reduced tax receipts."[234] In addition to fixing short-run problems, the amendments sought to eliminate the medium-range deficit (over the next 25 years) and to reduce the projected long-range deficit (next 75 years) from more than 8% of taxable payroll to less than 1.5%. The basic approach was to (1) handle the short-term financing problem either through increased payroll taxes or infusions from the general fund; and (2) reduce and possibly eliminate the projected long-run deficit by modifying the benefit formula to stabilize replacement rates.

Neither house of Congress gave much attention to an Administration proposal to authorize use of general revenues for Social Security during periods of high unemployment (the so-called "counter cyclical" use of general revenues). Instead, to meet the short-run problem the new law mostly increased Social Security tax rates and the taxable earnings base and somewhat reduced expenditures. The final bill contained "decoupling" procedures, which also had been supported by the Ford Administration, for correcting a basic flaw in the benefit computation formula, and thereby largely reduced the long-run problem. P.L. 95-216 also liberalized the earnings test by providing a five-step ad hoc increase in the earnings limits for recipients age 65 and over (the limit for persons under age 65 continued to be adjusted only for increases in average wages after 1978); eliminated the earnings test for recipients aged 70 and over (reduced from age 72), beginning in 1982; reduced spousal benefits for government annuitants whose government jobs were not covered by Social Security; and liberalized the treatment of divorced and widowed recipients.

1. House Action

Legislation that incorporated the Administration's recommendations (H.R. 8218) was introduced on July 12, 1977, by Mr. Burke (D-MA), chairman of the House Ways and Means Committee's Social Security Subcommittee. After reworking the Administration's package, the Subcommittee made recommendations to the full committee that were introduced by Chairman Ullman (D-OR) on September 27, 1977, as H.R. 9346. On October 6, 1977, the full committee approved a financing plan combining payroll tax increases with basic changes in benefits and coverage. H.R. 9346, was reported to the House on October 12, 1977. The House floor debate on H.R. 9346 began on October 26, 1977.[235]

a. On October 26, 1977, The House considered an amendment from the Committee on Post Office and Civil Service.[236] The amendment would have deleted the provision in the Ways and Means Committee bill covering federal, state, local, and nonprofit employees under Social Security.

b. Mr. Fisher (D-VA) offered a substitute for the Post Office and Civil Service Committee amendment. The Fisher substitute provided that federal employees would continue to be exempt from the Social Security system and that state and local governments and nonprofit organizations would continue to have the option of electing to cover their employees. While the amendment deleted mandatory coverage of these employees, the bill retained a provision requiring a study of mandatory coverage to be conducted jointly by the Civil Service Commission, the Departments of Treasury and Health, Education, and Welfare, and the Office of Management and Budget. Many Members

Social Security: Major Decisions in the House and Senate Since 1935   53

endorsed the concept of universal mandatory Social Security coverage, but supporters of the Fisher amendment asserted that a study of the universal coverage issue should be conducted first. Opponents, on the other hand, argued that the committee bill, by postponing the extension of coverage until 1982, allowed sufficient time to work out details.[237] In order to make up for the revenue loss due to deletion of the mandatory coverage provisions, the amendment also provided for greater increases in the Social Security tax rate and wage base than those included in the committee bill. The Administration, as well as representatives of many groups that would have been affected by the coverage extension, lobbied for the Fisher amendment.[238] Mr. Fisher's substitute amendment was agreed to by a vote of 386 (129-R, 257-D) to 38 (14-R, 24-D).[239] The House then adopted the Post Office and Civil Service Committee amendment, as amended by the Fisher amendment, by a vote of 380 (124-R, 256-D) to 39 (14-R, 25-D).[240]

c. On October 26, 1977, Mr. Pickle (D-TX) offered an amendment to strike another committee provision authorizing standby loans to the OASDI system from general revenues whenever trust fund reserves dipped below 25% of a year's outgo. Mr. Pickle argued that any use of general treasury funds for Social Security undermined the contributory nature of the program. He remarked that he did not want to see the Social Security program turned into a "welfare or need program." The Pickle amendment was rejected by a vote of 196 (122-R, 74-D) to 221 (15-R, 206-D).[241]

d. On October 26, 1977, Mr. Corman (D-CA) offered an amendment to eliminate the minimum Social Security benefit for new recipients. Mr. Corman said that the minimum benefit gave those who had paid very little in Social Security taxes a benefit "far in excess of his or her average monthly wage." He stated that his amendment restored "a measure of the social insurance principle of relating benefits to contributions." The amendment was rejected by a vote of 131 (68-R, 63-D) to 271 (64-R, 207-D).[242]

e. On October 27, 1977, Mr. Ketchum (R-CA) offered an amendment to raise the earnings limitation on recipients over age 65 gradually and to phase it out completely in 1982. The amendment included a tax rate increase to meet the cost of the additional benefit payments. The amendment was adopted by a vote of 268 (139-R, 129-D) to 149 (1-R, 148-D).[243]

54 Gary Sidor

    f.   On October 27, 1977, Mr. Conable (R-NY) moved to recommit H.R. 9346 to the Ways and Means Committee with instructions to report out the bill with an amendment that mandated coverage of federal workers, diverted half of the HI portion of the Social Security tax to OASDI in 1980, and replaced the lost HI revenues with general revenues. Mr. Conable argued that an amendment containing the above would enable both the wage base and the tax rate to remain as scheduled under existing law. The recommittal motion was rejected by a vote of 57 (44-R, 13-D) to 363 (97-R, 266-D).[244]

    g.   H.R. 9346 passed the House on October 27, 1977, by a vote of 275 (40-R, 235-D) to 146 (100-R, 46-D).[245]

2. Senate Action

Preliminary hearings and mark-up sessions on financing and decoupling were held by the Senate Committee on Finance in the summer and fall of 1977, even though the House had not yet passed its Social Security bill.[246] Before H.R. 9346 was passed by the House, the Finance Committee had tentatively agreed that its amendments would be attached to H.R. 5322, an unrelated tariff bill that had originated in the House. H.R. 5322 was to be a convenient vehicle for putting the Senate Finance Committee proposals before the Senate promptly.[247]

    a.   When H.R. 9346 as passed by the House came up for debate on the Senate floor on November 2, 1977, Mr. Long (D-LA) introduced an amendment to substitute the Finance Committee Social Security proposals in H.R. 5322 for the House bill. The Finance Committee proposals included decoupling measures similar to those in the House bill. They also included provisions that would require employers to pay Social Security taxes on a higher wage base than employees and would reduce spousal benefits by the amount of a government pension that was based on work not covered by Social Security. Mr. Long's amendment was agreed to with no recorded vote.[248] Thus, the text of H.R. 5322 became H.R. 9346 as amended by the Senate.

    b.   On November 3, 1977, Mr. Curtis (R-NE) offered an amendment that would have kept the taxable wage base the same for employers and employees (at the level specified for employees in the committee proposal) but would have raised the tax rate above the committee-recommended levels. Mr. Curtis said his amendment would take care of the deficit in the Social Security fund. He stated that raising the

Social Security: Major Decisions in the House and Senate Since 1935   55

wage base would put half of the financing burden exclusively on the people with higher incomes.

Mr. Nelson (D-WI) acknowledged that the Curtis amendment would supply the necessary funding to keep the retirement system solvent, but stressed that the average worker would pay a higher tax under the Curtis plan than under the committee proposal. Mr. Nelson's motion to table the Curtis amendment lost by a vote of 44 (3-R, 41-D) to 45 (31-R, 14-D),[249] but the Senate then rejected the Curtis amendment, 40 (27-R, 13-D) to 50 (7-R, 43-D).[250]

c. On November 4, 1977, Mr. Goldwater (R-AZ) offered an amendment to lower the age at which the earnings test would no longer apply from 72 to 65. Mr. Goldwater said that his amendment would end the discrimination that allowed full benefits to relatively wealthy retirees who had unearned income in excess of $3,000, but reduced benefits for retirees who relied entirely on additional earned income to supplement their Social Security benefits. Opponents of the amendment said that it would provide a windfall to professionals who continued to work at lucrative jobs past retirement age.

Mr. Church (D-ID offered a substitute amendment to lower from 72 to 70 the age at which the earnings test would no longer apply. Mr. Goldwater's motion to table the Church amendment was rejected 33 (25-R, 8-D) to 53 (7-R, 46-D).[251] The Senate adopted the Church substitute amendment 59 (12-R, 47-D) to 28 (20-R, 8-D)[252] and then adopted the Goldwater amendment as amended by the Church substitute by a vote of 79 (30-R, 49-D) to 4 (4-D).[253]

d. An amendment offered by Mr. Church on November 4, 1977, to provide for semiannual COLAs (when the rate of inflation for a six-month period was 4% or greater) was adopted by a vote of 50 (11-R, 39-D) to 21 (15-R, 6-D).[254]

e. On November 4, 1977, Mr. Bayh (D-IN) offered an amendment to remove the earnings limit for blind persons collecting disability benefits and to set the number of quarters blind persons must work to qualify for disability benefit at six. The Bayh amendment was adopted by voice vote.[255]

f. The Senate passed H.R. 9346, as amended, by a vote of 42 (9-R, 33-D) to 25 (15-R, 10-D) on November 4, 1977.[256]

3. Conference Action

The conference agreement provided for higher payroll tax rates than those proposed by either the House or Senate. The House-approved authority for loans to the trust funds from general revenues was dropped, as was the Senate-passed proposal to raise the wage base for employers higher than that for employees. Rather than phase out the earnings test, as in the House-passed bill, the conferees agreed to raise, over five years, the earnings tests limit for the elderly (65 and older).

Despite numerous differences between the House and Senate versions of the bill, the Congressional Quarterly Almanac stated that the conferees resolved their differences "without trouble."[257] The main controversy involved provisions dealing with welfare programs and college tuition tax credits.

a. On December 15, 1977, the House agreed to the conference report by a vote of 189 (15-R, 174-D) to 163 (109-R, 54-D).[258] There was unease in the House because of the large tax increases. Mr. Conable (R-NY) claimed that more reasonable non-tax alternatives were available.

b. On December 15, 1977, Mr. Ullman (D-OR) stated that the conference report "responsibly faces up to the issues of Social Security, both short range and long range." Mr. Ullman also assured Members that he would "move as expeditiously as possible ... toward adopting a new revenue mechanism whereby we can back off from these major increases...."[259]

c. On December 15, 1977, the Senate passed the conference report with little controversy by a vote of 56 (17-R, 39-D) to 21 (14-R, 7-D).[260]

V. P.L. 96-265, Social Security Disability Amendments of 1980

H.R. 3236, the Social Security Disability Amendments of 1980, was signed by President Carter on June 9, 1980. H.R. 3236 changed the Social Security disability insurance program in four major ways: (1) it placed a new limit on family benefits to prevent Social Security benefits from exceeding the worker's previous average earnings; (2) it provided incentives for recipients to return to work; (3) it required a higher percentage of federal reviews of new disability awards and more frequent periodic state-level reexamination of existing recipients; and (4) it modified the administrative relationship between the federal government and states. The amendments also made similar changes

Social Security: Major Decisions in the House and Senate Since 1935   57

in disability payments under the SSI program and established federal standards for "medigap" insurance policies sold by private insurance companies to supplement federal Medicare health insurance.

1. House Action

The House Ways and Means Committee's Subcommittee on Social Security held public hearings in February and March 1979. Following these hearings, the Subcommittee held mark-up sessions on H.R. 2854, the Administration's proposals, and incorporated its recommendations into H.R. 3236, which was introduced on March 27, 1979. After considering the Subcommittee's recommendations, the full Committee on Ways and Means reported the bill to the House on April 23, 1979. Action on the bill was delayed as several major groups raised questions about the legislation, and controversy arose as to the rules under which the bill would be considered on the House floor. Many of the interested parties wanted an opportunity to consider several of the provisions separately when H.R. 3236 was considered on the floor, rather than to vote for or against the bill as a whole. The Rules Committee held hearings on June 6 and 7, 1979, and reported out on June 7, 1979, H.Res. 310, which provided for a modified rule and one hour of debate on H.R. 3236. The rule provided that the only amendments that would be in order would be those recommended by the Ways and Means Committee (which were not amendable) and an amendment offered by Mr. Simon (D-IL) that would delay the implementation of a provision affecting vocational rehabilitation funding by one year. Despite the passage of the rule, "the opposition coalition was able to block floor consideration of the measure for 3 months."[261] Floor debate on H.R. 3236 did not begin until September 6, 1979.[262]

> a.   On September 6, 1979, the House agreed to the Ways and Means Committee and Mr. Simon's amendments[263] and passed H.R. 3236 by a vote of 235 (108-R, 127-D) to 162 (36-R, 126-D).[264]

2. Senate Action

In October 1979, the Senate Finance Committee held hearings on proposed disability legislation. The committee completed its markup on November 7, 1979, and reported H.R. 3236 to the Senate on November 8, 1979. On December 5, 1979, the Senate began floor debate. Final debate, which occurred in late January 1980, centered primarily on the provision to establish a lower limit on family benefits.[265]

a. On January 30, 1980, Mr. Metzenbaum's (D-OH) amendment to increase the limit on disability benefits from 85 to 100% of the worker's previous average earnings was defeated by a vote of 47 (7-R, 40-D) to 47 (31-R, 16-D).[266]

b. On January 30, 1980, Mr. Bayh (D-IN) offered an amendment to exempt terminally-ill applicants from the waiting period. The amendment was limited to people who, in the opinion of two doctors, would probably die within a year. Mr. Bayh said it was cruel to deny assistance to desperately ill people on the basis of an arbitrary waiting period that lasted longer than most of them were likely to live.

Mr. Long (D-LA) said elimination of the waiting period for one group would eventually lead to its elimination for all disabled persons, at a cost of $3 billion a year. Mr. Long also argued that the amendment was not germane since there was nothing in the bill relating to the waiting period for benefits. The amendment was ruled out of order but the Senate voted 37 (19-R, 18D) to 55 (17-R, 38-D) against the ruling of the chair,[267] and then adopted the Bayh amendment by a vote of 70 (25-R, 45-D) to 23 (12-R, 11-D).[268]

c. On January 31, 1980, the Senate passed H.R. 3236, with amendments, by a vote of 87 (35-R, 52-D) to 1 (1-D).[269]

3. Conference Action

On May 13, 1980, the conference committee reported the bill.[270] On the key issue of limiting future family benefits, the conferees combined the Senate limit of 85% of the worker's previous average work earnings and the House provision limiting benefits to no more than 150% of the worker's basic individual benefit.[271] The conferees also made a modification to the medigap provision (added by the Senate) and dropped the Senate amendment regarding the waiting period for the terminally ill, calling for a study of the issue instead.

a. On May 22, 1980, the House passed H.R. 3236, as agreed to by the conferees, by a vote of 389 (147-R, 242-D) to 2 (2-D).[272]

b. On May 29, 1980, the Senate passed the conference report on H.R. 3236 by a voice vote.[273]

Social Security: Major Decisions in the House and Senate Since 1935   59

W. P.L. 96-403, Reallocation of OASl and Dl Taxes

On October 9, 1980, H.R. 7670, the Reallocation of Social Security Taxes Between OASl and Dl Trust Funds, was signed into law by President Carter. Although the Social Security Amendments of 1977 did, in part, remedy the program's financing problems, high inflation increased Social Security benefits and higher than expected unemployment reduced income to the trust funds. The outlook for the OASI program, in particular, was deteriorating fairly rapidly. H.R. 7670 shifted revenues from the Disability Insurance Trust Fund to the Old-Age and Survivors Trust Fund during 1980 and 1981 so that adequate reserves could be maintained in both trust funds at least through the end of calendar year 1981.

1. House Action
On July 21, 1980, Mr. Pickle (D-TX) moved to suspend the rules and pass H.R. 7670. In his remarks, Mr. Pickle said that "the bill we bring today is a deliberate step both to insure the stability of the trust funds and to provide the Congress the time it will need to make any further changes necessary." He also stated that "Reallocation, the mechanism used in H.R. 7670, has been the traditional way of redistributing the OASDI tax rates when there have been changes in the law and in the experience of programs and in order to keep all the programs on a more or less even reserve ratio.... Reallocation means that the formula for allocating the incoming payroll tax receipts is changed in the law so that funds will flow into the various funds in a different mix than currently projected."[274]

    a. On July 21, 1980, the House suspended the rules and passed H.R. 7670. There was no roll call vote.[275]

2. Senate Action
    a. On September 25, 1980, H.R. 7670 was passed by unanimous consent.[276]

X. P.L. 96-473, Retirement Test Amendments[277]

On October 19, 1980, H.R. 5295 was signed by President Carter. It made various changes in the earnings test provisions enacted in 1977 and limited the circumstances under which Social Security benefits could be paid to prisoners.

Before enactment of P.L. 96-473, two earnings tests applied to Social Security benefits. One was an annual test, the other a monthly test. If a recipient earned more than the annual limit, his benefits were reduced $1 for every $2 of excess earnings until all Social Security benefits were withheld. Under the monthly earnings test, however, if a person's earnings were less than one-twelfth of the annual amount, he or she could get full benefits for that month, regardless of annual earnings.[278] The 1977 provision eliminating the monthly earnings test was designed with retirees in mind. However, the language as enacted applied to all classes of recipients affected by the earnings limitation. Generally, these recipients are likely to get a job and have substantial earnings in the year their benefits end. If these earnings were over the annual earnings limitation, some of the benefits they already received in the year become overpayments and had to be repaid.[279] P.L. 96-473 modified this by allowing individuals who received a dependent's benefit (a child or student's benefit, mother's benefit, or father's benefit) to use the monthly earnings test in the year in which their entitlement to such benefits ended. P.L. 96-473 also allowed all recipients to qualify for at least 1 "grace year" in which the monthly earnings test applies, and made other changes relating to the earnings test for the self-employed, particularly those whose incomes were often in "deferred" forms.

In addition, P.L. 96-473 prohibited payment of Social Security disability insurance benefits or of student benefits (based on any kind of Social Security status) to prisoners convicted of a felony, except where the individual is participating in a court-approved rehabilitation program (but allowed benefits to be paid to their dependents); disallowed impairments that arise from or are aggravated by the commission of a crime to be considered in determining whether a person is disabled; and disallowed impairments developed while an individual is in prison to be considered in determining disability while the person remains in prison.

1. House Action

On July 23, 1979, the House Ways and Means Committee's Subcommittee on Social Security held a hearing on the Social Security earnings test. In the spring of 1980, Congress also was concerned with the issue of paying Social Security benefits to prisoners. The Subcommittee on Social Security held hearings on the subject, and numerous bills prohibiting payments to prisoners were introduced.

    a.   On December 19, 1979, Mr. Long (D-LA) in discussing the earnings test as amended by the 1977 amendments said, "The purpose of the

Social Security: Major Decisions in the House and Senate Since 1935 61

change was to simplify the test and make more evenhanded the treatment of those who had similar amounts of annual earnings but differences in monthly work patterns. Several categories of recipients have been experiencing unforeseen problems with the new annual earnings test, however, and have been disadvantaged by it. H.R. 5295 is designed to correct those inequities."[280]

   b. On December 19, 1979, H.R. 5295, as amended, was passed unanimously by the House, 383 to 0.[281]

2. Senate Action

On April 21, 1980, the Senate Finance Committee's Subcommittee on Social Security held a hearing on the Social Security earnings test. During the spring of 1980, the Subcommittee also held hearings on the subject of denying Social Security benefits to prisoners. When S. 2885, the 1981 Budget Reconciliation bill, was reported out of the Senate Finance, it included a provision that prohibited payment of Social Security disability benefits to prisoners convicted of crimes. The Finance Committee also included this measure in H.R. 5295.

   a. On September 30, 1980, the Senate passed H.R. 5295, with amendments, by unanimous consent.[282]

3. House Concurrence

   a. On October 1, 1980, Mr. Conable (R-NY) remarked "The only amendment that we are asking to be attached here that goes to the Senate is an amendment that changes the word "crime" to the words "crime in the nature of a felony," so that it would apply only to more serious crimes and not possibly to traffic infractions and things of that sort."[283]

   b. On October 1, 1980, the House concurred in the Senate amendments with an amendment by unanimous consent.[284]

4. Senate Concurrence

   a. On October 1, 1980, Mr. Byrd's motion that the Senate concur with the House amendment to the Senate amendment was agreed to by voice vote.[285]

Y. P.L. 97-35, The Omnibus Budget Reconciliation Act of 1981

H.R. 3982, the Omnibus Budget Reconciliation Act of 1981, was signed into law (P.L. 97-35) by President Reagan on August 13, 1981. It included most of the Social Security changes proposed as part of the President's 1982 budget, as well as some added by the House. The Social Security provisions were among many outlay reduction measures intended to constrain federal expenditures. The Administration argued that the benefits it targeted for elimination or reduction were not directed at the basic goals of the program, and it did not consider them to have been "earned." The budget proposals eliminated the minimum Social Security benefit for both current and future recipients,[286] phased out benefits for students in postsecondary schools (age 18 and older, except for those under age 19 still in high school), made lump-sum death benefits available only to a spouse who was living with the worker or a spouse or child eligible for immediate monthly survivor benefits, and reduced benefits for those whose Social Security disability payments and certain other public pensions exceed 80% of pre-disability earnings. The amendments also eliminated reimbursement of the cost of state vocational rehabilitation services from the trust funds except where it could be shown that the services had resulted in the disabled person leaving the rolls; postponed the lowering of the earnings test exempt age (from 72 to 70) until 1983; ended parents' benefit when the youngest child reaches age 16; and provided that workers and their spouses would not receive benefits unless they meet the requirements for entitlement throughout the month. These last three provisions were initiatives added by the Ways and Means Committee.

1. Senate Action[287]

Because the Social Security legislation was considered in the context of the budget and reconciliation processes, there was virtually simultaneous consideration of the proposals by the House and the Senate. After final adoption (May 21, 1981) of the First Concurrent Budget Resolution, both the House and the Senate were acting within similar reconciliation guidelines.[288]

> a. On June 10, 1981, the Finance Committee reported its recommendations for spending reductions. These were included by the Senate Budget Committee in S. 1377, the Omnibus Budget Reconciliation Act of 1981, which was reported by the Budget Committee to the Senate on June 17, 1981. The Social Security

Social Security: Major Decisions in the House and Senate Since 1935   63

proposals included in S. 1377 were basically those proposed by the Administration with some minor modifications.

b. On June 22-25, 1981, the Senate debated S. 1377. The most controversial aspect of the bill relating to the Social Security program was the elimination of the minimum benefit for people already on the benefit rolls. On June 23, 1981, Mr. Riegle (D-MI) offered an amendment that would have eliminated the minimum benefit only for future recipients. The amendment was defeated by a vote of 45 (4-R, 41-D) to 53 (48-R, 5-D).[289]

c. On June 25, 1981, the Senate passed S. 1377, with the Finance Committee's Social Security proposals, by a vote of 80 (52-R, 28-D) to 15 (O-R, 15-D).[290]

2. House Action

The Ways and Means Committee recommendations, while touching on some of the same benefit categories as the Administration's proposals, were notably different. These proposals were incorporated by the Budget Committee into its version of the Omnibus Budget Reconciliation Act of 1981, H.R. 3982, which was reported to the House on June 19, 1981.

The adoption of the rule for floor consideration of H.R. 3982 became, in itself, a highly controversial issue. The Democratic leadership argued for allowing six separate votes on the grounds that this would allow for greater accountability for individual Members and avoid criticisms of "rubber-stamping" the Administration's proposals.[291] A bipartisan group of Members (generally supported by the Administration) argued instead for a rule that allowed only an up-or-down vote on a substitute for the Budget Committee bill sponsored by Mr. Gramm (D-TX) and Mr. Latta (R-OH).[292] Those arguing for the substitute said it would facilitate future conference agreement by bringing H.R. 3982 more closely in line with the President's original proposals and with S. 1377 then pending in the Senate.[293]

a. On June 25, 1981, the original rule for floor consideration of the bill was defeated by a vote of 210 (1-R, 209-D) to 217 (188-R, 29-D).[294]

b. A package of amendments by Mr. Latta, the so-called Gramm-Latta II alternative, called for (1) deletion of the Ways and Means' proposal to move the COLA from July to October and (2) changing the effective date of the Senate-passed minimum benefit proposal, affecting both current and future recipients, and (3) the Senate-passed student benefit phase-out proposal (which contained a faster phase-out than the Ways

64 Gary Sidor

and Means Committee version). The Gramm-Latta II alternative package passed the House on June 26, 1981, by a vote of 217 (188-R, 29-D) to 211 (2-R, 209-D).[295]

c. On June 26, 1981, the House passed the Omnibus Budget Reconciliation Act of 1981 by a vote of 232 (185-R, 47-D) to 193 (5-R, 188-D).[296]

3. Conference Action

The passage of the alternative budget package resulted in House-passed Social Security measures that were very similar to the Administration's original proposals and to those in the Senate-passed reconciliation bill. On July 13, 1981, the Senate voted to substitute the reconciliation proposals from S. 1377 for those passed by the House in H.R. 3982 and to go to conference to resolve the differences.[297]

On July 30, 1981, Mr. Bolling (D-MO), chairman of the House Rules Committee, threatened to prevent the conference agreement from being brought to the House floor for final approval until something could be worked out to modify the minimum benefit provision. An agreement was worked out permitting a bill that would modify the minimum benefit provision to be brought to the House floor before the vote on the reconciliation conference report. This bill was H.R. 4331, the Social Security Amendments of 1981. (See following section for further details.)

a. On July 31, 1981, both the House and the Senate approved the conference report on the 1981 Budget Reconciliation bill, the House by a voice vote and the Senate by a vote of 80 (49-R, 31-D) to 14 (1-R, 13-D).[298]

Z. P.L. 97-123, The Social Security Amendments of 1981

H.R. 4331, the Social Security Amendments of 1981, was signed by President Reagan on December 29, 1981. The amendments restored the minimum benefit for current recipients, but eliminated it for people becoming eligible for benefits after December 31, 1981 (see discussion of P.L. 97-35 above). In July 1981, as part of P.L. 97-35, Congress had enacted the elimination of the minimum benefit effective in April 1982. However, the public outcry was so great that both houses and the Administration thought it prudent to reconsider the measure.[299] H.R. 4331 also allowed the financially

Social Security: Major Decisions in the House and Senate Since 1935   65

troubled OASI trust fund to borrow from the healthier disability insurance and hospital insurance trust funds until December 31, 1982. The law specified that the borrowing could not exceed amounts needed to pay full benefits for six months and provided for repayment of any amounts borrowed. OASI borrowed $17.5 billion from the two trust funds late in December 1982, an amount limited to that necessary to keep benefits flowing until June 1983.

In addition, the bill (1) allowed members of religious orders who had taken a vow of poverty and were covered by Social Security before enactment of the bill to continue to become eligible for the minimum benefit during the next 10 years; (2) extended the payroll tax to the first six months of sick pay; (3) made it a felony to alter or counterfeit a Social Security card; and (4) allowed the Department of Health and Human Services access to recorded Social Security numbers to prevent ineligible prisoners from receiving disability benefits.

1. House Action

On July 21, 1981, the House, by a vote of 405 (176-R, 229-D) to 13 (10-R, 3-D),[300] adopted a non-binding resolution (H.Res. 181) urging that steps be taken "to ensure that Social Security benefits are not reduced for those currently receiving them." After the conference report on the reconciliation bill was filed, the House Rules Committee Chairman Richard Bolling (D-MO) held up the reconciliation bill in his committee in an effort to restore the minimum benefit. An agreement was subsequently reached whereby the budget bill would be reported out of the Rules Committee intact, and a separate bill to restore the minimum benefit for all current and future recipients (H.R. 4331) would be taken up by the House before the vote on the budget bill.[301] The House passed H.R. 4331 on July 31, 1981. It repealed the section of P.L. 97-35 that eliminated the minimum benefit, thereby reinstating the minimum benefit for current and future recipients.

a.   On July 31, 1981, the House passed H.R. 4331 by a vote of 404 (172-R, 232-D) to 20 (17-R, 3-D).[302]

2. Senate Action

When H.R. 4331 was sent to the Senate, Mr. Riegle (D-MI), Mr. Moynihan (D-NY), and Mr. Kennedy (D-MA) moved to have the Senate immediately consider it. The Senate's presiding officer ruled the motion out of order, and the ruling was upheld by a vote of 57 to 30,[303] thereby permitting consideration of the bill by the Finance Committee and delaying a Senate vote until October.

The bill reported by the Finance Committee in September 1981 included provisions that restored the minimum benefit for current recipients, except for those with government pensions, whose so-called "windfall" Social Security benefits would be reduced dollar for dollar by the extent their government pension exceeded $300 a month. The bill provided that members of religious orders who became eligible for Social Security in 1972 could remain eligible for the minimum benefit for the next 10 years. To offset the cost of restoring the minimum benefit, the Senate agreed to apply the payroll tax to the first six months of all sick pay received and to lower the maximum family retirement and survivor benefit to 150% of the worker's primary insurance amount (PIA). The bill also allowed inter-fund borrowing.

a. On October 14, 1981, the Senate by a voice vote agreed to (1) Mr. Danforth's (R-MO) amendment to override provisions of the federal Privacy Act to allow access to prison records so that disability payments to ineligible inmates could be stopped;[304] and (2) Mr. Baucus' (D-MT) amendment to make it a felony to alter or counterfeit a Social Security card.[305]

b. On October 15, 1981, Mr. Dole's (R-KS) amendment to apply the Social Security payroll tax to the first six months of all employer-financed sick pay, except that paid as insurance, was accepted by voice vote.[306]

c. On October 15, 1981, Mr. Moynihan's (D-NY) amendment requiring counterfeit-proof Social Security cards was agreed to by voice vote.[307]

d. On October 15, 1981, Mr. Eagleton (D-MO) offered an amendment to repeal a provision of the Economic Recovery Tax Act of 1981 (P.L. 97-34) that had reduced windfall profit taxes on newly discovered oil, and then use these tax savings to build an emergency reserve for the Social Security trust funds. The amendment was tabled 65 (42-R, 23-D) to 30 (7-R,23-D).[308]

e. On October 15, 1981, by a unanimous vote of 95 (48-R, 47-D) to 0, the Senate passed H.R. 4331, as amended.[309]

3. Conference Action

The Congressional Quarterly Almanac states that the major dispute of the conference was whether to pay for the cost of restoring the minimum benefit by tax increases or by benefit cuts. The conferees finally agreed to accept only

Social Security: Major Decisions in the House and Senate Since 1935   67

the sick pay tax "on the condition that inter-fund borrowing be allowed for just one year."[310] The conference agreement restored the minimum benefit to recipients eligible for benefits before 1982, and it rejected the Senate provisions (1) to reduce the minimum for those also receiving government pensions above $300 per month and (2) to limit further family benefits in OASI cases.

- a. The Senate agreed to the conference report on December 15, 1981, by a vote of 96 (50-R, 46-D) to 0.[311]
- b. The House agreed to the conference report on December 16, 1981, by a vote of 412 (181-R, 231-D) to 10 (7-R, 3-D).[312]

AA. P.L. 97-455, An Act Relating to Taxes on Virgin Island Source Income and Social Security Disability Benefits

President Reagan signed H.R. 7093 on January 12, 1983. In March 1981, the Administration began implementing the continuing disability investigation process mandated (beginning in 1982) under the 1980 amendments (P.L. 96-265), with the result that thousands of recipients lost their benefits, although many were restored upon appeal to an administrative law judge. P.L. 97-455 was a "stopgap" measure to remedy some of the perceived procedural inequities in the disability review process. It provided, temporally, an opportunity for individuals dropped from the rolls before October 1, 1983, to elect to receive DI and Medicare benefits while they appealed the decision; June 1984 was to be the last month for which such payments could be made.[313] The DI benefits would have to be repaid if the appeal were lost. The measure also required the Department of Health and Human Services to provide, as of January 1, 1984, face-to-face hearings during reconsideration of any decision to terminate disability benefits. Previously, recipients did not have such a meeting until they appeared before an administrative law judge. The bill also required the Secretary to report to Congress semiannually on the rate of continuing disability reviews and terminations; and gave the Secretary authority to decrease the number of disability cases sent to State agencies for review.

1. Senate Action[314]
On September 28, 1982, the Finance Committee marked up S. 2942, which contained a number of continuing disability review provisions. The

chairman, Mr. Dole (R-KS), asked that S. 2942 be attached to a House-passed bill (H.R. 7093) dealing with Virgin Islands taxation. Thus, H.R. 7093, with provisions of S. 2942, was reported to the Senate on October 1, 1982.

    a. On December 3, 1982, Mr. Heinz (R-PA) said, "... this emergency legislation does not completely solve the problem of the unfair terminations of hundreds of thousands of disabled individuals ... nonetheless. It means that in the immediate future, at least, individuals who have been wrongly terminated will not be financially ruined because they have been deprived of their benefits during a lengthy appeals process."[315]

    b. On December 3, 1982, the Senate passed H.R. 7093 by a vote of 70 (43-R, 27-D) to 4 (1-R, 3-D).[316]

2. House Action

On September 20, 1982, the House passed H.R. 7093 by voice vote. This version of the bill contained no Social Security provisions.[317]

    a. On December 14, 1982, the House amended the Senate-passed version of H.R. 7093 and passed it by unanimous consent.[318] H.R. 7093 was then sent back to the Senate for consideration of the added amendments. These amendments required the Secretary to (1) provide face-to-face hearings during reconsideration of any decision to terminate disability benefits; (2) advise recipients of what evidence they should bring to and what procedures they should follow at the reconsideration hearing; and (3) provide that, for a five-year period beginning December 1, 1982, only one-third of a spouse's government pension would be taken into account when applying the government pension offset provision enacted in 1977.

3. Conference Action

The bill as agreed to by the conferees was identical to the House-passed bill, except for the modification in the government pension offset provision.

    a. The House passed the conference report on H.R. 7093 on December 21, 1982, by a vote of 259 (115-R, 144-D) to 0.[319]

    b. The Senate passed the report by a voice vote on December 21, 1982.[320]

BB. P.L. 98-21, The Social Security Amendments of 1983

H.R. 1900, the Social Security Amendments of 1983, was signed by President Reagan on April 20, 1983. The latest projections showed that the OASDI program was projected to run out of funds by mid-1983, and to need about $150 billion to $200 billion to provide reasonable assurance that it would remain solvent for the rest of the decade.[321] Once this short-run problem was addressed, the program was projected to be adequately financed for about 35 years. However, beginning about 2025, the effects of the retirement of the baby-boom was projected to plunge the system into deficit again. The National Commission on Social Security Reform, a bipartisan panel appointed by President Reagan and congressional leaders, was formed to seek a solution to the system's financing problems. On January 15, 1983, a majority of the Commission members reached agreement on a package of changes.

Conforming to most of the recommendations in the Commission's package, the 1983 amendments: put new federal employees and all nonprofit organization employees under the OASDI program as of January 1, 1984; prohibited state and local and nonprofit agencies from terminating Social Security coverage; moved the annual cost-of-living adjustments in benefits from July to January of each year (which caused a delay of six months in 1983); made up to one-half of the benefits received by higher income recipients subject to federal income taxation; gradually raised the full benefit retirement age from 65 to 67 early in the next century; increased benefits for certain groups of widow(er)s; liberalized the earnings test; increased the delayed retirement credit; reduced benefits for workers also getting pensions based on noncovered employment; called for the earlier implementation of scheduled payroll tax increases; and substantially raised the tax rates on the self-employed. P.L. 98-21 also stipulated that beginning with the FY1993 budget, income and expenditures for OASDI and HI would no longer be included in federal budget totals. The 1983 amendments also stipulated that only two-thirds of a spouse's government pension would be taken into account when applying the government pension offset provision, eliminated remaining gender-based distinctions, and made numerous additional technical changes in the law.

1. House Action

On March 4, 1983, the Ways and Means Committee reported out H.R. 1900. The bill included most of the recommendations of the National Commission, numerous additional relatively minor Social Security provisions, and other measures mostly related to long-run financing issues, along with provisions affecting the Medicare and Unemployment Insurance programs.

On March 9, 1983, the House debated H.R. 1900. Proponents of the bill maintained that, although there were many provisions that individuals or certain groups might find troublesome, there was an overriding need to deal quickly and effectively with the Social Security financing issues. Opponents questioned whether this was the best way to solve the system's projected financial difficulties. Many favored raising the retirement age instead of increasing payroll taxes.

a. On March 9, 1983, Mr. Pickle's (D-TX) amendment calling for increases in the age at which "full" retirement benefits (i.e., unreduced for early retirement) are payable to 66 by 2009 and to 67 by 2027 was approved by a vote of 228 (152-R, 76-D) to 202 (14-R, 188-D).[322] Early retirement at age 62 would be maintained but at 70% of full benefits (instead of 80%), becoming fully effective after the "full retirement age" reached 67.

Mr. Pepper (D-FL) then offered a substitute amendment to raise the OASDI tax rate from 6.20% to 6.73% beginning in 2010. The amendment was rejected by a vote of 132 (1-R, 131-D) to 296 (16-R, 131-D).[323] Had the amendment passed, it would have superseded Mr. Pickle's amendment.

b. The House passed H.R. 1900, as it had been amended, by a vote of 282 (97-R, 18-D) to 148 (69-R, 79-D)[324] on March 9, 1983.

2. Senate Action

The Senate Finance Committee reported out S. 1 on March 11, 1983. As with the House bill, the committee adopted long-term financing measures along the lines of the recommendations of the National Commission and provisions affecting the Medicare and Unemployment Insurance programs.

The full Senate began consideration of H.R. 1900 on March 16, 1983. Seventy-two amendments were offered to the bill on the floor; the Senate adopted 49 of them. The following were among the major amendments debated.

a. On March 23, 1983, Mr. Long (D-LA) offered an amendment to make coverage of newly hired federal employees contingent upon enactment of a supplemental civil service plan for them. It was passed by a voice vote.[325]

Social Security: Major Decisions in the House and Senate Since 1935   71

b. An amendment to the Long amendment by Mr. Stevens (R-AL) and Mr. Mathias (R-MD) to exclude federal workers from coverage altogether was rejected by a vote of 12 (8-R, 4-D) to 86 (46-R, 40-D) on March 23, 1983.[326]

c. Mr. Stevens' amendment to the Long amendment to require the creation of a supplemental civil service retirement program by October 1985, while granting new employees wage credits toward such a plan in the meantime, was rejected 45 (41R, 4-D) to 50 (12-R, 38-D) on March 23, 1983.[327]

d. The Senate passed H.R. 1900 on March 23, 1983, by a vote of 88 (47-R, 41-D) to 9 (6-R, 3-D).[328]

3. Conference Action[329]

On March 24, 1983, conferees agreed to the final provisions of H.R. 1900. The primary issue was how to solve the system's long-run financial problems. The House measure called for a two-year increase in the retirement age, while the Senate bill proposed to increase the retirement age to 66, eliminate the earnings test, and cut initial benefit payments 5%. Another major difference was a provision in the Senate bill delaying coverage of new federal employees until a supplemental civil service retirement plan could be developed. House conferees charged that if the change were made, no revenues from the proposed coverage could be counted on for the Social Security bailout plan since, if such a plan were not subsequently developed, federal workers might escape coverage altogether.

The conferees agreed to the House retirement age change. Senate conferees then agreed to recede on the federal employee coverage issue.

a. On March 24, 1983, the House passed the conference report by a vote of 243 (80-R, 163-D) to 102 (48-R, 54-D).[330]

b. On March 25, 1983, the Senate passed H.R. 1900, as agreed to in the conference report, by a vote of 58 (32-R, 26-D) to 14 (8-R, 6-D).[331]

CC. P.L. 98-460, Social Security Disability Benefits Reform Act of 1984

On October 9, 1984, President Reagan signed H.R. 3755, the Social Security Disability Benefits Reform Act of 1984. P.L. 98-460 ended three years of controversy over the Administration's efforts to rid the Disability

Insurance program of ineligible recipients through an expanded periodic review process. The expanded reviews had been authorized by the 1980 disability amendments.[332]

Shortly after implementation of periodic review, the public and Congress began to criticize the process. The major complaints were the large number of persons dropped from the Dl rolls, of whom many had been receiving benefits for years and had not expected their cases to be reviewed; the great increase in the number of cases subjected to continuing disability reviews; and the number of cases in which recipients were erroneously dropped from the rolls. More than half of those removed from the rolls were reinstated upon appeal, fueling complaints that many terminations were unjustified. Advocacy groups for the disabled raised questions about the Social Security Administration's termination policies and procedures and petitioned Congress for legislative relief.[333] In addition, concerns about the disability process were raised by the federal courts and the states.

P.L. 98-460 provided that (1) with certain exceptions, benefit payments can be terminated only if the individual has medically improved and can engage in substantial gainful activity; (2) benefit payments can be continued until a decision by the administrative law judge in cases where a termination of benefits for medical reasons is being appealed; (3) reviews of all mental impairment disabilities be delayed until regulations stipulating new medical listings for mental impairments are published; (4) in cases of multiple impairments, the combined effect of all the impairments must be considered in making a disability determination; (5) the Department of Health and Human Services Secretary initiate demonstration projects providing personal appearance interviews between the recipient and state agency disability examiner in potential termination cases and potential initial denials; (6) the Secretary issue uniform standards, binding at all levels of adjudication, for disability determinations under Social Security and SSI disability; (7) the Secretary federalize disability determinations in a state within six months of finding that a state is not in substantial compliance with federal laws and standards; and (8) the qualifications of representative payees be more closely examined, and that the Secretary establish a system of annual accountability monitoring where benefit payments are made to someone other than a parent or spouse living in the same household with the recipient. It also established a temporary statutory standard for the evaluation of pain and directed that a study of the problem of evaluating pain be made by a commission to be appointed by the Secretary.

1. House Action

On March 14, 1984, the House Committee on Ways and Means reported H.R. 3755 with amendments.

    a. During debate on H.R. 3755, Mr. Conable (R-NY) remarked that the intent of the 1980 legislation, requiring continuing disability reviews, was meritorious, but the results were not what the drafters intended. Mr. Conable further stated, "Not only were ineligible recipients terminated, but some eligible recipients were taken from the rolls, as well. Many, especially those with mental impairments, suffered duress and the economic hardship of interrupted benefits." Mr. Conable also said, "Both Congress and the administration have taken remedial steps ... we approved P.L. 97-455, which, on an interim basis, provided for the continuation of benefits during an appeal of an adverse decision ... H.R. 3755 represents the next step."[334]

       The sponsor of H.R. 3755, Mr. Pickle (D-TX), said, "In the past 3 years nearly half a million disabled recipients have been notified that their benefits will end. Far too often this notice has been sent in error, and corrected only at the recipient's expense ... we who serve on the Social Security Subcommittee have heard those pleas from the disabled, from Governors, and from those who must administer this program in the states ... for over a year now we have carefully drafted legislation to bring order to the growing chaos ... This bill does not attempt to liberalize the disability program. It does restore order and humanity to the disability review process."[335]

    b. On March 27, 1984, the House passed H.R. 3755 by a vote of 410 (160-R, 250-D) to 1 (1-R).[336]

2. Administrative Action

Six months before legislation was enacted, Secretary Heckler imposed a moratorium on periodic continuing disability reviews. The Secretary said:

> Although we have made important progress in reforming the review process with Social Security, the confusion of differing court orders and state actions persists. The disability program cannot serve those who need its help when its policies are splintered and divided. For that reason, we must suspend the process and work together with Congress to regain order and consensus in the disability program.[337]

3. Senate Action

On May 16, 1984, the Finance Committee approved S. 476. Major provisions of the bill allowed disabled persons to continue collecting Social Security benefits if their medical condition had not improved since they were determined disabled. The major difference between the medical improvement provision in S. 476 and H.R. 3755 was that the Senate bill stated that the recipient bore the burden of proof that his or her condition had not improved.

a. On May 22, 1984, Mr. Cohen (R-ME), one of the sponsors of S. 476, said, "The need for fundamental change in the disability reviews has been evident for some time. Since the reviews began, more than 12,000 individuals have filed court actions challenging the Social Security Administration's termination of their benefits. An additional 40 class action suits had been filed as of last month. The legislation before the Senate today would end this chaos and insure an equitable review process."[338]

b. Mr. Levin (D-MI), another sponsor, said, "It has taken us 3 years to come to grips with the problems in the disability review process as a legislative body. And while it was long in coming, I am pleased with the final outcome. The bill I, along with Senator Cohen and others introduced on February 15, 1983, S. 476, as reported by the Finance

Committee contains the essential ingredients to the development of a fair and responsible review process."[339]

c. On May 22, 1984, the Senate passed H.R. 3755, after substituting the language of S. 476 for the House-passed version, 96 (52-R, 44-D) to 0.[340]

4. Conference Action

On September 19, 1984, the conferees filed the conference report. The conference committee generally followed the House version of the medical improvement standard (with some modifications) and added the requirement that any continuing disability review be made on the basis of the weight of the evidence with regard to the person's condition.

a. On September 19, 1984, the House and Senate passed H.R. 3755 unanimously; 402 to 0 in the House,[341] and 99 to 0 in the Senate.[342]

DD. P.L. 99-177, Public Debt Limit—Balanced Budget and Emergency Deficit Control Act of 1985

The Balanced Budget and Emergency Deficit Control Act, which was included as Title II of H.J.Res. 372, increasing the national debt, was signed by President Reagan on December 12, 1985. The act stipulated that budget deficits must be decreased annually, and under certain circumstances required across-the-board cuts of non-exempt programs by a uniform percentages to achieve this result. Under the act, if annual deficit amounts were larger than the law established, a formula would be used to reduce the deficit annually until it reached zero in FY1991. This part of P.L. 99-177 generally is referred to by the names of its sponsors—Senators Gramm (R-TX), Rudman (R-NH), and Hollings (D-SC).[343] The Gramm-Rudman-Hollings Act accelerated the "off-budget" treatment of OASDI, as prescribed by P.L. 98-21, from FY1993 to FY1986. (However, Social Security income and outgo still would be counted toward meeting Gramm-Rudman-Hollings deficit reduction targets.) The HI trust fund was not affected (i.e., not to be separated from the budget until FY1993). In addition, the act exempted Social Security benefits (including COLAs) from automatic cuts and required the Secretary of the Treasury to restore to the trust funds any interest lost as a result of 1984 and 1985 debt ceiling constraints, and to issue to the trust funds obligations bearing interest rates and maturities identical to those of securities redeemed between August 31, 1985, and September 30, 1985.

1. House Action
a. On August, 1, 1985, the House approved the debt-limit increase, unamended, as part of the FY1986 budget resolution (S.Con.Res. 32) by a vote of 309 (127-R, 182-D) to 119 (52-R, 67-D).[344]

2. Senate Action
a. On October 9, 1985, the Senate adopted the Gramm-Rudman-Hollings amendment to H.J.Res. 372 (Balanced Budget and Emergency Control Act of 1985) by a vote of 75 (48-R, 27-D) to 24 (4-R, 20-D).[345]
b. On October 10, 1985, the Senate passed H.J.Res. 372, with amendments, by a vote of 51 (38-R, 13-D) to 37 (8-R, 29-D).[346]

3. Conference Action

On November 1, 1985, the conference report was filed in disagreement. The House asked for another conference on November 6, 1985, the Senate agreeing on November 7, 1985. The second conference report was filed on December 10, 1985.

a. On December 11, 1985, both the House and the Senate agreed to the conference report, the House by a vote of 271 (153-R, 118-D) to 154 (24-R, 130-D)[347] and the Senate by a vote of 61 (39-R, 22-D) to 31 (9-R, 22-D).[348]

EE. S.Con.Res. 32, Proposed COLA Constraints in FY1986 Budget Resolution

In 1985, the Senate voted to skip the 1986 COLA for various federal programs, including Social Security, when it passed S.Con.Res. 32, the first concurrent budget resolution for FY1986. However, the House-passed version had no COLA freeze, and the proposal was dropped in conference.

a. In his FY1986 Budget submitted in January 1985, President Reagan proposed that there be no COLA for several al federal benefit programs, among them civil service and military retirement, in 1986. However, Social Security was exempted from the proposal. In considering S.Con.Res. 32, the first concurrent budget resolution for FY1986 (which involves the goal-setting stage of the congressional budget process) on March 14 the Senate Budget Committee, by a vote of 11 (11-R, 0-D) to 10 (0-R, 10-D)[349] added Social Security to the list of programs whose COLAs were to be skipped in 1986. The Social Security portion of the COLA "freezes," as they were called, was estimated to yield $22 billion in savings over the FY1986-FY1988 period, and larger savings thereafter. An alternative COLA cutback proposal emerged shortly thereafter, as part of a substitute deficit-reduction package developed by the Administration and the Senate Republican leadership. Instead of freezing COLAs in the affected federal retirement programs for 1 year, it would have limited the COLAs for the next 3 years to 2% per year plus any amount by which inflation exceeded the Administration's assumptions (its assumptions at that time suggested that inflation would hover in the high 3% or

Social Security: Major Decisions in the House and Senate Since 1935   77

low 4% range). It further included a guarantee provision under which the affected COLAs could not be less than 2%. It, too, would have resulted in about $22 billion in Social Security savings over the following 3 years (as well as higher savings in later years).

1. Senate Action

a. When the Senate took up the Budget Committee's first budget resolution, it rejected both the COLA freeze and the alternative COLA limitation by agreeing on May 1, 1985, by a vote of 65 (19-R, 46-D) to 34 (33-R, 1-D)[350] to an amendment by Senator Dole (R-KS), for Senators Hawkins (R-FL) and D'Amato (R-NY), to provide for full funding of Social Security COLAs.

b. However, on May 10, 1985, after considering many amendments, the Senate adopted by a vote of 50 (49-R, 1-D) to 49 (4-R, 45-D)[351] an entirely revised budget package, introduced by Senator Dole, which incorporated the original COLA freeze recommended by the committee.

c. Subsequently, the Senate considered an amendment by Senator Moynihan (D-NY) to provide a full Social Security COLA in January 1986, but it was tabled by a vote of 51 (49-R, 2-D) to 47 (3-R, 44-D).[352]

d. The final budget resolution, passed by a voice vote, assumed later enactment of the 1986 COLA freezes, including one affecting Social Security.

2. House Action

The House-passed version of the FY1986 first budget resolution, H.Con.Res. 152, assumed that full COLAs would be paid in all federal benefit programs.

a. On May 22, 1985, the House rejected an amendment by Mr. Dannemeyer (R-CA) to limit Social Security COLAs to 2% per year for the 3-year period FY1986-FY1988 by a vote of 382 (135-R, 247-D) to 39 (39-R, 0-D)[353]

b. On May 23, 1985, the House also rejected by a vote of 372 (165-R, 207-D) to 56 (15-R, 41-D) an amendment offered by Representative Leath (D-TX) to freeze 1986 COLAs for Social Security, federal retirement, and veterans' compensation while adding back 20% of the anticipated savings to programs that aid needy elderly and disabled people.[354]

c. Provisions of the House-passed resolution were inserted in S.Con.Res. 32, in lieu of the Senate-passed measures, which was approved by a vote of 258 (24-R, 234-D) to 170 (155-R, 15-D) on May 23, 1985.[355]

3. Conference Action

Conferees for the House and Senate met throughout June and July 1985 to work out an agreement on a deficit reduction package. Among the number of ideas that surfaced were proposals to delay the Senate-passed COLA freezes until 1987, means test the COLAs, make both the COLAs and adjustments to income tax brackets effective every other year (instead of annually), and increase the amount of Social Security benefits that would be subject to income taxes. Ultimately, however, agreement could not be reached on any form of Social Security constraint, and the conference agreement on the First Concurrent Resolution on the Budget for FY1986, passed on August 1, 1985, did not assume any such savings.

FF. P.L. 99-509, The Omnibus Budget Reconciliation Act of 1986

President Reagan signed H.R. 5300, the Omnibus Budget Reconciliation Act of 1986, on October 21, 1986. During 1986, inflation slowed to a rate that made it unlikely that it would reach the 3% threshold necessary to provide a COLA in that year. P.L. 99-509 permanently eliminated the 3% requirement, which enabled a 1.3% COLA to be authorized for December 1986.

1. Senate Action

The Senate Finance Committee, as part of its budget provisions incorporated in S. 2706, the Omnibus Budget Reconciliation Act of 1986, included a measure that would have provided a Social Security COLA in January 1987 no matter how low inflation turned out to be, i.e., it permanently eliminated the 3% requirement.

a. The Senate approved S. 2706 on September 20, 1986, by a vote of 88 (50-R, 38-D) to 7 (0-R, 7-D).[356]

Social Security: Major Decisions in the House and Senate Since 1935   79

2. House Action

The House Ways and Means Committee, as part of its budget reconciliation provisions incorporated in H.R. 5300, its version of the Omnibus Budget Reconciliation Act of 1986, included a similar measure.

    a.   The House passed H.R. 5300 with this measure on September 24, 1986, by a vote of 309 (99-R, 210-D) to 106 (71-R, 35-D).[357]

3. Conference Action

The conference report on H.R. 5300, including the COLA provision, was approved by both houses on October 17, 1986, by a vote of 305 (112-R, 193-D) to 70 (R-51, D-19) in the House and 61 (33-R, 28-D) to 25 (10-R, 15-D) in the Senate.[358]

GG. P.L. 100-203, The Omnibus Budget Reconciliation Act of 1987

H.R. 3545, the Omnibus Budget Reconciliation Act of 1987, was signed into law on December 22, 1987, by President Reagan. Several of its provisions affected Social Security. P.L. 100-203 extended FICA coverage to military training of inactive reservists, the employer's share of all cash tips, and several other categories of earnings; lengthened from 15 to 36 months the period during which a disability recipient who returns to work may become automatically re-entitled to benefits; and extended the period for appeal of adverse disability decisions through 1988.

1. House Action

H.R. 3545 was a bill to meet the deficit reduction targets set by the FY1988 budget resolution (H.Con.Res. 93). Earlier, in July, the Ways and Means Committee also had approved changes in Social Security. Two of these provisions—extending coverage to military training of inactive reservists and group term life insurance—had been requested by President Reagan. In addition, the committee agreed to lengthen from 15 to 36 months the period during which a disability recipient who returns to work may become automatically re-entitled to benefits, to extend the period for appeal of adverse disability decisions through 1988, and to cover certain agricultural workers, children and spouses in family businesses.

80 Gary Sidor

a. The house passed H.R. 3545 on October 29, 1987, by a vote of 206 (1-R, 205-D) to 205 (164-R, 41-D).[359]

2. Senate Action

When the Finance Committee approved H.R. 3545 on December 3, 1987, it included the House Social Security coverage provisions.

a. On December 10, 1987, the Senate rejected an amendment by Ms. Kassebaum (R-KS) that would have limited the 1988 Social Security COLA to 2%, by a vote of 71 (34-R, 37-D) to 25 (11-R, 14-D).[360]
b. On December 11, 1987, the Senate approved H.R. 3545 by a voice vote.

3. Conference Action

The conference committee generally accepted the House-passed version of H.R. 3545.

a. On December 21, 1987, the House passed the conference report by a vote of 237 (44-R, 193-D) to 181 (130-R, 51-D).[361]
b. On December 21, 1987, the Senate passed the conference report by a vote of 61 (18-R, 43-D) to 28 (23-R, 5-D).[362]

HH. P.L. 100-647, The Technical and Miscellaneous Revenue Act of 1988

On November 10, 1988, President Reagan signed H.R. 4333, the Technical and Miscellaneous Revenue Act of 1988. In addition to various tax measures the bill contained several provisions affecting Social Security. Among these, H.R. 4333 provided interim benefits to individuals who have received a favorable decision upon appeal to an Administrative Law Judge but whose case has been under review by the Appeals Council for more than 110 days; extended the existing provision for continued payment of benefits during appeal; denied benefits to Nazis who are deported; and lowered the number of years of substantial Social Security-covered earnings that are needed to begin phasing out the windfall benefit formula (which applies to someone receiving a pension from noncovered employment) from 25 to 20 years.

Social Security: Major Decisions in the House and Senate Since 1935   81

1. House Action

On July 14, 1988, the Ways and Means Committee approved a "tax corrections" bill, H.R. 4333, that also included some measures affecting Social Security.

    a.   The house passed H.R. 4333 on August 4, 1988, by a vote of 380 (150-R, 230-D) to 25 (19-R, 6-D).[363]

2. Senate Action

The Finance Committee adopted about half of the House Social Security provisions.

    a.   The Senate approved H.R. 4333 on October 11, 1988, by a vote of 87 (38-R, 49-D) to 1 (0-R, 1-D).[364]

3. Conference Action

The conference committee generally accepted the House-passed version of H.R. 4333.

    a.   On October 21, 1988, the House passed the conference report by a vote of 358 (150-R, 208-D) to 1 (0-R, 1-D).[365]

    b.   On October 21, 1988, the Senate passed the conference report by a voice vote.

II. P.L. 101-239, The Omnibus Budget Reconciliation Act of 1989

On December 19, 1989, President Bush signed H.R. 3299, the Omnibus Budget Reconciliation Act of 1989. Among other things, its Social Security provisions extended benefits to children adopted after the worker became entitled to benefits, regardless of whether the child was dependent on the worker before the worker's entitlement; again extended the existing provision for continued payment of benefits during appeal; increased the calculation of average wages, used for purposes of computing of benefits and the maximum amount of earnings subject to FICA tax, by including deferred compensation; and, beginning in 1990, required that SSA provide estimates of earnings and future benefits to all workers over age 24.

1. House Action

When the Ways and Means Committee considered H.R. 3299 on October 5, 1989, it proposed several Social Security-related measures. Among these was a provision making SSA an independent agency, raising the Special Minimum benefit by $35 a month, increasing the earnings test limits for recipients over age 64, extending benefits to children adopted after the worker became entitled to benefits, regardless of whether the child was dependent on the worker before the worker's entitlement, again extending the existing provision for continued payment of benefits during appeal, and including deferred compensation in the determination of average wages for purposes of determining benefits and the maximum amount of earnings subject to the FICA tax.

    a.   On October 5, 1989, the House passed H.R. 3299 by a vote of 333 (R-146, D-187) to 91 (R-28, D-63).[366]

2. Senate Action

The Finance Committee approved its version of H.R. 3299 on October 3, 1989. Like the House version, it included an increase in the maximum amount of earnings subject to the FICA tax, but specifically earmarked the revenue therefrom to pay for proposed increases in the earnings test limits. It also approved making SSA an independent agency, but with a single administrator as opposed to a three-person board in the House version. However, because it was thought that a "clean bill" would improve chances of passage, the bill was stripped of its Social Security provisions before it reached the floor.

    a.   The senate approved its version of H.R. 3299 on October 13, 1989, by a vote of 87 (R-40, D-47) to 7 (R-2, D-5).[367]

3. Conference Action

In conference, most of the House provisions were accepted (the major exclusion was making SSA an independent agency). Although neither version of H.R. 3299 included it, a provision was added that, beginning in 1990, required that SSA provide estimates of earnings and future benefits to all workers over age 24.

    a.   On November 22, 1989 (legislative day November 21), the House approved the conference report by a vote of 272 (R-86, D-186) to 128 (R-81, D-47).[368] The Senate approved it the same day by a voice vote.

Social Security: Major Decisions in the House and Senate Since 1935   83

JJ. P.L. 101-508, The Omnibus Budget Reconciliation Act of 1990

On November 5, 1990, President Bush signed H.R. 5835, the Omnibus Budget Reconciliation Act of 1990.Among its Social Security provisions, it made permanent a temporary provision, first enacted in 1984 and subsequently extended, that provides the option for recipients to choose to continue to receive disability and Medicare benefits while their termination is being appealed; liberalized the definition of disability for disabled widow(er)s by making it consistent with that for disabled workers; extended benefits to spouses whose marriage to the worker is otherwise invalid, if the spouse was living with the worker before he or she died or filed for benefits; removed the operation of the trust funds from budget deficit calculations under the Gramm-Rudman-Hollings Act; established separate House and Senate procedural safeguards to protect trust fund balances; extended coverage to employees of state and local governments who are not covered by a retirement plan; and raised the maximum amount of earnings subject to HI taxes to $125,000, effective in 1991, with raises thereafter indexed to increases in average wages.

1. House Action

In 1990, the congressional agenda was dominated by the debate over how to reduce a large budget deficit, which, under the Gramm-Rudman Hollings (GRH) sequestration rules, would have required billions of dollars of cuts in many federal programs. The administration's FY1991 budget contained several Social Security measures, the most prominent of which was to extend Social Security coverage to state and local government workers not covered by a retirement plan. The Ways and Means Social Security Subcommittee included some of them in a package of Social Security provisions it forwarded to the full committee. For several months budget negotiations stalled, as the democratic majority in Congress disagreed with the administration's position that the deficit should be reduced entirely with spending cuts. As a result of a budget "summit" between congressional and administration leaders, an agreement was reached in which the President would put tax increases on the table and the Congress would consider spending cuts in entitlements, including Social Security and Medicare. The resulting bill reported from the Budget Committee on October 15, H.R. 5835, extended Social Security coverage to state and local government workers not covered by a retirement plan and raised the maximum amount of earnings subject to HI taxes to $100,000, effective in 1991. However, the same day the Ways and Means Committee reported out H.R. 5828, a bill making miscellaneous and technical amendments to the Social Security Act, that incorporated most of the provisions that had earlier been approved by the Social Security Subcommittee.

    a.   On October 16, 1990, the House approved H.R. 5835 by a vote of 227 (10-R, 217-D) to 203 (163-R, 40-D).[369]

2. Senate Action

During 1990, the debate about Social Security was largely dominated by a proposal by Senator Moynihan (D-NY) to cut the Social Security payroll tax and return the program to true pay-as-you-go financing. The driving force behind the proposal was the growing realization that the rapid rise in Social Security yearly surpluses, caused by payroll tax revenues that exceeded the program's expenditures, were significantly reducing the size of the overall federal budget deficit. This had led to charges that the Social Security trust funds were being "raided" to finance the rest of government and "masking" the true size of the deficit. In S. 3167, Senator Moynihan proposed that the payroll tax rate be scheduled to fall and rise with changes in the program's costs.

    a.   On October 10, 1990, Senator Moynihan asked that the Senate vote on S. 3167. While the Senate leadership agreed to bring the bill to the floor, a point of order was raised against it on the basis that it violated the Budget Act. Although a majority of Senators voted to override the point of order, 54 (R-12, D-42) to 44 (31-R, 13-D), the measure fell short the 60 votes required.[370]

    b.   When the Senate considered H.R. 5835 on October 18, 1990, it accepted by a vote of 98 (43-R, 55-D) to 2 (2-R, 0-D) an amendment by Senators Hollings (D-SC) and Heinz (R-PA) to remove Social Security from GRH budget deficit calculations.[371]

    c.   On October 19, 1990 (legislative day October 18), the Senate passed the budget reconciliation bill by a vote of 54 (23-R, 31-D) to 46 (22-R, 24-R).[372]

3. Conference Action

    a.   On October 27, 1990 (legislative day October 26), the House passed the conference report on H.R. 5835 by a vote of 228 (47-R, 181-D) to 200 (126-R, 74-D).[373]

Social Security: Major Decisions in the House and Senate Since 1935   85

b. On October, 27, 1990, the Senate passed the conference report by a vote of 54 (19-R, 35-D) to 45 (25-R, 20-D)[374]

KK. P.L. 103-66, The Omnibus Budget Reconciliation Act of 1993

On August 10, 1993, President Clinton signed H.R. 2264, the Omnibus Budget Reconciliation Act of 1993. Effective in 1994, H.R. 2264: made up to 85% of Social Security benefits subject to the income tax for recipients whose income plus one-half of their benefits exceed $34,000 (single) and $44,000 (couple); and eliminated the maximum taxable earnings base for HI, i.e., subjected all earnings to the HI tax, effective in 1994.

As part of his plan to cut the Federal fiscal deficit, President Clinton proposed in his first budget that the proportion of benefits subject to taxation should be increased from 50% to 85%, effective in 1994. His budget document said this would "move the treatment of Social Security and railroad retirement Tier I benefits toward that of private pensions" and would generate $32 billion in new tax revenues over five years. The proceeds would not be credited to the Social Security trust funds, as under current law, but to the Medicare Hospital Insurance program, which had a less favorable financial outlook than did Social Security. Doing so also would have avoided procedural obstacles that could have been raised in the budget reconciliation process. The budget also proposed that the maximum taxable earnings base for HI be eliminated entirely beginning in 1994.

Both proposals, especially the increase in the taxation of benefits, were opposed vigorously by the Republican minority. Critics maintained that the increase was unfair as it changed the rules in the middle of the game, penalizing recipients who relied on old law and who cannot change past work and savings decisions. Regardless of abstract arguments about tax principles, many recipients regard increased taxation as simply a reduction in the benefits they had been promised. They regarded taxation of benefits as an indirect means test, which would weaken the "earned right" nature of the program, and make it more like welfare, where need determines the level of benefits. Finally, they maintained that it grossly distorts marginal tax rates and provides a strong disincentive for many recipients to work.[375]

1. House Action

H.Con.Res. 64, the FY1994 Concurrent Budget Resolution, included the additional revenue from the President's proposal.

  a. On March 18, 1993, the House passed H.Con.Res. 64 by a vote of 243 (0-R, 242-D, 1-I) to 183 (172-R, 11-D), which included the additional revenue from the President's proposal.[376]

2. Senate Action

The Senate devoted six days of debate to H.Con.Res. 64 at the end of March.

  a. On March 24, 1993, the Senate rejected by a vote of 47 (43-R, 4-D) to 52 (0-R, 52-D) an amendment by Senator Lott (R-MS) that would have deleted from the resolution the revenue projected from the President's proposal.[377]
  b. On March 24, 1993, the Senate approved, by a vote of 67 (12-R, 55-D) to 32 (31-R, 1-D), an amendment by Senators Lautenberg (D-NJ) and Exon (D-NE) expressing the sense of the Senate that the revenues set forth in the resolution assume that the Finance Committee would make every effort to find alternative sources of revenue before imposing additional taxes on the Social Security benefits of recipients with threshold incomes of less than $32,000 (single) and $40,000 (couples). The thresholds for taxing 50% of benefits were to remain at the current law levels of $25,000 and $32,000.[378]
  c. On March 25, 1993, the Senate approved H.Con.Res. 64 by a vote of 54 (0-R, 54-D) to 45 (43-R, 1-D).[379]

3. Conference Action

On March 31, 1993, the House approved the conference report on H.Con.Res. 64 by a vote of 240 (0-R, 239-D, 1-I) to 184 (172-R, 12-D).[380] On April 1, 1993, the Senate approved the conference report by a vote of 55 (0-R, 55-D) to 45 (43-R, 2-D).[381] It included the sense of the Senate resolution.

4. House Action

On May 13, 1993, by a party-line vote of 24-14, the House Committee on Ways and Means approved the President's proposal, but modified it so that the additional proceeds would be credited to the General Fund instead of to

Medicare. This measure was included in H.R. 2264, the 1993 Omnibus Budget Reconciliation Act.

    a.   On May 27, 1993, the House passed H.R. 2264 by a vote of 219 (0-R, 218-D, 1-I) to 213 (175-R, 38-D).[382]

5. Senate Action

On June 18, 1993, by a party-line vote of 11-9, the Finance Committee approved H.R. 2264, but included the Lautenberg-Exon amendment to raise the taxation thresholds to $32,000 (single) and $42,000 (couple).

    a.   On June 24, 1993, the Senate rejected, by a vote of 46 (41-R, 5-D) to 51 (1-R, 50-D), an amendment by Senator Lott to delete the taxation of benefits provision.[383]

    b.   It also rejected, by a vote of 46 (3-R, 43-D) to 51 (40-R, 11-D) an amendment by Senator DeConcini to increase the 85% thresholds to $37,000 (single) and $54,000 (couple),[384] and, by a vote of 41 (40-R, 1-D) to 57 (3-R, 54-D) an amendment by Senator McCain to direct that the proceeds of increased taxation of benefits be credited to the Social Security trust funds.[385]

    c.   On June 24, 1993, the Senate approved, by a vote of 50 (0-R, 50-D) to 49 (43-R, 6-D) the Budget Reconciliation bill. It included the Lautenberg-Exon amendment creating second-tier thresholds of $32,000 and $40,000.[386]

6. Conference Action

On July 14, 1993, the House adopted, by a vote of 415 to 0, an amendment by Representative Sabo (D-MN) to instruct its conferees on the bill to accept the Senate version of taxation of benefits.[387]

    a.   When the House and Senate versions of the budget package were negotiated in conference, the conferees modified the Senate taxation of Social Security benefits provision by setting the second tier thresholds at $34,000 (single) and $44,000 (couple). The measure was included in the final version of the reconciliation bill passed by the House on August 5, 1993, by a vote of 218 (0-R, 217-D, 1-I) to 216 (175-R, 41-D).[388]

    b.   On August 6, 1993, the Senate passed H.R. 2264 by a vote of 51 (0-R, 51-D) to 50 (44-R, 6-D).[389]

LL. P.L. 103-296, The Social Security Administrative Reform Act of 1994

President Clinton signed H.R. 4277, the Social Security Administrative Reform Act of 1994, on August 15, 1994. P.L. 103-296 established the Social Security Administration (SSA) as an independent agency, effective March 31, 1995; and restricted DI and SSI benefits payable to drug addicts and alcoholics by creating sanctions for failing to get treatment, limiting their enrollment to three years, and requiring that those receiving DI benefits have a representative payee (formerly required only of SSI recipients). Representatives of the Clinton Administration initially opposed making SSA an independent agency, but President Clinton supported H.R. 4277's final passage.

Interest in making SSA independent began in the early 1970s, when Social Security's impact on fiscal policy was made more visible by including it in the federal budget. During congressional budget discussions in the early 1980s proponents of independence wanted to insulate Social Security from benefit cuts designed to meet short-term budget goals rather than policy concerns about Social Security. Many argued that making the agency independent would help insulate it from political and budgetary discussions, would lead to better leadership, and reassure the public about Social Security's long-run survivability.

Opponents argued that Social Security's huge revenue and outlays should not be isolated from policy choices affecting other HHS social programs, and that its financial implications for the economy and millions of recipients should be evaluated in conjunction with other economic and social functions of the government. They further believed that making SSA independent would not necessarily resolve its administrative problems, which were heavily influenced by ongoing policy changes to its programs resulting from legislation and court decisions.

Starting in 1986, a number of attempts were made in Congress to make SSA independent. Various Administrations generally opposed the idea, and a disagreement persisted between the House and Senate over how such an agency should be administered. The House preferred an approach under which an independent SSA would be run by a three-member bipartisan board; the Senate preferred an approach where it would be run by a single administrator.

Social Security: Major Decisions in the House and Senate Since 1935   89

1. House Action

On May 12, 1994, the Ways and Means Committee reported out H.R. 2264 (incorporating the three-member bipartisan board approach), introduced by Representative Jacobs (D-IN).

    a.   The House passed H.R. 2264 on May 17, 1994, by a vote of 413-0.[390]

2. Senate Action

On January 25, 1994, the Senate Finance Committee reported out S. 1560 (incorporating the single-administrator approach), introduced by Senator Moynihan (D-NY).

    a.   The Senate passed S. 1560 by voice vote on March 2, 1994.
    b.   On May 23, 1994, the Senate approved H.R. 4277, after striking its language and substituting that of S. 1560, by voice vote.

3. Conference Action

Conferees reached an agreement on July 20, 1994, under which SSA would be run by a single administrator appointed for a six-year term, supported by a seven-member bipartisan advisory board.

    a.   The Senate passed the agreement by voice vote on August 5, 1994.
    b.   The House passed the agreement on August 11, 1994, by a vote of 431-0.[391]

MM. P.L. 103-387, The Social Security Domestic Reform Act of 1994

President Clinton signed H.R. 4278, Social Security Domestic Reform Act of 1994, on October 22, 1994. H.R. 4278: raised the threshold for Social Security coverage of household employees from remuneration of $50 in wages a quarter to $1,000 a year, which would rise thereafter with the growth in average wages; and reallocated taxes from the OASI fund to the DI fund.

In early 1993, the issue of coverage of domestic workers burst into public awareness when several Cabinet nominees revealed that they had failed to report the wages they had paid to childcare providers. Subsequent media scrutiny made it apparent that under-reporting of household wages was common. It also highlighted that householders were supposed to be reporting even occasional work such as babysitting and lawn mowing. As the threshold had not been changed for 43 years, the question naturally arose of whether it should be raised.

1. House Action

Several measures were introduced in the 103rd Congress that would have raised the threshold by varying amounts. On March 22, 1994, Mr. Andrew Jacobs (D-IN) introduced H.R. 4105, which would have raised the threshold to $1,250 a year in 1995, to be indexed thereafter to increases in average wages.

    a.   This measure was included in H.R. 4278, approved by the House on May 12, 1994, by a vote of 420-0.[392]

2. Senate Action

When the Senate considered H.R. 4278 on May 25, 1994, it struck the House language and substituted the text of S. 1231, a bill by Senator Moynihan (D-NY) which would have raised the annual threshold to the same level as that needed to earn a quarter of coverage ($620 in 1994) and exempted from Social Security taxes the wages paid to domestic workers under the age of 18.

    a.   The Senate passed the revised version of H.R. 4278 on May 25, 1994, by unanimous consent.

3. Conference Action

On October 5, 1994, conferees agreed to a measure that raised the threshold for Social Security coverage of household workers to $1,000, effective in 1994. The measure also provided that the threshold would rise in the future, in $100 increments, in proportion to the growth in average wages in the economy (it rose to $1,100 in 1998, $1,200 in 2000, and $1,300 in 2001).[393]

    a.   On October 6, 1994, the conference report was approved in the House by a vote of 423-0.

    b.   The same day, the Senate approved the conference report by unanimous consent.

NN. P.L. 104-121, The Senior Citizens Right to Work Act of 1996

On March 29, 1996, President Clinton signed H.R. 3136, the Senior Citizens Right to Work Act of 1996. H.R. 3136: raised the annual earnings test exempt amount, for recipients who have attained the full retirement age, over a period of seven years, reaching $30,000 in 2002; prohibited DI and SSI eligibility to individuals whose disability is based on drug addiction or alcoholism; tightened eligibility requirements for entitlements to benefits as a stepchild; and, as a way to produce program savings that would help compensate for the increased costs to the Social Security system due to liberalizing the earnings test, provided funds for additional continuing disability reviews.

On September 27, 1994, 300 Republican congressional candidates presented a "Contract with America" that listed 10 proposals that they would pursue if elected. One of the proposals, the "Senior Citizens Equity Act," included a measure to increase the earnings test limits, for those over age 64, over a period of five years, reaching $30,000 in 2000. After the Republican victory in the election, the Senior Citizens Equity Act was sponsored by 131 Members in H.R. 8, introduced January 4, 1995.Although the House approved the measure as part of H.R. 1215, it was not included in the Balanced Budget Reconciliation bill (H.R. 2491) passed by the Congress on November 20, 1995.

1. House Action

On November 28, 1995, the Social Security Subcommittee of the Ways and Means Committee approved H.R. 2684, the Senior Citizens Right to Work Act, introduced by Chairman Bunning, (R-KY) that gradually would increase the earnings test limits for those aged 65-69 to $30,000 in 2002. The full committee approved H.R. 2684 by a vote of 31-0 on November 30, 1995.

a. The House approved H.R. 2684 on December 5, 1995, by a vote of 411 (230-R, 180-D, 1-I) to 4 (0-R, 4-D).[394]
   On March 21, 1996, reportedly with the agreement of the Administration, a modified version of H.R. 2684 was included in H.R. 3136, the Contract with America Advancement Act of 1996, introduced by Mr. Archer (D-TX). H.R. 3136, also included an increase in the debt ceiling and other measures. The part of H.R. 3136 relating to the earnings test was similar to H.R. 2684, but modified to

slow the rise in the exempt amounts during the first five years of the phase-in.

  a. On March 28, 1996, H.R. 3136 was passed by the House by a vote of 328 (201-R, 127-D) to 91 (30-R, 60-D, 1-I).[395]

2. Senate Action

On December 14, 1995, the Senate Committee on Finance approved S. 1470, a bill similar to H.R. 2684.

  a. On March 28, 1996, H.R. 3136 was passed by the Senate by unanimous consent.

OO. P.L. 106-170, The Ticket to Work and Work Incentives Improvement Act of 1999

President Clinton signed H.R. 1180, the Ticket to Work and Work Incentive Act of 1999, on December 17, 1999. H.R. 1180 provided disabled recipients with vouchers they can use to purchase rehabilitative services from public or private providers and extended Medicare coverage for up to 4.5 additional years for disabled recipients who work.

In the 1990s, there was a growing movement to mitigate what was seen as a fundamental dilemma faced by many disabled Social Security recipients. The dilemma was that, while the disabled were encouraged to try to leave the Social Security rolls by attempting to work, in doing so they faced a limited choice in seeking rehabilitation services and a potentially serious loss of Medicare and Medicaid benefits. Proponents of providing greater work opportunity argued that incentives for the disabled to attempt to work should be enhanced.

1. House Action

  a. On October 19, 1999, the House approved H.R. 1180, The Ticket to Work and Work Incentives Improvement Act of 1999, introduced By Representative Vic Lazio (R-NY), by a vote of 412 (206-R, 205-D, 1-I) to 9 (9-R, 0-D).[396]

2. Senate Action

  a. On June 16, 1999, the Senate passed a similar bill, S. 331, the Work Incentives Improvement Act of 1999, introduced by Senator James S.

Jeffords (R-VT), by a vote of 99-0.[397] On October 21, 1999, the Senate passed H.R. 1180, after striking its language and substituting that of S. 331, by unanimous consent.

3. Conference Action

a. On November 18, 1999, the House adopted the conference report by a vote of 418 (212-R, 205-D, 1-I) to 2 (0-R, 2-D).[398]

b. On November 19, 1999, the Senate adopted the conference report by a vote of 95 (51-R, 44-D) to 1 (1-R, 0-D).[399]

PP. P.L. 106-182, The Senior Citizens Right to Work Act

President Clinton signed H.R. 5, the Senior Citizens Right to Work Act, on April 7, 2000. H.R. 5 eliminated the earnings test for recipients who have attained the full retirement age, effective in 2000.

The earnings test has always been one of the most unpopular features of the Social Security program. Critics said it was unfair and inappropriate to impose a form of "means" test for a retirement benefit that has been earned by a lifetime of contributions to the program, that it has a strong negative effect on work incentives, and that it can hurt elderly individuals who need to work to supplement their Social Security benefits. Defenders of the provision said that it is a reasonable means of executing the purpose of Social Security. Because the system is social insurance that protects workers from loss of income due to the retirement, death, or disability of the worker, they consider it appropriate to withhold benefits from workers who show by their substantial earnings that they have not in fact "retired." Also, they argued that eliminating or significantly liberalizing the benefit would primarily help those who do not need help (i.e., the better-off).

However, over the years probably the main impediment to eliminating the earnings test was its negative effect on the financial status of the program and on current federal budgets, which perennially were in deficit. By 2000, the federal budget was running large surpluses, so major alterations to the test were deemed affordable. Also, it was projected that eliminating the test would have no negative impact on Social Security's long-range financing because of offsetting savings. The ground work for this offsetting effect had been laid in 1983, when Congress increased the Delayed Retirement Credit (DRC). The DRC increases benefits for retirees by a certain percentage for each month they do not receive benefits after they attain their full retirement age. The 1983 legislation provided for a long phase-in of the increase in the DRC, so that its ultimate rate would not be achieved until 2008. At that point it would be "actuarial," meaning that the additional benefits a person would receive over his or her lifetime due to the DRC would be approximately equal to the value of the benefits lost due to the earnings test. Thus, the long-range cost of eliminating the earnings test for those above the full retirement age would be offset by the savings produced by fewer payments of DRCs. Because there was no threat to Social Security's long-range solvency and the short range costs were judged to be affordable, the momentum to repeal the test for those at or over the retirement age was overwhelming.

1. House Action

    a.   On March 1, 2000, the House approved H.R. 5, a bill that would eliminate the earnings test for recipients who have attained the full retirement age, introduced by Representative Sam Johnson (R-TX), by a vote of 422-0.[400]

2. Senate Action

    a.   On March 22, 2000, the Senate approved H.R. 5, with a modification to the monthly exempt amounts in the year of attaining the full retirement age, by a vote of 100-0.[401]

3. Conference Action

    a.   On March 28, 2000, the house approved the Senate version of H.R. 5 by a vote of 419-0.[402]

QQ. P.L. 108-203, The Social Security Protection Act of 2004

President Bush signed H.R. 743, the Social Security Protection Act of 2004, on March 2, 2004. The measure included various provisions designed to reduce fraud and abuse in the Social Security[403] and Supplemental Security Income (SSI) programs. Among other changes, H.R. 743 imposed stricter standards on individuals and organizations that serve as representative payees for Social Security and SSI recipients; made nongovernmental representative payees liable for misused funds and subjected them to civil monetary penalties; tightened restrictions on attorneys who represent Social Security and SSI disability claimants; limited assessments on attorney fee payments; prohibited fugitive felons from receiving Social Security benefits; modified

Social Security: Major Decisions in the House and Senate Since 1935   95

the *last day rule* under the Government Pension Offset provision; and required certain noncitizens to have authorization to work in the United States at the time a Social Security Number is assigned, or at some later time, to gain insured status under the Social Security program. Several major provisions of the new law are described below.[404]

The Social Security Administration (SSA) may designate a "representative payee" to accept monthly benefit payments on behalf of Social Security and SSI recipients who are physically or mentally incapable of managing their own funds, or on behalf of children under age 18. Before P.L. 108-203, SSA was required to reissue benefits misused by an individual or organizational representative payee only in cases where the Commissioner of Social Security found that SSA negligently failed to investigate or monitor the payee. The new law eliminated the requirement that the reissuance of benefits be subject to a finding of negligence on the part of SSA. As a result, SSA is required to reissue any benefits misused by an individual representative payee who represents 15 or more recipients, or by an organizational representative payee. In addition, the new law made nongovernmental representative payees (i.e., those other than federal, state, and local government agencies) liable for the reimbursement of misused funds. Under the new law, SSA has the authority to impose a civil monetary penalty (up to $5,000 for each violation) and an assessment (up to twice the amount of misused benefits) on representative payees who misuse benefits. The new law included a number of other provisions aimed at strengthening the accountability of representative payees.

Social Security and SSI disability claimants may choose to have an attorney or other qualified individual represent them in proceedings before SSA, and the claimant representative may charge a fee for his or her services. The fee, which is subject to limits, must be authorized by SSA. If a *Social Security* disability claimant is awarded past-due benefits and his or her representative is an *attorney*, SSA withholds the attorney's fee payment from the benefit award and sends the payment directly to the attorney. To cover the administrative costs associated with the fee withholding process for attorney representatives of Social Security disability claimants, SSA withholds an assessment of up to 6.3% from the attorney's fee. Before P.L. 108-203, if the claimant representative was not an attorney, or the claim was for SSI benefits, SSA would send the full benefit award to the claimant and the claimant representative would be responsible for collecting his or her fee from the individual. The new law capped the assessment for processing attorney fee payments at the lesser of 6.3% of the attorney's fee and $75 (indexed to inflation); provided for a temporary (five-year) extension of the attorney fee withholding process to SSI claims; authorized a five-year demonstration project to extend the fee withholding process to non-attorney representatives in both Social Security and SSI claims; and required the General Accounting Office (now known as the Government Accountability Office) to study the fee payment process for claimant representatives.

Before P.L. 108-203, SSA was prohibited from paying *SSI* benefits only (not Social Security benefits) to fugitive felons (i.e., persons fleeing prosecution, custody, or confinement after conviction, and persons violating probation or parole). In addition, upon written request, SSA was required to provide information about these individuals (current address, Social Security Number, and photograph) to law enforcement officials. The new law prohibited SSA from paying *Social Security* benefits as well to fugitive felons and required SSA, upon written request, to provide information to law enforcement officials to assist in the apprehension of these individuals. The new law authorized the Commissioner of Social Security to pay, with good cause, SSI and Social Security benefits previously denied because of an individual's status as a fugitive felon.[405]

If an individual receives a government pension from work that was not covered by Social Security, his or her Social Security spousal or widow(er) benefit is reduced by an amount equal to two-thirds of the non-covered government pension, under a provision known as the Government Pension Offset (GPO). Before P.L. 108-203, a state or local government employee who was not covered by Social Security would be exempt from the GPO if he or she worked in a Social Security-covered government position on the *last day of employment*. That is, under the *"last day rule,"* a non-covered state or local government employee could avoid having his or her Social Security spousal or widow(er) benefit reduced under the GPO by switching to a Social Security-covered government position for one day (or longer). Under the new law, a state or local government employee must be covered by Social Security for at least the *last 60 calendar months of employment* to be exempt from the GPO.[406]

Before P.L. 108-203, a noncitizen was not required to have authorization to work in the United States at any point to qualify for Social Security benefits. Under the new law, a noncitizen who is assigned a Social Security Number (SSN) in *2004 or later* is required to have work authorization at the time the SSN is assigned, or at some later time, to gain insured status under the Social Security program. Specifically, if the individual obtains work authorization at some point, *all* of his or her Social Security-covered earnings count toward qualifying for benefits (all authorized and unauthorized earnings). If the individual never obtains authorization to work in the United States, *none* of his or her Social Security-covered earnings count toward qualifying for benefits. A noncitizen who was assigned an SSN *before 2004* is not subject to the work authorization requirement established under the new law (i.e., all of the individual's Social Security-covered earnings count toward qualifying for benefits, regardless of his or her work authorization status).[407]

1. House Action

   a. On April 2, 2003, the House approved H.R. 743, The Social Security Protection Act of 2003, introduced by Representative E. Clay Shaw (R-FL), by a vote of 396 (219-R, 176-D, 1-I) to 28 (3-R, 25-D).[408]

2. Senate Action

   a. On September 17, 2003, the Senate Finance Committee approved an amendment in the nature of a substitute to H.R. 743, as passed by the House, by a voice vote.

   b. On December 9, 2003, the Senate approved H.R. 743, with an amendment that substituted for the version of the bill approved by the Senate Finance Committee, by unanimous consent.

3. House Response to Senate Action

   a. On February 11, 2004, the House agreed to the Senate version and passed H.R. 743 (renamed the Social Security Protection Act of 2004), by a vote of 402 (221-R, 180-D, 1-I) to 19 (4-R, 15-D).[409]

RR. P.L. 111-312, The Tax Relief, Unemployment Insurance Reauthorization, and Job Creation Act of 2010

President Obama signed H.R. 4853, the Tax Relief, Unemployment Insurance Reauthorization, and Job Creation Act of 2010, on December 17, 2010. Section 601 of the law reduced, in 2011 only, the Social Security portion of the payroll tax applied to both the wages and salaries of FICA-covered workers and to the net earnings of SECA-covered self-employed workers, by two percentage points. The Social Security initiative was just one among other provisions included in the legislation intended to stimulate the economy by creating jobs, extending public payments to the unemployed, and providing workers with more disposable income.

The act temporarily reduced the FICA tax rate from 6.2% of covered earnings to 4.2% for employees, and the SECA tax rate from 12.4% of covered net self-employed earnings to 10.4%. The law did not change the FICA rate for employers in 2011, which remained at 6.2%.

Net revenue to the Social Security trust funds was not impacted by P.L. 111-312. Any decline in tax revenue in 2011 attributed to the act was covered by appropriate transfers from the General Fund of the U.S. Treasury.

1. House Action

On March 17, 2010, the House approved H.R. 4853, under suspension of the rules by voice vote. The bill, introduced by Representative James Oberstar (D-MN), at the time was known as the ultimately unrelated *"Federal Aviation Administration Extension Act of 2010."*

2. Senate Action

On September 23, 2010, the Senate passed the bill, with an amendment in the nature of a substitute to H.R. 4853, as passed by the House, by unanimous consent. The Senate's amendment, still focused on the aviation industry, was titled the *"Airport and Airway Extension Act of 2010, Part III."*

3. House Action

After a few days of debate on tax relief and the economy in early December, the House moved to strip out all aviation provisions in H.R. 4853 and subsequently used the bill as a vehicle for tax relief measures. On December 2, 2010, the House agreed to adopt an amendment to H.R. 4853, as amended by the Senate, by a vote of 234 (231-D, 3-R) to 188 (168-R, 20-D).[410]

4. Senate Action

The Senate immediately began deliberation of its version of tax relief in response to the House amendment to the Senate amendment of H.R. 4853. On December 9, 2010, the Senate produced a new substitute to H.R. 4853, in the form of yet another amendment. This version included a provision to grant a one year partial payroll tax "holiday" to workers and the self-employed in 2011. The holiday was packaged as a two percentage point reduction in the FICA and SECA payroll tax rates. On December 15, 2010, the Senate approved this new version of the bill, by a vote of 81 (43-D, 37-R, 1-I) to 19 (13-D, 5-R, 1-I).[411]

Social Security: Major Decisions in the House and Senate Since 1935   99

5. House Action

On December 17, 2010, the House approved the latest Senate version of H.R. 4853 (officially, the Senate amendment to the House amendment to the Senate amendment of H.R. 4853). The House approved the measure by a vote of 277 (139-D, 138-R) to 148 (112-D, 36-R).[412]

SS. P.L. 112-78, The Temporary Payroll Tax Cut Continuation Act of 2011

President Obama signed H.R. 3765, the Temporary Payroll Tax Cut Continuation Act of 2011, on December 23, 2011. Section 101 of the law extended the expiring temporary Social Security payroll tax contribution rates that were provided in P.L. 111-312, the Tax Relief, Unemployment Insurance Reauthorization, and Job Creation Act of 2010 (P.L. 111-312), effective in calendar year 2011, into calendar year 2012. In addition to the Social Security payroll tax provisions, P.L. 112-78 also included extensions of unemployment insurance and health provisions, as well as provisions relating to mortgage fees and the construction of a transcontinental oil pipeline.

Specifically, the Social Security portion of the payroll tax applied to the covered net earnings of SECA-covered self-employed workers remained reduced throughout 2012 at 10.4%, down from the SECA tax rate of 12.4%. The act also extended the 2011 temporary reduction of the FICA tax rate on employee covered earnings from 6.2% to 4.2% through February 2012 only.

Throughout 2011, several proposals were introduced to extend the 2011 temporary payroll tax reductions through calendar year 2012. H.R. 3630 received attention as the vehicle for a year-long extension, which had bipartisan and bicameral support, but the bill stalled as respective versions advanced by the House and Senate differed on how to replace revenue lost as a result of the payroll tax rate reductions. Ultimately, H.R. 3765 emerged as a short-term compromise, and it extended the payroll tax reductions for two months. The year-long extension of payroll tax cuts through calendar year 2012 is addressed in Section TT of this report, when Congress revisited H.R. 3630 after the adoption of H.R. 3765 into P.L. 112-78.

1. House Action

    a.   On December 23, 2011, the House approved H.R. 3765, introduced by Representative Dave Camp (R-MI) without objection.

100 Gary Sidor

2. Senate Action

    a.   On December 23, 2011, the Senate approved H.R. 3765 by unanimous consent.

TT. P.L. 112-96, The Middle Class Tax Relief and Job Creation Act of 2012

President Obama signed H.R. 3630, the Middle Class Tax Relief and Job Creation Act of 2012, on February 22, 2012. Section 1001 of the law further extended, through 2012, expiring reduced Social Security payroll tax contribution rates first provided in the Tax Relief, Unemployment Insurance Reauthorization, and Job Creation Act of 2010 (P.L. 111-312).

The payroll tax rate reductions of the Tax Relief, Unemployment Insurance Reauthorization, and Job Creation Act of 2010, addressed above in Section RR, were initially intended to be applied only in 2011. These rate reductions were extended for an additional two months, through February 2012, by the Temporary Payroll Tax Cut Continuation Act of 2011 (P.L. 112-78). The Middle Class Tax Relief and Job Creation Act of 2012 further extended the rate reductions through the end of calendar year 2012.

In addition to the Social Security payroll tax provisions, P.L. 112-96 also included extensions of unemployment insurance, health, and welfare provisions, as well as provisions relating to the retirement contributions for federal employees and to public safety programs.

In the second session of the 112th Congress, the House and Senate came to an agreement on how to pay for the provisions in H.R. 3630, and the legislation advanced with the filing of a conference report on February 16, 2012. The temporary payroll tax rates extended under P.L. 112-96 expired at the end of 2012. The tax rates returned to 6.2% of covered earnings for employees and 12.4% of covered net earnings for the self-employed in 2013.

1. House Action

    a.   On December 13, 2011, the House approved H.R. 3630, the Middle Class Tax Relief and Job Creation Act of 2011, introduced by Representative Dave Camp (R-MI), by a vote of 234 (224-R, 10-D) to 193 (14-R, 179-D).[413]

Social Security: Major Decisions in the House and Senate Since 1935 101

2. Senate Action

a. On December 17, 2011, the Senate approved its version of H.R. 3630, as an amendment in the nature of a substitute and renamed the Temporary Payroll Tax Cut Continuation Act of 2011 by Majority Leader Harry Reid (D-NV), by a vote of 89 (49-D, 39-R, 1-I) to 10 (2-D, 7-R, 1-I).[414]

3. House Action

a. On February 17, 2012, the House agreed to the conference report of the bill, now identified as the Middle Class Tax Relief and Job Creation Act of *2012*, by a vote of 293 (146-R, 147-D) to 132 (91-R, 41-D).[415]

4. Senate Action

a. On February 17, 2012, the Senate agreed to the conference report by a vote of 60 (45-D, 14-R, 1-I) to 36 (5-D, 30-R, 1-I).[416]

End Notes

[1] U.S. Congress, House Committee on Ways and Means, *The Social Security Bill*, report to accompany H.R. 7260, 74th Cong., 1st sess., Report no.615 (Washington, GPO, 1935), p. 44.

[2] Edwin E. Witte, *The Development of the Social Security Act* (University of Wisconsin Press, 1963), p. 98. (Hereinafter cited as Witte, *The Development of the Social Security Act*.)

[3] *Congressional Record*, April 18, 1935, House, p. 5958. The vote on the Townsend plan amendment was not taken by roll call, but by division. A division vote is taken as follows: Members in favor of a proposal stand and are counted by a presiding officer; then Members opposed stand and are counted. There is no record of how individual Members voted. The Members voting for the Townsend plan, however, were listed in newspapers. The majority of Members who voted for the Townsend plan were conservative Republicans who opposed the entire Social Security bill. Witte, *The Development of the Social Security Act*, p. 99.

[4] *Congressional Record*, April 18, 1935, House, in floor remarks by Mr. Lundeen, p. 5965.

[5] *Congressional Record*, April 18, 1935, House, p. 5969. In the House, Members would file past tellers and be counted as for or against a measure, but they were not recorded by name. The teller vote has not been used in the House in many years and was never used in the Senate.

[6] *Congressional Record*, April 18, 1935, House, in floor remarks by Mr. Treadway, p. 5990. Also see, *Congressional Record*, April 12, 1935, House, p. 5531.

[7] *Congressional Record*, April 18,1935, House, in floor remarks by Mr. Jenkins, p. 5993.

[8] *Congressional Record*, April 18, 1935, House, p. 5994.

[9] *Congressional Record*, April 19, 1935, p. 6068.

[10] *Congressional Record*, April 12, 1935, House, in floor remarks by Mr. Treadway, p. 5531.

[11] *Congressional Record*, April 19, 1935, House, in floor remarks by Mr. Treadway, p. 6053.

[12] *Congressional Record*, April 19, 1935, House, Roll call no. 56, not voting 29, p. 6068-6069.

[13] *Congressional Record*, April 19, 1935, House, Roll call no. 57, not voting 25, p. 6069-6070.

[14] *Congressional Record*, June 17, 1935, Senate, p. 9427-9437.

[15] *Congressional Record,* June 19, 1935, Senate, not voting 9, p. 9631.

[16] *Congressional Record,* June 17,1935, Senate, in floor remarks by Mr. Hastings, p. 9422.

[17] *Congressional Record,* Senate. June 19,1935, not voting 17, p. 9648.

[18] *Congressional Record,* June 19, 1935, Senate, p. 9650.

[19] *Congressional Record,* June 19, 1935, Senate, not voting 12, p. 9646.

[20] The issue, however, does not appear to have emerged in subsequent Social Security legislation. It has been said that deferring the Clark amendment was crucial to the passage of the bill (Derthick, Martha, *Policymaking for Social Security.* The Brookings Institution, 1979, p. 282). (Hereinafter cited as Derthick, *Policymaking for Social Security.*)

[21] *Congressional Record,* July 17, 1935, House, Roll call no. 132, not voting 83, pp. 11342-11343.

[22] *Congressional Record,* July 17, 1935, House, Roll call no. 133, not voting 95, p. 11343.

[23] *Congressional Record,* July 17, 1935, Senate, p. 11310.

[24] *Congressional Record,* August 8, 1935, House, p. 12760.

[25] *Congressional Record,* August 9, 1935, Senate, pp. 12793-12794.

[26] *Congressional Record,* August 9, 1935, Senate, p. 12794.

[27] The PIA was the basic benefit amount for a worker who began receiving benefits at the age of 65.

[28] Benefits can be paid to workers or their dependents or survivors only if the worker is "insured" for these benefits. Insured status is measured in terms of "quarters of coverage." A person who had one year of coverage for every two years after 1936 and before death or reaching the age of 65 was fully insured.

[29] The Townsend movement, led by a California doctor named Francis E. Townsend, began in 1934, survived for some 20 years, and was at its peak in the 1935-1941 period, according to Derthick, *Policymaking for Social Security,* p. 193.

[30] U.S. Congress, House Committee on Ways and Means, *Economic Security Act,* hearings on H.R. 4120, 74th Cong., 1st sess., January 21-31 and February 1, 2, 4-8, and 12, 1935 (Washington, GPO, 1935), p. 680.

[31] *Congressional Record,* June 6, 1939, House, p. 6681.

[32] Witte, *The Development of the Social Security Act,* pp. 95-96.

[33] *Congressional Record,* June 1, 1939, House, Roll call no. 85, not voting 29, pp. 6524-6525.

[34] *New York Times,* June 2, 1939, Editorial page.

[35] U.S. Congress, House Committee on Ways and Means, *Social Security Amendments of 1939,* report to accompany H.R. 6635, 76th Cong., 1st sess., H.Rept. no. 728 (Washington, GPO, 1939), p. 113.

[36] *Congressional Record,* June 9, 1939, House, p. 6935.

[37] *Congressional Record,* June 9, 1939, House, p. 6936.

[38] *Congressional Record,* June 9, 1939, House, pp. 6937-6939.

[39] *Congressional Record,* June 10, 1939, House, p. 6970.

[40] *Congressional Record,* June 10. 1939, House, Roll call no. 91, not voting 63, pp. 6970-6971.

[41] *Congressional Record,* July 13, 1939, Senate, not voting 31, p. 9023.

[42] *Congressional Record,* July 13, 1939, Senate, p. 9030.

[43] *Congressional Record,* July 13, 1939, Senate, not voting 31, p. 9031.

[44] *Congressional Record,* August 4, 1939, House, p. 11092.

[45] *Congressional Record,* August 5, 1939, Senate, not voting 33, p. 11146.

[46] *Congressional Record,* January 19, 1944, Senate, in floor statement by Mr. Vandenberg, p. 374

[47] *Congressional Record,* January 19, 1944, Senate, p. 374.

[48] *Congressional Record,* October 9, 1942, Senate, pp. 7983-7984.

[49] Derthick, *Policymaking for Social Security,* p. 237.

[50] Social Security Administration, "Social Security Legislation. January-June 1948: Legislative History and Background" (by) Wilbur Cohen and James L. Calhoon, *Social Security Bulletin,* vol. 11, no. 7, July 1948, pp. 3-11.

[51] Ibid.

Social Security: Major Decisions in the House and Senate Since 1935   103

[52] *Congressional Record,* April 6, 1948, House, p. 4134.

[53] *United States v. Silk* (67 S. Ct. 1463), *Harrison v. Grayvan Lines, Inc.* (67 S. Ct. 1463), and *Bartels v. Birmingham* (67 S. Ct. 1547).

[54] *Congressional Record,* March 4, 1948, House, p. 2143.

[55] *Congressional Record,* February 27, 1948, House, Roll call no.18, not voting 103, pp. 1908-1909.

[56] *Congressional Record,* March 23, 1948. Senate, p. 3267

[57] *Congressional Record,* June 4. 1948, Senate, not voting 16, p. 7134

[58] *Congressional Record,* June 4, 1948, House, p. 7215.

[59] *Congressional Record,* April 6, 1948, House, p. 4134.

[60] *Congressional Record,* June 14. 1948, House, p. 8188.

[61] *Congressional Record,* April 14, 1948, House, Roll call no. 44, not voting 93, p. 4432.

[62] *Congressional Record,* April 20, 1948, Senate, not voting 12, p. 4594.

[63] *Congressional Record,* June 14, 1948, House, Roll call no. 105, not voting 57, p. 8191.

[64] *Congressional Record,* June 14, 1948, Senate, not voting 19, p. 8093.

[65] Several subsequent pieces of legislation during the early 1950s extended these wage credits to periods of service up to December 31, 1956. The 1967 amendments gave military wage credits of $300 per calendar quarter of service after 1967 (amended in 1972 to be effective in 1957). The 1977 amendments gave wage credits of $100 per $300 of basic pay, up to a maximum of $1,200 credit per year, beginning in 1978.

[66] U.S. Congress, House Committee on Ways and Means, *Social Security Act of 1949,* report to accompany H.R. 6000, 81st Cong., 1st sess., H.Rept. 1300 (Washington, GPO, 1949), p. 157-165.

[67] *Congressional Record,* October 4, 1949, House, Roll call no. 215, not voting 106, p. 13819.

[68] *Congressional Record,* October 5, 1949, House, Roll call no. 217, not voting 84, pp. 13972-13973.

[69] *Congressional Record,* October 5, 1949, House, Roll call no. 218, not voting-84, pp. 13973-13974.

[70] U.S. Congress, Senate Committee on Finance, *Social Security Act Amendments of 1950,* report to accompany H.R. 6000, 81st Cong., 2nd sess., May 17, 1950, H.Rept.1669 (Washington, GPO, 1950), p. 2.

[71] *Congress and the Nation: 1945-1964,* Washington, Congressional Quarterly Inc., 1965, p. 1243.

[72] *Congressional Record,* June 20, 1950, Senate, p. 8904.

[73] *Congressional Record,* June 20, 1950, Senate, not voting 15, p. 8883.

[74] *Congressional Record,* June 20, 1950, Senate, not voting 13, p. 8889.

[75] *Congressional Record,* June 20, 1950, Senate, p. 8883.

[76] *Congressional Record,* June 20, 1950, Senate, p. 8878.

[77] *Congressional Record,* June 20,1950, Senate, not voting 13, p. 8910.

[78] A motion for the previous question, when carried, has the effect of stopping all debate and amendments, forcing a vote on the pending matter. This parliamentary maneuver is used only in the House.

[79] *Congressional Record,* August 16, 1950, House, Roll call no. 242, not voting 55, p. 12673.

[80] *Congressional Record,* August 17, 1950, House, p. 12718.

[81] *Congressional Record,* May 19, 1952, House, Roll call no. 79, not voting 139, pp. 5483-5484.

[82] *Congressional Record,* June 16, 1952, House, p. 7293.

[83] *Congressional Record,* June 17, 1952, House, Roll call no. 106, not voting 46, p. 7387.

[84] *Congressional Record,* June 26, 1952, Senate, p. 8141.

[85] *Congressional Record,* June 26, 1952, Senate, p. 8155.

[86] U.S. Congress, Conference Committee, 1952. *Social Security Act Amendments of 1952,* conference report to accompany H.R. 7800, 82nd Cong., 2nd sess., July 1952, H.Rept. 2491 (Washington, GPO, 1952), p. 9.

[87] *Congressional Record,* July 5, 1952, House, p. 9670. Also see, *Congressional Record,* July 5, 1952, Senate, p. 9523.

[88] *Congressional Record,* June 1, 1954, House, in floor remarks by Mr. Smith, p. 7423.

[89] *Congressional Record,* House. June 1, 1954, Roll call no.77, not voting 87, p. 7425.

[90] The American Dental Association (ADA) and the American Medical Association (AMA) strongly opposed Social Security coverage for their groups. The AMA said it was incompatible with the free enterprise system. *Congressional Record,* August 13, 1954, Senate, in floor remarks by Mr. Millikin (R-CO), p. 14422.

[91] *Congressional Record,* June 1, 1954, House, Roll call no. 78, not voting 68, p. 7468.

[92] Social Security Administration, "Social Security Act Amendments of 1954: A Summary and Legislative History," [by] Wilbur J. Cohen, Robert M. Ball, and Robert J. Myers, *Social Security Bulletin,* vol. 17, no. 9, September 1954, p. 3-18.

[93] *Congressional Record,* August 13, 1954, Senate, p. 14442.

[94] *Congressional Record,* August 13, 1954, Senate, p. 14433.

[95] *Congressional Record,* August 13, 1954, Senate, p. 14435.

[96] *Congressional Record,* August 13, 1954, Senate, p. 14444.

[97] *Congressional Record,* August 13, 1954, Senate, p. 14419.

[98] *Congressional Record,* August 13, 1954, Senate, p. 14446.

[99] *Congressional Record,* August 20, 1954, House, p. 15544. Also, *Congressional Record,* August 20, 1954, Senate, p. 15414.

[100] P.L. 881-84th Congress, the Servicemen's and Veterans' Survivor Benefit Act (H.R. 7089), extended coverage of the OASDI system to members of the uniformed services on active duty on a permanent contributory basis beginning in 1957. It was signed into law on August 1, 1956.

[101] *Congressional Record,* July 18, 1955, House, Roll call no. 119, not voting 29, pp. 10798-10799.

[102] Mr. Folsom stated that until the ultimate costs were known, whether it was possible to make disability determinations good enough to avoid "fraudulent' claims for benefits, and whether disability pensions might discourage individual rehabilitative efforts, adding disability insurance to OASI would risk "overburdening and thus wrecking" the Social Security system. *Congress and the Nation: 1945-1964,* p. 1251.

[103] *Congressional Record,* July 17, 1956, Senate, not voting 4, p. 13056.

[104] *Congressional Record,* July 17, 1956, Senate, not voting 3, p. 13073.

[105] *Congressional Record,* July 17, 1956, Senate, not voting 6, p. 13103.

[106] *Congressional Record,* July 26, 1956, House, p. 14828.

[107] *Congressional Record,* July 26, 1956, Senate, p. 15107.

[108] *Congressional Record,* July 31, 1958, House, p. 15740.

[109] *Congressional Record,* July 31, 1958, House, Roll call no. 149, not voting 54, pp. 15775-15776.

[110] *Congressional Record,* August I5, 1958, Senate, p. 17798.

[111] *Congressional Record,* August 16, 1958, Senate, not voting 11, pp. 17971-17972.

[112] *Congressional Record,* August 16, 1958, Senate, p. 17985.

[113] *Congressional Record,* August 16, 1958, Senate, p. 18005.

[114] *Congressional Record,* August 16, 1958, Senate, p. 18008.

[115] *Congressional Record,* August 16, 1958, Senate, p. 17986.

[116] *Congressional Record,* August 16, 1958, Senate, p. 17982.

[117] *Congressional Record,* August 16, 1958, Senate, not voting 17, p. 18014.

[118] *Congressional Record,* August 19, 1958, House, p. 18540.

[119] See Social Security Online: Chronology, March 31, 1960, http://www.ssa.gov/history/1960.html.

[120] *Congressional Record,* June 22, 1960, House, in floor remarks by Mr. Thompson, p. 13846.

[121] *Congressional Record,* June 22, 1960, House, in floor remarks by Mr. Thompson, p. 13845.

Social Security: Major Decisions in the House and Senate Since 1935 105

[122] *Congressional Record,* June 23, 1960, House, Roll call no. 143, not voting 24, pp. 14054-14055.

[123] *Congressional Record,* August 23, 1960, Senate, Roll call no. 305, not voting 5, p. 17176.

[124] *Congressional Record,* August 23, 1960, Senate, Roll call no. 307, not voting 5, p. 17220.

[125] *Congressional Record,* August 23, 1960, Senate, p. 17234.

[126] *Congressional Record,* August 23, 1960, Senate, Roll call no. 309, not voting 7, p. 17235.

[127] *Congressional Record,* August 26, 1960, House, Roll call no. 197, not voting 44, p. 17893.

[128] *Congressional Record,* August 29, 1960, Senate, Roll call no. 314, not voting 15, p. 18096.

[129] Social Security Administration, "Social Security Amendments of 1961: Summary and Legislative History," [by] Wilbur J. Cohen and William L. Mitchell, *Social Security Bulletin,* v. 24, no. 9, September 1961, p. 8.

[130] *Congress and the Nation: 1945-1964,* p. 1255.

[131] *Congressional Record,* April 20, 1961, House, in floor remarks by Mr. Curtis, p. 6471.

[132] *Congressional Record,* April 20, 1961, House, p. 6492.

[133] *Congressional Record,* April 20, 1961, House, p. 6495.

[134] *Congressional Record,* April 20, 1961, House, Roll call no. 40, not voting 17, p. 6495.

[135] *Congressional Record,* June 26, 1961, Senate, p. 11309.

[136] *Congressional Record,* June 26, 1961, Senate, p. 11314.

[137] *Congressional Record,* June 26, 1961, Senate, in floor remarks by Mr. Kerr, p. 11310.

[138] *Congressional Record,* June 26, 1961, Senate, Roll call no. 83, not voting 11, p. 11318.

[139] *Congressional Record,* June 26, 1961, Senate, p. 11325.

[140] *Congressional Record,* June 26, 1961, Senate, p. 11327.

[141] *Congressional Record,* June 26, 1961, Senate, Roll call no. 85, not voting 10, p. 11328.

[142] *Congressional Record,* June 29, 1961, House, p. 11791, and, *Congressional Record,* June 29, 1961, Senate, p. 11693.

[143] *Congressional Record,* July 29, 1964, House, Roll call no.193, not voting 35, pp. 17298-17299.

[144] *Congressional Record,* August 31, 1964, Senate, p. 21103.

[145] *Congressional Record,* August 31, 1964, Senate, p. 21086.

[146] *Congressional Record,* September 2, 1964, Senate, Roll call no. 558, not voting 7, p. 21318.

[147] *Congressional Record,* September 3, 1964, Senate, Roll call no. 561, not voting 12, p. 21553.

[148] Social Security Administration, "Social Security Legislation," *Commissioner's Bulletin,* no. 17, October 3, 1964.

[149] President Johnson flew to Independence, Missouri, to sign H.R. 6675 in the presence of Harry S. Truman, the first President to propose a national health insurance program.

[150] *Congressional Quarterly Almanac: 1965,* Washington, Congressional Quarterly, Inc, p. 236.

[151] *Congressional Record,* April 8, 1965, House, Roll call no. 70, not voting 5, pp. 7443-7444.

[152] *Congressional Record,* April 8, 1965, House, Roll call no. 71, not voting 5, p. 7444.

[153] *Congressional Record,* July 7, 1965, Senate, Roll call no. 165, not voting 18, p. 15835.

[154] *Congressional Record,* July 8, 1965, Senate, Roll call no. 166, not voting 15, p. 15869.

[155] *Congressional Record,* July 8, 1965, Senate, Roll call no. 167, not voting 9, p. 15909.

[156] *Congressional Record,* July 8, 1965, Senate, Roll call no. 168, not voting 8, p. 15927.

[157] *Congressional Record,* July 7, 1965, Senate, p. 15794.

[158] *Congressional Record,* July 8, 1965, Senate, p. 15904.

[159] *Congressional Record,* July 9, 1965, Senate, p. 16115.

[160] *Congressional Record,* July 9, 1965, Senate, p. 16130.

[161] *Congressional Record,* July 9, 1965, Senate, p. 16138.

[162] *Congressional Record,* July 9, 1965, Senate, Roll call no. 170, not voting 10, p. 16100.

[163] *Congressional Record,* July 9, 1965, Senate, Roll call no. 174, not voting 8, p. 16119.

[164] *Congressional Record,* July 9, 1965, Senate, Roll call no. 175, not voting 11, p. 16126.

[165] *Congressional Record,* July 9, 1965, Senate, Roll call no. 176, not voting 11, p. 16157.

[166] *Congressional Record,* July 27, 1965, House, Roll call no. 203, not voting 11, pp. 18393-18394.

106   Gary Sidor

[167] *Congressional Record,* July 28, 1965, Senate, Roll call no.201, not voting 6, p. 18514.

[168] *Congressional Record,* February 23, 1966, House, Roll call no. 20, not voting 41, pp. 3719-3720.

[169] *Congressional Record,* March 8, 1966, Senate, in floor remarks by Mr. Prouty, pp. 5289-5292.

[170] *Congressional Record,* March 8, 1966, Senate, Roll call no. 46, not voting 12, p. 5298.

[171] *Congressional Record,* March 8, 1966, Senate, Roll call no. 47, not voting 15, p. 5298.

[172] *Congressional Record,* March 8, 1966, Senate, Roll call no. 48, not voting 13, p. 5301.

[173] *Congressional Record,* March 9, 1966, Senate, Roll call no. 52, not voting 12, p. 5485.

[174] *Congressional Record,* March 15, 1966, House, Roll call no. 36, not voting 41, p. 5801.

[175] *Congressional Record,* March 15, 1966, Senate, Roll call no. 57, not voting 23, p. 5960.

[176] Social Security Administration, "Social Security Amendments of 1967: Summary-and Legislative History," [by] Wilbur J. Cohen and Robert M. Ball, *Social Security Bulletin,* vol. 31, no. 2, February 1968.

[177] *Congressional Record,* August 17, 1967, House, p. 23132.

[178] *Congressional Record,* August 17, 1967, House, Roll call no. 222, not voting 3, p. 23132.

[179] *Congressional Record,* November 17, 1967, Senate, Roll call no. 327, not voting 32, p. 33078.

[180] *Congressional Record,* November 17, 1967, Senate, Roll call no. 329, not voting 46, p. 33119.

[181] *Congressional Record,* November 21, 1967, Senate, Roll call no. 335, not voting 24, p. 33496.

[182] *Congressional Record,* November 21, 1967, Senate, Roll call no. 337, not voting 20, p. 33510.

[183] *Congressional Record,* November 21, 1967, Senate, Roll call no. 349, not voting 27, p. 33587.

[184] *Congressional Record,* November 22, 1967, Senate, Roll call no. 350, not voting 16, p. 33637.

[185] *Congressional Record,* December 13, 1967, House, Roll call no. 439, not voting 38, p. 36393.

[186] *Congressional Record,* December 15, 1967, Senate, Roll call no.392, not voting 24, p. 36924.

[187] *Congressional Record,* August 7, 1969, House, Roll call No. 149, not voting 7, pp. 22808-22809.

[188] *Congressional Record,* December 5, 1969, Senate, Roll call no. 179, not voting 13, p. 37247.

[189] *Congressional Record,* December 5, 1969, Senate, Roll call no. 177, not voting 10, p. 37240.

[190] *Congressional Record,* December 5, 1969, Senate, Roll call no. 175, not voting 9, p. 37230.

[191] *Congressional Record,* December 11, 1969, Senate, Roll call no. 223, not voting 6, p. 38396.

[192] *Congressional Record,* December 22.1969, House, Roll call no. 351, not voting 50, pp. 40899-40900.

[193] *Congressional Record,* December 22, 1969, Senate, Roll call no. 273, not voting 23, p. 40718.

[194] *Congressional Record,* May 21, 1970, House, Roll call no. 136, not voting 53, pp. 16587-16588.

[195] *Congressional Record,* December 29, 1970, Senate, Roll call no. 455, not voting 19, p. 43868.

[196] *Congressional Quarterly Almanac*; 1971, p. 421-425.

[197] *Congressional Record,* March 12, 1971, Senate, p. 6374.

[198] *Congressional Record,* March 12, 1971, Senate, Roll call no. 20, not voting 18, p. 6381.

[199] *Congressional Record,* March 12, 1971, Senate, Roll call no. 23, not voting 20, p. 6390.

[200] *Congressional Record,* March 16, 1971, House, Roll call no. 20, not voting 68, pp. 6741-6742.

[201] *Congressional Record,* March 16, 1971, Senate, Roll call no. 24, not voting 24, p. 6688.

[202] *Congressional Quarterly Almanac*: 1972, p. 399.

[203] *Congressional Record,* February 23, 1972, House, p. 5269-5270.

[204] *Congressional Record,* June 27, 1972, House, Roll call no. 237, not voting 53, pp. 22558-22559.

[205] *Congressional Record,* June 29, 1972, Senate, Roll call no. 266, not voting 11, p. 23294.

[206] *Congressional Record,* June 30, 1972, Senate, Roll call no. 267, not voting 13, pp. 23511-23512.

[207] *Congressional Record,* June 30, 1972, Senate, Roll call no. 268, not voting 13, p. 23512.

[208] *Congressional Record,* June 30, 1972, Senate, Roll call no. 272, not voting 19, p. 23545.

[209] *Congressional Quarterly Almanac*: 1972, pp. 402-403.

[210] *Congressional Record,* June 30, 1972, House, Roll call no. 259, not voting 95, p. 23738.

Social Security: Major Decisions in the House and Senate Since 1935 107

[211] *Congressional Record,* June 30, 1972, House, Roll call no. 260, not voting 95, pp. 23738-23739.

[212] *Congress and the Nation: 1969-1972,* Vol. III, p. 619.

[213] Under P.L. 92-336, the tax rates had been reduced over then existing scheduled increases through 2010; rates under P.L. 92-603 advanced the tax rate schedule and raised the out-year rates.

[214] *Congressional Record,* June 22, 1971, House, Roll call no. 157, not voting 13, p. 21463.

[215] *Congressional Record,* September 27, 1972, Senate, Roll call no. 478, not voting 19, p. 32488.

[216] *Congressional Record,* September 28, 1972, Senate, p. 32720.

[217] *Congressional Record,* September 29, 1972, Senate, Roll call no. 484, not voting 25, p. 32905.

[218] *Congressional Record,* September 29, 1972, Senate, Roll call no. 485, not voting 27, p. 32907.

[219] *Congressional Record,* September 30, 1972, Senate, Roll call no. 488, not voting 46, p. 33000.

[220] *Congressional Record,* September 27, 1972, Senate, p. 32485.

[221] *Congressional Record,* October 5, 1972, Senate, Roll call no. 536, not voting 27, p. 33995.

[222] *Congressional Record,* October 17, 1972, Senate, Roll call no. 455, not voting 122, p. 36936.

[223] *Congressional Record,* October 17, 1972, Senate, Roll call no. 567, not voting 39, p. 36825.

[224] P.L. 93-66 also increased the earnings test threshold amount from $2,100 to $2,400 for 1974.

[225] *Congressional Record,* November 15, 1973, House, Roll call no. 592, not voting 22, p. 37159.

[226] *Congressional Quarterly Almanac:* 1973, p. 573.

[227] *Congressional Record,* November 15, 1973, House, Roll call no. 592, not voting 22, p. 37159.

[228] *Congressional Record,* November 29, 1973, Senate, Roll call no. 527, not voting 13, p. 38645.

[229] *Congressional Record,* November 29, 1973, Senate, Roll call no. 528, not voting 15, pp. 38645-38646.

[230] *Congressional Record,* November 30, 1973, Senate, Roll call no. 540, not voting 24, p. 38975.

[231] *Congressional Quarterly Almanac:* 1973, p. 577-580.

[232] *Congressional Record,* December 21,1973, Senate, Roll call no. 613, not voting 34, p. 43115. Note: The Congressional Quarterly vote breakdown indicates 66 in favor (21-R, 45-D) and 0 opposed.

[233] *Congressional Record,* December 21, 1973, House, Roll call no. 719, not voting 118, p. 43230.

[234] *Congressional Quarterly Almanac: 1977,* p. 161.

[235] Social Security Administration, "Social Security Amendments of 1977: Legislative History and Summary of Provisions," prepared by John Snee and Mary Ross, Office of Program Evaluation and Planning, *Social Security Bulletin,* vol. 41, no. 3, March 1978, p. 6-9. (Hereinafter cited as "Social Security Amendments of 1977: Legislative History.")

[236] When H.R. 9346 was introduced it was referred solely to the Ways and Means Committee. The chairman of the Post Office and Civil Service Committee, Mr. Nix (D-PA), concerned over the Social Security coverage of federal employees under the bill, persuaded the Speaker to give his Committee sequential referral of the bill. The Committee on Post Office and Civil Service unanimously voted to amend the bill to strike Social Security coverage of federal employees. However, under the rule for floor debates the bill as reported by the Ways and Means Committee was to be the vehicle for floor consideration. The Post Office and Civil Service Committee amendment was considered as a floor amendment to the Ways and Means Committee bill.

[237] *Congressional Quarterly Almanac:* 1977, p. 165.

[238] Ibid.

[239] *Congressional Record,* October 26, 1977, House, Roll call no. 697, not voting 10, p. 35315.

[240] *Congressional Record,* October 26, 1977, House, Roll call no. 698, not voting 15, pp. 35315-35316.

[241] *Congressional Record,* October 26, 1977, House, Roll call no. 700, not voting 17, p. 35323.

[242] *Congressional Record,* October 26, 1977, House, Roll call no. 701, not voting 32, p. 35326.

[243] *Congressional Record,* October 27, 1977, House, Roll call no. 704, not voting 17, p. 35394.

[244] *Congressional Record,* October 27, 1977, House, Roll call no. 705, not voting 14, p. 35406.

[245] *Congressional Record,* October 27, 1977, House, Roll call no. 706, not voting 13, pp. 35406-35407.

[246] "Social Security Amendments of 1977: Legislative History." p. 9.

[247] Ibid., pp. 10-11.

[248] *Congressional Record,* November 2, 1977, Senate, p. 36449.

[249] *Congressional Record,* November 3, 1977, Senate, Roll call no. 611, not voting 11, p. 36763.

[250] *Congressional Record,* November 3, 1977, Senate, Roll call no. 612, not voting 10, p. 36764.

[251] *Congressional Record,* November 4, 1977, Senate, Roll call no. 620, not voting 14, pp. 37130-37131.

[252] *Congressional Record,* November 4, 1977, Senate, Roll call no. 621, not voting 13, p. 37132.

[253] *Congressional Record,* November 4, 1977, Senate, Roll call no. 622, not voting 17, p. 37132.

[254] *Congressional Record,* November 4, 1977, Senate, Roll call no. 627, not voting 29, p. 37162.

[255] *Congressional Record,* November 4, 1977, Senate, p. 37141.

[256] *Congressional Record,* November 4, 1977, Senate, Roll call no. 631, not voting 31, p. 37199-37200.

[257] *Congressional Quarterly Almanac:* 1977, p. 171.

[258] *Congressional Record,* December 15,1977, House, Roll call no. 782, not voting 81, p. 39035.

[259] *Congressional Record,* December 15, 1977, House, in floor remarks by Mr. Ullman, pp. 39007-39008.

[260] *Congressional Record,* December 15, 1977, Senate, Roll call no. 636, not voting 22, pp. 39152-39153

[261] *Congressional Quarterly Almanac,* 1979, p. 505.

[262] Social Security Administration, "Social Security Disability Amendments of 1980: Legislative History and Summary of Provisions," *Social Security Bulletin,* vol. 44, no. 4, April 1981, p. 14-23. (Hereinafter cited as "Social Security Disability Amendments of 1980: Legislative History.")

[263] *Congressional Record,* September 6, 1979, House, p. 23398 and p. 23401.

[264] *Congressional Record,* September 6, 1977, House, Roll call no.447, not voting 37, pp. 23401-23402.

[265] "Social Security Disability Amendments of 1980: Legislative History." pp. 23-24.

[266] *Congressional Record,* January 30, 1980, Senate, Roll call no.23, not voting 6, p. 1231.

[267] *Congressional Record,* January 30, 1980, Senate, Roll call no. 18, not voting 8, p. 1203.

[268] *Congressional Record,* January 30, 1980, Senate, Roll call no. 19, not voting 7, p. 1207.

[269] *Congressional Record,* January 31, 1980, Senate, Roll call no. 27, not voting 12, p. 1411.

[270] "Social Security Disability Amendments of 1980: Legislative History." p. 24.

[271] *Congressional Quarterly Almanac:* 1980, p. 437.

[272] *Congressional Record,* May 22, 1980, House, Roll call no. 253, not voting 42, pp. 12175-12176.

[273] *Congressional Record,* May 29, 1980, Senate, p. 12628.

[274] *Congressional Record,* July 21, 1980, House, in floor remarks by Mr. Pickle, p. 18827.

[275] *Congressional Record,* July 21, 1980, House, p. 18830.

[276] *Congressional Record,* September 25, 1980, Senate, p. 27297.

[277] Other Social Security measures were taken up by the Congress in 1980. On December 5, 1980, President Carter signed H.R. 7765, the Omnibus Reconciliation Act of 1980 (P.L. 96-499), which limited the maximum number of months of retroactive entitlement to OASI benefits from 12 months to 6 months. Also, both the House and Senate passed resolutions expressing disapproval of the Social Security Advisory Council's recommendation that half of Social Security benefits be made subject to federal income tax. House Concurrent Resolution 351 was approved by the House on July 21, 1980, by a vote of 384 to 1, and Senate Resolution 432 was approved by the Senate on August 4, 1980, by voice vote.

[278] *Congressional Quarterly Almanac,* 1980, p. 295.

Social Security: Major Decisions in the House and Senate Since 1935 109

[279] U.S. Congress, House Committee on Ways and Means, *Earnings Test for Social Security Recipients*, report to accompany H.R. 5295, 96th Cong., 1st sess., October 19, 1979, H.Rept. 96-537 (Washington, GPO, 1979).

U.S. Congress, Senate Committee on Finance, *Amendments to the Social Security Program*, report to accompany H.R. 5295, 96th Cong., 2nd sess., September 24, 1980, H.Rept. 96-987 (Washington, GPO, 1980).

[280] *Congressional Record*, December 19, 1979, House, p. 36961.

[281] *Congressional Record*, December 19, 1979, House, Roll call no. 751, not voting 50, p. 36969.

[282] *Congressional Record*, September 30, 1980, Senate, p. 28195.

[283] *Congressional Record*, October 1, 1980, House, pp. 8676-28677.

[284] *Congressional Record*, October 1, 1980, House, p. 28677.

[285] *Congressional Record*, October 1, 1980, Senate, p. 28881.

[286] The minimum benefit is the smallest benefit (before actuarial or earnings test reduction) payable to a worker or from which benefits to his survivors/dependents will be determined. In 1977, the minimum benefit was frozen at $122 per month for workers who became disabled or died after 1978, or reached age 62 after 1983. However, the 1981 legislation eliminated the minimum benefit for all people becoming eligible for benefits in January 1982 or later (except it exempted for 10 years certain members of religious orders who have taken a vow of poverty—these people have their benefits computed under the regular benefit computation rules). People already eligible for benefits before 1982 are able to continue receiving the minimum benefit.

[287] The Senate action is given first because the Senate passed the bill before the House did.

[288] "Social Security Administration, Omnibus Budget Reconciliation Act of 1981: Legislative History and Summary of OASDI and Medicare Provisions," [by] John A. Svahn, *Social Security Bulletin*, vol. 44, no.10, October 1981, p. 7. (Herineafter cited as "Omnibus Budget Reconciliation Act of 1981: Legislative History.")

[289] *Congressional Record*, June 23, 1981, Senate, Roll call no. 160, not voting 2, p. 13304.

[290] *Congressional Record*, June 25, 1981, Senate, Roll call no. 182, not voting 5, p. 13933.

[291] "Omnibus Budget Reconciliation Act of 1981: Legislative History," p. 11.

[292] Ibid.

[293] Ibid.

[294] *Congressional Record*, June 25, 1981, House, Roll call no. 104, not voting 4, pp. 14078-14079.

[295] *Congressional Record*, June 26, 1981, House, Roll call no. 111, not voting 4, pp. 14681-14682.

[296] *Congressional Record*, June 26, 1981, House, Roll call no. 113, not voting 6, pp. 14794-14795.

[297] "Omnibus Budget Reconciliation Act of 1981: Legislative History," p. 13.

[298] *Congressional Record*, July 31,1981, Senate, Roll call no. 247, not voting 6, p. 19144.

[299] *Congressional Quarterly Almanac*, 1981, p. 117.

[300] *Congressional Record*, July 21,1981, House, Roll call no. 145, not voting 15, pp. 16659-16660.

[301] *Congressional Quarterly Almanac*, 1981, p. 119-120.

[302] *Congressional Record*, July 31, 1981, House, Roll call no. 189, not voting 10, pp. 18899-18900.

[303] *Congressional Record*, July 31, 1981, Senate, Roll call no. 248, not voting 12, p. 19148.

[304] *Congressional Record*, October 14, 1981, Senate, p. 23967.

[305] *Congressional Record*, October 14, 1981, Senate, p. 23971.

[306] *Congressional Record*, October 15, 1981, Senate, p. 24107.

[307] *Congressional Record*, October 15, 1981, Senate, p. 24108.

[308] *Congressional Record*, October 15, 1981, Senate, Roll call no. 312, not voting 5, pp. 24096-24097.

[309] *Congressional Record*, October 15, 1981, Senate, Roll call no. 315, not voting 5, p. 24120.

110 Gary Sidor

[310] *Congressional Quarterly Almanac*, 1981, p. 121.

[311] *Congressional Record,* December 15, 1981, Senate, Roll call no. 486, not voting 4, p. 31309.

[312] *Congressional Record,* December 16, 1981, House, Roll call no. 365, not voting 11, p. 31699.

[313] P.L. 98-118 extended until December 7, 1983, the period for which the provisions continuing payment of Social Security disability benefits during appeal were applicable.

[314] In a departure from format, the Senate action is given first because the Senate passed the bill (with regard to Social Security provisions) before the House did.

[315] *Congressional Record,* daily edition, December 3, 1982, Senate, p. S13857.

[316] *Congressional Record,* daily edition, December 3, 1982, Senate, Roll call no. 394, not voting 26, p. S13869.

[317] *Congressional Record,* daily edition, September 20, 1982, House, p. H7219.

[318] *Congressional Record,* daily edition, December 14, 1982, House, p. H9665.

[319] *Congressional Record,* daily edition, December 21, 1982, House, Roll call no. 487, not voting 174, pp. HI0679-H10680.

[320] *Congressional Record,* daily edition, December 21, 1982, Senate, p. S15966.

[321] Based on estimates by the National Commission on Social Security Reform.

[322] *Congressional Record,* daily edition, March 9, 1983, House, Roll call no. 22, not voting 3, pp. H1064-H1065.

[323] *Congressional Record,* daily edition, March 9, 1983, House, Roll call no. 24, not voting 5, p. H1079.

[324] *Congressional Record,* daily edition, March 9, 1983, House, Roll call no. 26, not voting 3, pp. H1080-H1081.

[325] *Congressional Record,* daily edition, March 23, 1983, Senate, p. S3711.

[326] *Congressional Record,* daily edition, March 23, 1983, Senate, Roll call no. 47, not voting 2, p. S3714.

[327] *Congressional Record,* daily edition, March 23, 1983, Senate, Roll call no. 48, not voting 4, p. S3720.

[328] *Congressional Record,* daily edition, March 23, 1983, Senate, Roll call no. 53, not voting 3, p. S3775.

[329] *Congressional Quarterly Almanac: 1983*, p. 226.

[330] *Congressional Record,* daily edition, March 24, 1983, House, Roll call no. 47, not voting 88, p. H1787.

[331] *Congressional Record,* daily edition, March 24, 1983, Senate, Roll call no. 54, not voting 28, p. S4104.

[332] *Congressional Quarterly Almanac*, 1984, p. 160.

[333] Social Security Administration, "Social Security Disability Benefits Reform Act of 1984: Legislative History and Summary of Provisions," *Social Security Bulletin*, vol. 48, no. 4, April 1985, p. 12. (Hereinafter cited as "Social Security Disability Benefits Reform Act of 1984: Legislative History.")

[334] *Congressional Record,* daily edition, March 27, 1984, House, in floor remarks by Mr. Conable, p. H1958.

[335] *Congressional Record,* daily edition, March 27, 1984, House, in floor remarks by Mr. Pickle, p. H1959.

[336] *Congressional Record,* daily edition, March 27, 1984, House, Roll call no. 55, not voting 22, pp. H1992-H1993.

[337] Social Security Disability Benefits Reform Act of 1984: Legislative History, p. 27.

[338] *Congressional Record,* daily edition, May 22, 1984, Senate, in floor remarks by Mr. Cohen, p. S6213-S6214.

[339] *Congressional Record,* daily edition, May 22, 1984, Senate, in floor remarks by Mr. Levin, p. 86230.

[340] *Congressional Record,* daily edition, May 22, 1984, Senate, Roll call no. 109, not voting 4, p. S6241.

Social Security: Major Decisions in the House and Senate Since 1935 111

[341] *Congressional Record,* daily edition, September 19, 1984, House, Roll call no. 404, not voting 30, pp. H9838-H9839.

[342] *Congressional Record,* daily edition, September 19, 1984, Senate, Roll call no. 243, not voting 1, p. 11477.

[343] In July 1986 the Supreme Court ruled that the automatic budget-cutting procedures in the legislation referred to as Gramm-Rudman-Hollings were unconstitutional.

[344] *Congressional Record,* daily edition, August 1, 1985, House, Roll call no. 290, call no. 290, not voting 5, pp. H7166-H7167.

[345] *Congressional Record,* daily edition, October 9, 1985, Senate, Roll call no. 213, not voting 1, p. S12988.

[346] *Congressional Record,* daily edition, October 10, 1985, Senate, Roll call no. 222, not voting 12, p. S13114.

[347] *Congressional Record,* daily edition, December 11, 1985, House, Roll call no. 454, not voting 9, pp. H11903-H11904.

[348] *Congressional Record,* daily edition, December 11, 1985, Senate, Roll call no. 371, not voting 6, pp. S17443-S17444.

[349] *Congressional Quarterly Almanac,* 99th Cong. 1st sess., 1985, vol. XLT, p. 447.

[350] *Congressional Record,* May 1, 1985, Senate, Roll call no. 35, not voting 1, p. 10075.

[351] *Congressional Record,* May 9, 1985, Senate, Roll call no. 72, not voting 2, p. 11475. The initial vote was 49 to 49, which necessitated that Vice President Bush cast the tie-breaking vote.

[352] *Congressional Record,* May 9, 1985, Senate, Roll call no. 73, not voting 2, p. 11477.

[353] *Congressional Record,* May 22, 1985, House, Roll call no. 124, not voting 13, p. 13066.

[354] *Congressional Record,* May 23, 1985, House, Roll call no. 129, not voting 5, p. 13387.

[355] *Congressional Record,* May 23, 1985, House, Roll call no. 131, not voting 6, p. 13407.

[356] *Congressional Record,* September 20, 1985, Senate, Roll call no. 277, not voting 5, p. 24918.

[357] *Congressional Record,* September 24, 1986, House, Roll call no. 408, not voting 17, p. 26024.

[358] *Congressional Record,* October 17, 1986, House, Roll call no. 487, not voting 57, p. 32978 and *Congressional Record,* October 17, 1986, Senate, Roll call no. 358, not voting 14, p. 33313.

[359] *Congressional Record,* October 29, 1987, House, Roll call no. 392, not voting 22, p. 30237.

[360] *Congressional Record,* December 10, 1987, Senate, Roll call no. 405, not voting 4, p. 34882.

[361] *Congressional Record,* December 21, 1987, House, Roll call no. 508, not voting 15, p. 37088.

[362] *Congressional Record,* December 21, 1987, Senate, Roll call no. 419, not voting 11, p. 37712.

[363] *Congressional Record,* August 4, 1988, House, Roll call no. 266, not voting 26, p. 20502.

[364] *Congressional Record,* October 11, 1988, Senate, Roll call no. 366, not voting 12, p. 29792.

[365] *Congressional Record,* October 21, 1988, House, Roll call no. 463, not voting 72, p. 33116.

[366] Congressional Record, October 5, 1989, House, Roll call no. 274, not voting 8, p. 23393.

[367] *Congressional Record,* October 13, 1989, Senate, Roll call no. 243, not voting 6, p. 24605.

[368] *Congressional Record,* November 21, 1989, House, Roll call no. 379, not voting 33, p. 31127.

[369] *Congressional Record,* October 16, 1990, House, Roll call no. 475, not voting 3, p. 29923.

[370] *Congressional Record,* October 10, 1990, Senate, Roll call no. 262, not voting 2, p. 28190.

[371] *Congressional Record,* October 18, 1990, Senate, Roll call no. 283, not voting 0, p. 30640.

[372] *Congressional Record,* October 18, 1990, Senate, Roll call no. 292, not voting 0, p. 30731.

[373] *Congressional Record,* October 26, 1990, House, Roll call no. 528, not voting 5, p. 35253.

[374] *Congressional Record,* October 27, 1990, Senate, Roll call no. 326, not voting 1, p. 36278.

[375] Subsequently, after the Republicans gained control of the House of Representatives, the House twice passed legislation that would repeal the 1993 increase in taxation of benefits. Repeal of the 1993 provision was part of the Republican "Contract with America," and was approved by the House as part of the omnibus budget reconciliation bill (H.R. 2491) but was not included in the final law. On July 27, 2000, the House of Representatives approved H.R. 4865, which, effective in 2001, would repeal the 1993 provision, thus lowering the maximum amount of benefits subject to taxation from 85% to 50%, and replace the

112   Gary Sidor

resulting reduced revenue to Medicare with general fund transfers. In neither instance were these measures approved by the Senate.

[376] *Congressional Record,* March 18, 1993, House, Roll call no. 85, not voting 4, p. 5674.

[377] *Congressional Record,* March 24, 1993, Senate, Roll call no. 57, not voting 1, p. 6142.

[378] *Congressional Record,* March 24, 1993, Senate, Roll call no. 58, not voting 1, p. 6149.

[379] *Congressional Record,* March 25, 1993, Senate, Roll call no. 83, not voting 1, p. 6408.

[380] *Congressional Record,* March 31, 1993, House, Roll call no. 127, not voting 6, p. 6964.

[381] *Congressional Record,* April 1, 1993, Senate, Roll call no. 94, not voting 0, p. 7215.

[382] *Congressional Record,* May 27, 1993, House, Roll call no. 199, not voting 0, p. 11952.

[383] *Congressional Record,* June 24, 1993, Senate, Roll call no. 169, not voting 3, p. 14028.

[384] *Congressional Record,* June 24, 1993, Senate, Roll call no. 172, not voting 2, p. 14069.

[385] *Congressional Record,* June 24, 1993, Senate, Roll call no. 184, not voting 2, p. 14107.

[386] *Congressional Record,* June 24, 1993, Senate, Roll call no. 190, not voting 2, p. 14172. The initial vote was 49 to 49, which necessitated that Vice President Gore cast the tie-breaking vote.

[387] *Congressional Record,* July 14, 1993, House, Roll call no. 329, not voting 19, p. 15670.

[388] *Congressional Record,* August 5, 1993, House, Roll call no. 406, not voting 0, p. 19476.

[389] *Congressional Record,* August 6, 1993, Senate, Roll call no. 247, not voting 0, p. 14107. The initial vote was 50 to 50, which necessitated that Vice President Gore cast the tie-breaking vote.

[390] *Congressional Record,* May 17, 1994, House, Roll call no. 177, not voting 20, p. 10603.

[391] *Congressional Record,* August 11, 1994, House, Roll call no. 392, not voting 3, p. 21535.

[392] *Congressional Record,* May 12, 1994, House, Roll call no. 169, not voting 15, p. 10028.

[393] *Congressional Record,* October 6, 1994, House, Roll call no. 494, not voting 11, p. 28504.

[394] *Congressional Record,* December 5, 1995, House, Roll call no. 837, not voting 17, p. H13974.

[395] *Congressional Record,* March 28, 1996, House, Roll call no. 102, not voting 12, p. 6940.

[396] *Congressional Record,* October 19, 1999, House, Roll call no. 513, not voting 12, p. 10273.

[397] *Congressional Record,* June 16, 1999, Senate, Roll call no. 169, not voting 1, p. S7064.

[398] *Congressional Record,* November 18, 1999, House, Roll call no. 611, not voting 15, p. H12832.

[399] *Congressional Record,* November 19, 1999, Senate, Roll call no. 372, not voting 4, p. S14986.

[400] *Congressional Record,* March 1, 2000, House. Roll call no. 27, not voting 13, p. H603.

[401] *Congressional Record,* March 22, 2000, Senate. Roll call no. 42, not voting 0, p. S1540.

[402] *Congressional Record,* March 28, 2000, House, Roll call no. 79, not voting 16, p. H1450.

[403] The Social Security program is also known by its formal name—the Old-Age, Survivors, and Disability Insurance (OASDI) program.

[404] For more information, see the summary of P.L. 108-203 available on the SSA website at http://www.ssa.gov/ legislation/legis_bulletin_030404.html, and CRS Report RL32089, *The Social Security Protection Act of 2004 (H.R. 743),* by Dawn Nuschler.

[405] For more information on this topic and a related decision by the United States Court of Appeals for the Second Circuit in December 2005, see CRS Report RL33394, *Social Security Administration: Suspension of Benefits for Fugitive Felons and the Agency's Response to the Fowlkes Decision,* by Scott D. Szymendera and Kathleen S. Swendiman.

[406] For more information, see CRS Report RL32453, *Social Security: The Government Pension Offset (GPO),* by Christine Scott.

[407] For more information, see CRS Report RL32004, *Social Security Benefits for Noncitizens,* by Dawn Nuschler and Alison Siskin.

[408] *Congressional Record,* April 2, 2003, House, Roll call no. 102, not voting 10, pp. H2668- H2669.

[409] *Congressional Record,* February 11, 2004, House, Roll call no. 23, not voting 11, pp. H477- H478.

[410] *Congressional Record,* December 2, 2010, House, Roll call no. 604, not voting 12, pp. H7889-H7890.

Social Security: Major Decisions in the House and Senate Since 1935 113

[411] *Congressional Record,* December 15, 2010, Senate, Roll call no. 276, p. S10255.

[412] *Congressional Record,* December 17, 2010, House, Roll no. 647, not voting. 8, pp. H8594-H8595.

[413] *Congressional Record*, December 13, 2011, House, Roll call no. 923, not voting 6, p. H8824.

[414] *Congressional Record*, December 17, 2011, Senate, Roll call no. 232, not voting 1, pp. S8748-9.

[415] *Congressional Record*, February 17, 2012. House Roll call no. 72, not voting 8, p. H926.

[416] *Congressional Record*, February 17, 2012. Senate Roll call no. 22, not voting 4, p. S892.

In: Social Security
Editor: Trevor L. Grover

ISBN: 978-1-60021-438-7
© 2014 Nova Science Publishers, Inc.

Chapter 2

SOCIAL SECURITY REFORM: CURRENT ISSUES AND LEGISLATION[*]

Dawn Nuschler

SUMMARY

Social Security reform is an issue of ongoing interest to policy makers. In recent years, Social Security program changes have been discussed in the context of negotiations on legislation to increase the federal debt limit and reduce federal budget deficits. For example, in August 2011, the Budget Control Act of 2011 (P.L. 112-25) established a Joint Select Committee on Deficit Reduction tasked with recommending ways to reduce the deficit by at least $1.5 trillion over the fiscal year period 2012 to 2021. Social Security program changes were among the measures discussed by the Joint Committee. The Joint Committee, however, did not reach agreement on a legislative proposal by the statutory deadline. Looking ahead, Social Security program changes could again be considered as part of any future negotiations on broad deficit reduction legislation or as stand-alone Social Security legislation.

The spectrum of ideas for reform ranges from relatively minor changes to the pay-as-you-go social insurance system enacted in the 1930s to a redesigned, "modernized" program based on personal savings and investments modeled after IRAs and 401(k)s. Proponents of the fundamentally different

---

[*] This is an edited, reformatted and augmented version of a Congressional Research Service publication, CRS Report for Congress RL33544, dated January 15, 2014.

approaches to reform cite varying policy objectives that go beyond simply restoring long-term financial stability to the Social Security system. They cite objectives that focus on improving the adequacy and equity of benefits, as well as those that reflect different philosophical views about the role of the Social Security program and the federal government in providing retirement income. However, the system's projected long-range financial outlook provides a backdrop for much of the Social Security reform debate in terms of the timing and degree of recommended program changes.

On May 31, 2013, the Social Security Board of Trustees released its latest projections showing that the trust funds will be exhausted in 2033 and an estimated 77% of scheduled annual benefits will be payable with incoming receipts at that time (under the intermediate projections). The primary reason is demographics. Between 2015 and 2035, the number of people aged 65 and older is projected to increase by about 65%, while the number of workers supporting the system (people aged 20-64) is projected to increase by about 6%. In addition, the trustees project that the system will run a cash flow deficit each year of the 75-year projection period. When current Social Security tax revenues are insufficient to pay benefits and administrative costs, federal securities held by the trust funds are redeemed and Treasury makes up the difference with other receipts. When there are no surplus governmental receipts, policy makers have three options: raise taxes or other income, reduce other spending, and/or borrow from the public. Public opinion polls show that less than 50% of respondents are confident that Social Security can meet its long-term commitments. There is also a public perception that Social Security may not be as good a value for future retirees. These concerns, and a belief that the nation must increase national savings, have led to proposals to redesign the system. At the same time, others suggest that the system's financial outlook is not a "crisis" in need of immediate action. Supporters of the current program structure point out that the trust funds are projected to have a positive balance until 2033 and that the program continues to have public support and could be affected adversely by the risk associated with some of the reform ideas. They contend that only modest changes are needed to restore long-range solvency to the Social Security system.

BACKGROUND

Social Security reform is an issue of interest to policy makers that arises in various contexts, from improving retirement security to reducing federal budget deficits. In 2011, for example, Social Security program changes were discussed by the Joint Select Committee on Deficit Reduction established by the Budget Control Act of 2011 (P.L. 112-25). The Joint Committee was tasked with recommending ways to reduce federal budget deficits by at least $1.5 trillion over the fiscal year period 2012 to 2021. Social Security program changes were among the measures considered by the Joint Committee; however, no agreement was reached on a legislative proposal by the statutory deadline. Social Security program changes could be considered in the future as part of broad deficit reduction legislation or as a stand-alone measure.

The Social Security reform debate reflects different approaches to reform. Some policy makers support restructuring the program through the creation of individual accounts (i.e., a pre-funded system in which benefits would be based increasingly on personal savings and investments). Supporters of individual accounts point to the system's projected long-range funding shortfall as a driver for change in conjunction with creating a system that would give workers a sense of "ownership" of their retirement savings. Other policy makers support maintaining the current structure of the program (i.e., a defined benefit system funded on a pay-as-you-go basis), pointing to the system's projected long-range financial outlook to support their view that the system is not in immediate "crisis" and that only modest program changes may be needed to extend trust fund solvency and provide for a potential increase in benefits.

Proponents of the fundamentally different approaches to reform (ranging from relatively minor changes to the current pay-as-you-go social insurance system to the creation of a "modernized" program based on personal savings and investments modeled after IRAs and 401(k)s cite varying policy objectives that go beyond simply restoring long-term financial stability to the system. They cite objectives that focus on improving the adequacy and equity of benefits, as well as those that reflect different philosophical views about the role of the Social Security program and the federal government in providing retirement income. However, the system's projected long-range financial outlook provides a backdrop for much of the Social Security reform debate in terms of the timing and degree of recommended program changes. For example, one of the key criteria used to evaluate any reform proposal is its projected impact on the Social Security trust funds. To place the discussion of Social Security reform issues into context, the report first looks at Social Security program financing and the long-range projections for the Social Security trust funds as reported by the Social Security Board of Trustees.[1] The report then looks at the various objectives and proposals for reform.

SOCIAL SECURITY PROGRAM FINANCING

Social Security, one of the largest federal programs, is a social insurance system that pays benefits to retired or disabled workers, their family members, and to the family members of deceased workers.[2] There are 57.9 million Social Security beneficiaries. Approximately 65% of beneficiaries are retired workers and 15% are disabled workers.

The remaining beneficiaries are survivors, or the spouses and children of retired or disabled workers.[3] Social Security covers an estimated 164.9 million workers.[4]

The Social Security program is funded by payroll taxes paid by covered workers and their employers, federal income taxes paid by some beneficiaries on a portion of their benefits, and interest income from the Social Security trust fund investments. Social Security tax revenues are invested in interest-bearing federal government securities (special issues) held by the Old-Age, Survivors, and Disability Insurance (OASDI) trust funds maintained by the U.S. Treasury Department.[5]

The revenues exchanged for the federal government securities are deposited into the Treasury's general fund and are indistinguishable from revenues in the general fund that come from other sources. Funds needed to pay Social Security benefits and administrative expenses come from the redemption or sale of federal government securities held by the trust funds.[6]

To place Social Security's finances into perspective, in 2012, the Social Security trust funds had receipts totaling $840 billion, expenditures totaling $786 billion, and a total surplus (a surplus including interest income) of $54 billion. The trust funds had a cash flow deficit (a deficit excluding interest income) of $55 billion.

At the end of 2012, the Social Security trust funds held assets totaling $2.7 trillion.[7] Because the assets held by the trust funds are federal government securities, the trust fund balance ($2.7 trillion in 2012) represents the amount of money owed to the Social Security trust funds by the general fund of the U.S. Treasury.

Social Security Financing on a Cash Flow Basis

From 1984 to 2009, Social Security generated surplus tax revenues. Surplus tax revenues and interest income credited to the trust funds in the form of federal government securities contributed to a growing trust fund balance.

Social Security Reform: Current Issues and Legislation   119

Table 1 shows the amount of annual surplus Social Security tax revenues collected by the federal government and used for other (non-Social Security) purposes from 1984 to 2009. Surplus Social Security tax revenues totaled $1.21 trillion (in nominal dollars) from 1984 to 2009. **Table 1** also shows total annual Social Security surpluses (including interest income) from 1984 to 2009.[8]

At the end of 2012, the trust funds were credited with assets totaling $2.7 trillion. Under the intermediate assumptions of the 2013 trustees report, the trust fund balance is projected to continue to increase, peaking at $2.9 trillion (in nominal dollars) at the end of 2020 ($2.4 trillion in constant 2013 dollars). Beginning in 2021, however, program expenditures are projected to exceed total income (tax revenues plus interest income) and trust fund assets will begin to be drawn down to help pay benefits and administrative expenses. The trustees project that the trust funds will continue to have a positive balance until 2033, allowing benefits scheduled under current law to be paid in full until that time.[9]

After the trust funds are exhausted, which is projected to occur in 2033, the program would operate using current Social Security tax revenues, which would be sufficient to pay an estimated 77% of benefit payments scheduled under current law in 2033 and an estimated 72% of scheduled benefits in 2087. (See **Table 2** and **Figure 1**.)

In 2010, Social Security began operating with an annual cash flow deficit (i.e., income excluding interest is less than expenditures). The trustees project that Social Security will operate with an annual cash flow deficit in each year of the 75-year projection period (2013-2087). When Social Security operates with a cash flow deficit, the program cashes in federal government securities to supplement current Social Security tax revenues.

General revenues are used to redeem the federal government securities held by the trust funds. When there are no surplus governmental receipts, the increased spending for Social Security from the general fund can only be paid for by the federal government raising taxes or other income, reducing other spending, and/or borrowing from the public (i.e., replacing bonds held by the trust funds with bonds held by the public). When total trust fund income (income including interest) is taken into account, the trustees project that Social Security will have a total surplus each year from 2013 to 2020.

Table 1. Surplus Social Security Tax Revenues and Total Social Security Surplus, Calendar Years 1984 to 2009 (in millions of nominal dollars)

Calendar Year	Payroll Tax Revenues	Revenues from Taxation of Benefits[a]	Total Tax Revenues	Cost	Surplus Tax Revenues (Total Tax Revenues Minus Cost)	Total Surplus (Including Interest Income)
1984	$180,067	$3,025	$183,092	$180,429	$2,663	$6,208
1985	194,149	3,430	197,579	190,628	6,951	11,088
1986	209,140	3,662	212,802	201,522	11,280	4,698
1987	222,425	3,221	225,646	209,093	16,553	21,946
1988	251,814	3,445	255,259	222,514	32,745	40,955
1989	274,189	2,534	276,723	236,242	40,481	53,206
1990	296,070	4,992	301,062	253,135	47,927	62,309
1991	301,711	6,054	307,765	274,205	33,560	55,471
1992	311,128	6,084	317,212	291,865	25,347	50,726
1993	322,090	5,616	327,706	308,766	18,940	46,812
1994	344,695	5,306	350,001	323,011	26,990	58,100
1995	359,021	5,831	364,852	339,815	25,037	59,683
1996	378,881	6,844	385,725	353,569	32,156	70,883
1997	405,984	7,896	413,880	369,108	44,772	88,560
1998	430,174	9,707	439,881	382,255	57,626	106,950
1999	459,556	11,559	471,115	392,908	78,207	133,673
2000	492,484	12,314	504,798	415,121	89,677	153,312
2001	516,393	12,715	529,108	438,916	90,192	163,088
2002	532,471	13,839	546,310	461,653	84,657	165,432
2003	533,519	13,441	546,960	479,086	67,874	152,799
2004	553,040	15,703	568,743	501,643	67,100	156,075
2005	592,940	14,916	607,856	529,938	77,918	171,821
2006	625,594	16,858	642,452	555,421	87,031	189,452
2007	656,121	18,585	674,706	594,501	80,205	190,388
2008	672,122	16,879	689,001	625,143	63,858	180,159
2009	667,257	21,884	689,141	685,801	3,340	121,689

Source: Table prepared by CRS based on data from the Social Security Administration, http://www.ssa.gov/ OACT/STATS/table4a3.html.

a. Some beneficiaries are required to pay federal income taxes on a portion of their benefits. For more information, see CRS Report RL32552, *Social Security: Calculation and History of Taxing Benefits.*

Social Security Reform: Current Issues and Legislation 121

Table 2. Projected Income and Outgo of the Social Security Trust Funds, Under Intermediate Assumptions, Calendar Years 2013-2032 (in billions of constant 2013 dollars)

Year	Tax Revenues (Non-Interest Income)	Interest Income	Total Income	Cost	Total Surplus/ Deficit[a]	Cash Flow Deficit[b]	Trust Fund Balance
2013	$752.2	$102.6	$854.8	$826.8	$28.0	-$74.6	$2,760.3
2014	782.7	96.1	878.8	856.1	22.7	-73.4	2,723.4
2015	814.3	93.3	907.6	884.2	23.4	-69.9	2,682.6
2016	848.4	93.4	941.8	916.0	25.8	-67.6	2,641.9
2017	882.2	94.9	977.2	949.2	28.0	-67.0	2,600.6
2018	913.3	97.1	1,010.4	982.8	27.6	-69.5	2,557.4
2019	938.3	98.2	1,036.5	1,018.5	18.0	-80.2	2,505.8
2020	960.1	98.3	1,058.4	1,055.5	2.9	-95.4	2,440.5
2021	981.1	97.3	1,078.3	1,090.5	-12.2	-109.4	2,361.8
2022	1,000.0	96.0	1,096.0	1,128.9	-32.9	-128.9	2,264.5
2023	1,016.7	97.7	1,114.4	1,167.0	-52.6	-150.3	2,150.3
2024	1,033.8	98.2	1,132.0	1,205.6	-73.6	-171.8	2,018.1
2025	1,051.0	97.1	1,148.1	1,244.3	-96.2	-193.3	1,866.9
2026	1,068.3	94.5	1,162.8	1,282.6	-119.8	-214.3	1,696.2
2027	1,086.0	90.0	1,176.0	1,320.7	-144.7	-234.7	1,505.3
2028	1,103.7	78.7	1,182.4	1,358.4	-176.0	-254.7	1,288.4
2029	1,121.4	66.0	1,187.4	1,395.2	-207.8	-273.8	1,045.5
2030	1,139.3	51.9	1,191.2	1,430.9	-239.7	-291.6	777.3
2031	1,157.6	36.4	1,194.0	1,465.2	-271.2	-307.6	484.9
2032[c]	1,176.2	19.5	1,195.7	1,498.5	-302.8	-322.3	169.0

Source: CRS, based on data from The 2013 Annual Report of the Board of Trustees of the Federal Old-Age and Survivors Insurance and Federal Disability Insurance Trust Funds, May 31, 2013, table VI.F7, available at http://www.socialsecurity. gov/OACT/TR/2013/lr6f7.html.

a. The total surplus/deficit for the year is equal to total income minus cost.

b. The *cash flow* deficit for the year is equal to tax revenues minus cost.

c. The Social Security trust funds are projected to be exhausted in 2033.

Stated another way, the emergence of annual cash flow deficits means that the program begins to rely on interest credited to the trust funds to meet annual program costs (to help pay benefits and administrative expenses). Interest is credited to the trust funds in the form of new special issue securities; it does not represent a financial resource for the federal government from outside sources. As previously noted, general revenues are used to redeem the federal government securities held by the Social Security trust funds to cover the difference between Social Security tax revenues and program costs. In the 2013 trustees report, the trustees project that the program's reliance on general revenues will be $95.4 billion in 2020 (in constant 2013 dollars). The program's reliance on general revenues will increase as the trust fund balance begins to be drawn down (starting in 2021 when program costs exceed total income). For example, the program's reliance on general revenues is projected to be $291.6 billion in 2030 (in constant 2013 dollars). Projected *total* Social Security surpluses and deficits, as well as projected *cash flow* deficits, for each year from 2013 to 2032 are shown in **Table 2** and **Figure 2**.

With respect to the program's reliance on general revenues, the program is relying on tax revenues collected for Social Security purposes in previous years (plus interest) that were used by the federal government at the time for other (non-Social Security) spending needs. The Social Security program draws on those previously collected Social Security tax revenues and interest income (accumulated trust fund assets) when current Social Security tax revenues fall below current program expenditures.

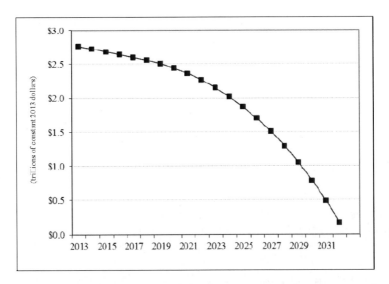

Figure 1. Projected Social Security Trust Fund Balances, Under the Intermediate Assumptions of the 2013Trustees Report, Calendar Years 2013-2032.

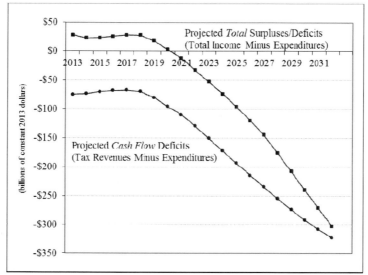

Source: Figures are based on data from The 2013 Annual Report of the Board of Trustees of the Federal Old-Age and Survivors Insurance and Federal Disability Insurance Trust Funds, May 31, 2013.

Figure 2. Projected Social Security Surpluses/Deficits, Under the Intermediate Assumptions of the 2013Trustees Report, Calendar Years 2013-2032.

Social Security Trust Fund Solvency

The trustees project that the Social Security trust funds will be exhausted in 2033, at which point incoming receipts will cover an estimated 77% of scheduled annual benefits.[10] The trustees also project that Social Security expenditures will exceed income by almost 20% on average over the next 75 years (2013-2087). Demographic changes are among the primary reasons for the system's projected funding shortfall. The first wave of the post-World War II baby boom generation began retiring in 2008, fertility rates continue to be lower than those experienced during the baby boom era (1946-1965), and life expectancy is projected to increase, factors that contribute to an older society. Between 2015 and 2035, the number of people aged 65 and older is projected to increase by about 65%, whereas the number of workers whose taxes will finance future benefits (people aged 20-64) is projected to increase by about 6%.[11] As a result, the number of workers supporting each Social Security beneficiary is projected to decline from 2.7 in 2015 to 2.1 in 2035.[12]

In addition, program design features contribute to the projected growth in program spending. For example, elements of the Social Security benefit formula are indexed to average wage growth, resulting in a projected increase in the value of initial monthly benefits for future retirees. Wage indexing allows initial monthly benefits to replace a constant proportion of pre-retirement earnings for future retirees, so that initial monthly benefits keep pace with rising living standards.

Program Costs and Income as a Percentage of Taxable Payroll

The cost of the Social Security program in 2013 is estimated to be $826.8 billion, an amount equal to 13.95% of workers' wages subject to the Social Security payroll tax (or taxable payroll).[13] The trustees project that program costs will increase to 16.98% of taxable payroll by 2035, decline to 16.78% in 2050, and then increase gradually to 18.01% in 2087.

By comparison, projections show relatively small increases in income rates over the period (annual income rates exclude interest income). As a percentage of taxable payroll, program income is projected to increase from 12.69% in 2013 to 13.25% in 2087. Income rates are projected to remain relatively stable over the period because the Social Security payroll tax rate (12.4% for employers and employees combined) is not scheduled to change under current law,[14] and income from the taxation of Social Security benefits is projected to increase gradually relative to taxable payroll as the proportion of beneficiaries who are required to pay federal income taxes on a portion of their benefits increases gradually over time.[15] As a result, the gap between income and expenditures is projected to increase over the period. By 2087, program costs are projected to exceed income by 36% (or an amount equal to 4.77% of taxable payroll). On average, over the 75-year period (2013-2087), the cost of the program is projected to exceed income by almost 20% (or an amount equal to 2.72% of taxable payroll). (See **Table 3.**)

Program Costs and Income as a Percentage of Gross Domestic Product

Social Security program costs and income are also evaluated as a share of U.S. economic output. The cost of the program is projected to increase from 5.06% of gross domestic product (GDP) in 2013 to 6.23% of GDP by 2035, declining to 6.05% of GDP by 2050. Costs are projected to remain between 6.0% and 6.2% of GDP through 2087.

Social Security Reform: Current Issues and Legislation 125

Table 3. Projected Social Security Income Rate, Cost Rate, and Balance as a Percentage of Taxable Payroll, Selected Calendar Years 2013-2087 (under the intermediate assumptions of the 2013 trustees report)

Year	Income Rate	Cost Rate	Balance
2013	12.69	13.95	-1.26
2015	12.86	13.97	-1.10
2020	12.97	14.26	-1.29
2025	13.07	15.48	-2.40
2030	13.13	16.49	-3.36
2035	13.16	16.98	-3.82
2040	13.17	16.96	-3.79
2045	13.17	16.83	-3.66
2050	13.17	16.78	-3.61
2055	13.18	16.91	-3.73
2060	13.20	17.14	-3.95
2065	13.21	17.36	-4.15
2070	13.22	17.58	-4.36
2075	13.23	17.72	-4.49
2080	13.23	17.76	-4.53
2085	13.24	17.91	-4.67
2087	13.25	18.01	-4.77
75 years: 2013-2087	13.88	16.60	-2.72

Source: The 2013 Annual Report of the Board of Trustees of the Federal Old-Age and Survivors Insurance and Federal Disability Insurance Trust Funds, May 31, 2013, table VI.F2 and table VI.F3.

Note: Annual income rates exclude interest income.

By comparison, program income as a percentage of GDP is projected to remain relatively stable over the period (annual income excludes interest income). Program income is projected to increase from 4.60% of GDP in 2013 to 4.87% in 2022. Program income as a percentage of GDP is then projected to decline gradually to 4.81% in 2040 and 4.56% in 2087. Program income is projected to decline as a share of GDP because wages subject to the Social Security payroll tax are projected to increase more slowly than other forms of employee compensation and other types of income. In 2087, the projected funding shortfall is an amount equal to 1.64% of GDP. On average, over the 75-year period (2013-2087), the projected funding shortfall is an amount equal to 0.98% of GDP. (See **Table 4**.)

**Table 4. Projected Social Security Income, Cost, and Balance as a
Percentage of Gross Domestic Product (GDP), Selected Calendar
Years 2013-2087
(under the intermediate assumptions of the 2013 trustees report)**

Year	Income	Cost	Balance
2013	4.60	5.06	-0.46
2015	4.67	5.07	-0.40
2020	4.84	5.32	-0.48
2025	4.86	5.75	-0.89
2030	4.84	6.08	-1.24
2035	4.83	6.23	-1.40
2040	4.81	6.19	-1.38
2045	4.78	6.10	-1.33
2050	4.74	6.05	-1.30
2055	4.72	6.05	-1.33
2060	4.69	6.09	-1.40
2065	4.66	6.12	-1.46
2070	4.63	6.16	-1.53
2075	4.61	6.17	-1.56
2080	4.58	6.15	-1.57
2085	4.56	6.17	-1.61
2087	4.56	6.20	-1.64
75 years: 2013-2087	5.01	6.00	-0.98

Source: The 2013 Annual Report of the Board of Trustees of the Federal Old-Age and
Survivors Insurance and Federal Disability Insurance Trust Funds, May 31, 2013,
table VI.F4, pp. 200-201, and online at http://www.socialsecurity.gov/OACT/
TR/2013/lr6f4.html. Income for individual years excludes interest on the trust
funds. Interest is implicit in the summarized value.

The projected long-range financial outlook for the Social Security system
is reflected in public opinion polls that show less than 50% of respondents are
confident in Social Security's ability to meet its long-term commitments.[16]
There is a growing public perception that Social Security may not be as good a
value in the future. Until recent years, retirees could expect to receive more in
benefits than they paid in Social Security payroll taxes. However, because
Social Security payroll tax rates have increased to cover the costs of the
maturing "pay-as-you-go" system, these ratios have become less favorable.
Such concerns, and a belief that the nation must increase national savings to

Social Security Reform: Current Issues and Legislation 127

meet the needs of an aging society, are among the factors behind reform efforts.

Supporters of the current program structure suggest that the issues confronting the system are not as serious as sometimes portrayed and believe there is no imminent crisis. They point out that the trust funds are projected to have a balance until 2033, there continues to be public support for the program, and there would be considerable risk in some of the reform ideas. They contend that relatively modest changes could restore long-range solvency to the system.[17]

BASIC DEBATE

The Social Security system has faced funding shortfalls in the past. In 1977 and 1983, Congress enacted a variety of measures to address the system's financial imbalance. These measures include constraints on the growth of initial benefit levels, a gradual increase in the full retirement age from 65 to 67 (i.e., the age at which unreduced benefits are first payable), payroll tax increases, taxation of benefits for higher-income beneficiaries, and extension of Social Security coverage to federal and nonprofit workers. Subsequently, projections showed the re-emergence of long-term deficits as a result of changes in actuarial methods and assumptions, and because program changes had been evaluated with respect to their effect on the *average* 75-year deficit. That is, while program changes were projected to restore trust fund solvency on average over the 75-year period, a period of surpluses was followed by a period of deficits.

Many policy makers believe that some type of action should be taken sooner rather than later. This view has been shared by the Social Security trustees and other panels and commissions that have examined the issue. In recent years, a wide range of interest groups have echoed this view in testimony before Congress. However, there is no consensus on whether the projections represent a "crisis." In 1977 and 1983, the trust fund balances were projected to fall to zero within a very short period (within months of the 1983 reforms). Today, the problem is perceived to be as many as 20 years away (based on the projected trust fund exhaustion date). Lacking a "crisis," the pressure to compromise is diffused and the issues and the divergent views about them have led to myriad complex proposals. In 1977 and 1983, the debate was not about fundamental reform. Rather, it revolved around how to raise the system's income and constrain costs. Today, the ideas range from restoring the system's solvency with as few alterations as possible to replacing it entirely with something modeled after IRAs or 401(k)s. This broad spectrum was reflected in the 1997 Social Security Advisory Council report, which presented three different reform plans. None of the plans was supported by a majority of the 13-member council. Similar diversity is reflected in the Social Security reform bills introduced in recent Congresses.

Push for Major Reform

Advocates of reform view Social Security as an anachronism, built on depression-era concerns about high unemployment and widespread "dependency" among the aged. They see the prospect of reform today as an opportunity to "modernize" the way society saves for retirement. They maintain that the vast economic, social and demographic changes that have transpired over the past 75 years require the system to change, and they point to changes made in other countries that now use market-based individual accounts to strengthen retirement incomes and bolster their economies by spurring savings and investments. They believe government-run, pay-as-you-go systems are unsustainable in aging societies. They prefer a system that allows workers to acquire wealth and provide for their retirement by investing in individual accounts.

Reform advocates also view it as a way to counter skepticism about the current system by giving workers a greater sense of "ownership" of their retirement savings. They contend that private investments would yield larger retirement incomes because stocks and bonds historically have provided higher returns than are projected from the current system. Some believe that individual accounts would address what they view as the system's contradictory mix of insurance and social welfare goals. Others maintain that creating a system of individual accounts would prevent the government from using any surplus Social Security tax revenues for other government spending. Recent stock market declines and the emergence of annual cash flow deficits for the Social Security system, however, have made investment-based proposals less popular among some policy makers in the near term.

Some, who do not necessarily seek a new system, view enactment of long-range Social Security constraints as one way to curb federal entitlement spending. The aging of society means that the cost of entitlement programs that aid the elderly will increase greatly in the future. The costs of the largest entitlement programs (Social Security, Medicare, and Medicaid) are directly linked to an aging population. Proponents of imposing constraints on these programs express concern that, if left unchecked, their costs will place pressure on the federal budget far into the future, consuming resources that could be used for other priorities and forcing future generations to bear a much higher tax burden.

As a matter of fairness, it has been pointed out that many current beneficiaries get back more than the value of their Social Security contributions, and far more than the baby boom generation will receive. They believe that to delay making changes to the program is unfair to current workers, who must pay for "transfer" payments that they characterize as "overgenerous" and unrelated to need, while facing the prospect that their own benefits may have to be scaled back severely. Others emphasize the system's projected long-range funding shortfall and contend that steps should be taken soon (e.g., raising the retirement age, restraining the growth of initial monthly benefits for future retirees, reducing cost-of-living adjustments, increasing the taxable wage base) so that changes can be phased-in, allowing workers more time to adjust their retirement expectations and plans to reflect what the program will be able to provide in the future. They maintain that more abrupt changes in taxes and benefits would otherwise be required.

Arguments for Retaining the Existing System

Those who favor a more restrained approach believe that the issues facing the system can be resolved with modest tax and spending changes, and that the program's critics are raising the specter that Social Security will "bankrupt the nation" to undermine public support and provide an excuse to incorporate individual accounts into the system. They contend that individual savings accounts would erode the social insurance nature of the program, which favors low-wage workers, the disabled, and survivors.

Others are concerned that switching to a new system of individual accounts would pose large transition problems by requiring younger workers to save for their own retirement while paying taxes to cover benefits for current retirees. Some doubt that it would increase national savings, arguing that higher government debt (resulting from the redirection of current payroll taxes to individual accounts) would offset the increased individual account savings. They also contend that the capital markets' inflow created by the accounts would make the markets difficult to regulate and potentially distort equity valuations. They point out that some of the countries that have moved to individual accounts did so to create capital markets. Such markets, they argue, are already well developed in the United States.

Some believe that a system of individual accounts would expose participants to excessive market risk for an income source that is essential to many of the nation's elderly. They say that the nation has a three-tiered retirement system (Social Security, private pensions, and personal assets) that already includes private savings and investment. They contend that while people may be willing and able to undertake some "risk" in the latter two tiers, Social Security (as the tier that provides a basic floor of protection) should be more stable. They further contend that the administrative costs of maintaining individual accounts could be very large and erode the value of the accounts.

SPECIFIC AREAS OF CONTENTION

System's Financial Outlook

There are conflicting views about the severity of Social Security's projected funding shortfall. Some maintain that the problem is more acute than portrayed under the traditional 75-year projections that show an average 75-year deficit equal to 2.72% of taxable payroll ($9.6 trillion in present value terms). They believe this view is supported by an alternative portrayal in the trustees' report that extends the projections indefinitely into the future. On an "infinite horizon" basis, the projected funding shortfall is equal to 4.0% of taxable payroll ($23.1 trillion in present value terms). They also point out that, in 2030, for example, the cost of the system is projected to exceed income by an amount equal to 3.36% of taxable payroll (costs are projected to exceed income by about 26%). By the end of the projection period (2087), however, the cost of the system is projected to exceed income by an amount equal to 4.77% of taxable payroll (costs are projected to exceed income by 36%). On a *pay-as-you-go basis*, the system would require more than a 20% change in taxes or expenditures over the next 75 years to cover projected program costs (over the next 75 years, *on average*, the cost of the system is projected to exceed income by almost 20%). In addition, they point out that the current 75-year actuarial deficit projected for the trust funds (2.72% of taxable payroll) is the largest actuarial deficit reported since prior to the 1983 Social Security Amendments.

They maintain that viewing the problem as 20 years away (because the trust funds are projected to have a positive balance until 2033) does not take into account the pressure Social Security will exert on the federal budget as annual cash flow deficits require the system to rely on assets held by the trust funds (federal government securities) to meet annual expenditures. The federal government securities held by the trust funds are redeemed with general revenues. Therefore, the government must rely on other financial resources to help pay Social Security benefits and administrative expenses, resources that could be used to finance other governmental functions.

Others maintain that, in contrast to earlier episodes of financial imbalance, the system has no "immediate" problem: the trust funds are projected to have a positive balance until 2033 and can pay benefits scheduled under current law (in full and on time) until then. For this reason, they maintain that policy makers have time to address changes to the Social Security program. They point out that there is inherent uncertainty surrounding the trust fund projections over a 75-year period, let alone the infinite horizon. Even if the 75-year projections hold, they point out for example that the average imbalance could be eliminated by increasing the combined employer and employee payroll tax rate during the period in a manner equivalent to an immediate increase of 2.66 percentage points (from the current level of 12.40% to 15.06%).

While acknowledging that the cost of the system is projected to represent a larger share of GDP in the future (increasing from 5.06% of GDP today to 6.23% of GDP by 2035), they point out that GDP would have risen in real terms. Moreover, while the ratio of workers to beneficiaries is projected to decline, they believe that employers are likely to respond with inducements for older workers to stay on the job longer. Phased retirements are becoming more prevalent, and some older workers view retirement as more than an all-or-nothing decision. In addition, they argue that Social Security program changes should not be considered in the context of broader deficit reduction efforts as policy makers look for ways to restrain federal budget deficits; rather, Social Security program changes should be considered separately.

Public Confidence

In recent years, public opinion polls have shown that a majority of Americans lack confidence in the system's ability to meet its future commitments. Younger workers are particularly skeptical. For example, in one recent poll of non-retired adults aged 18 or older, 70% of those in the 18-49 age group said they did not think the Social Security system would be able to pay them a benefit when they retire, compared with 34% in the 50 or older age group.[18]

Some observers express caution about inferring too much from polling data, arguing that public understanding of Social Security is limited and often inaccurate. They maintain that a major reason confidence is highest among older persons is that they have learned more about Social Security because they are more immediately affected by the program. Some believe that the annual Social Security Statements provided by the Social Security Administration (SSA) will make workers more aware of their estimated future benefits scheduled under current law and thus more trusting of the system.[19] Others suggest, however, that the skepticism is justified by the system's repeated financial difficulties and diminished "money's worth" for younger workers.

Doubts about Money's Worth

Until recent years, Social Security beneficiaries received more, often far more, than the value of the Social Security taxes they paid. However, because Social Security payroll tax rates have increased over the years and the full retirement age (the age at which unreduced benefits are first payable) is being increased gradually, it is becoming more apparent that Social Security will be less of a "good deal" for many future retirees. Some observers believe this discrepancy is inequitable and cite it as evidence that the system needs to be substantially restructured.

Others discount this phenomenon, viewing Social Security as a *social insurance* program serving social ends that transcend questions of whether some individuals fare better than others. For example, the program's anti-poverty features are designed to replace a higher proportion of earnings for lower-wage workers and provide additional benefits for workers with families. Some observers point out that current workers, who will receive less direct value from their taxes compared with current retirees, have in part been relieved from having to support their parents, and many elderly are able to live independently and with dignity. These observers contend that the value of these aspects of the program is not reflected in comparisons of taxes and benefits.

Debate over Individual Accounts

Social Security's projected long-range financial outlook, skepticism about the sustainability of the current system, and a belief that economic growth could be bolstered through increased savings have led to a number of proposals to incorporate individual accounts into the Social Security system, reviving a debate that dates back to the creation of the program in 1935. All three plans presented by the 1994-1996 Social Security Advisory Council featured program involvement in the financial markets. The first called upon Congress to consider authorizing investment of part of the Social Security trust funds in equities (on the assumption that stocks would produce a higher return to the system). The second would require workers to contribute an extra 1.6% of pay to individual accounts to make up for Social Security benefit reductions called for under the plan to restore the system's long-range solvency. The third would redesign the system by gradually replacing Social Security retirement benefits with flat-rate benefits based on length of service and individual accounts (funded with 5 percentage points of the current Social Security tax rate).[20]

The reform that Chile enacted in 1981, which replaced a troubled pay-as-you-go system with one requiring workers to invest part of their earnings in individual accounts through government-approved pension funds, has been reflected in a number of reform bills introduced in recent Congresses.[21] These measures would permit or require workers to invest some or all of their Social Security payroll taxes in individual accounts. Most call for future Social Security benefits to be reduced or forfeited. Similarly, the three options presented by the Social Security reform commission appointed by former President George W. Bush in 2001 would allow workers to participate in individual accounts and would reduce their future Social Security benefit by the projected value of the account based on an assumed (rather than the actual) rate of return.[22]

Another approach is reflected in bills that would require any budget surpluses to be used to finance individual accounts to supplement Social Security benefits for those who pay Social Security payroll taxes. Former President William Clinton's January 1999 reform plan would have allocated a portion of budget surpluses to individual accounts, supplemented by a worker's own contributions and a government match (scaled to income). In addition, the plan would have redirected a portion of budget surpluses, or the interest savings resulting therefrom, to the Social Security trust funds. Some of the funds would have been used to acquire stocks, similar to the approach suggested in one of the Advisory Council plans and some past legislation. Most of these approaches would require establishment of an independent board to invest some of the funds in stocks or corporate bonds and the remaining funds in federal securities.

Some individual account proponents believe that individual accounts would reduce future financial demands on government and reassure workers by giving them a sense of "ownership" of their retirement savings. Others believe that individual accounts would enhance workers' retirement income because stocks and bonds generally have provided higher rates of return than are projected from Social Security. In conjunction with this, they maintain that individual accounts would increase national savings and promote economic growth. Others maintain that individual accounts would prevent the government from using any surplus Social Security revenues to "mask" public borrowing, or for other spending or tax reductions. Generally, proponents of an individual account system express concern that "collective" investment of the Social Security trust funds in the markets would concentrate too much economic power in a government-appointed board.[23]

Opponents of individual accounts maintain that Social Security's projected long-range funding shortfall could be resolved without altering the fundamental nature of the program. They express concern that replacing Social Security with individual accounts would erode the social insurance aspects of the system that favor lower-wage workers, survivors and the disabled. Others are concerned that individual accounts would pose large transition problems by requiring younger workers to save for their own retirement while simultaneously paying taxes to support current beneficiaries, and would further exacerbate current budget deficits. Some doubt that individual accounts would increase national savings, maintaining that any increase in private savings would be offset by increased government borrowing. They also point out that the investment pool created by the accounts could be difficult to regulate and distort capital markets and equity valuations. Still others view it as exposing participants to excessive market risk for something as essential as core retirement benefits and, unlike Social Security, as providing poor protection against inflation.

Some prefer "collective" investment of the Social Security trust funds in the markets to potentially bolster their returns and spread the risks of poor performance broadly.

Maximum Taxable Earnings

Social Security payroll taxes are levied on Social Security-covered earnings up to a maximum amount set each year. In 2014, this maximum amount—the *contribution and benefit base* or the *taxable earnings base*—is $117,000. The taxable earnings base is adjusted each year based on average wage growth, if a Social Security cost-of-living adjustment (COLA) is payable. The taxable earnings base limits the amount of annual wages or self-employment income used to determine a worker's contributions to Social Security.[24] It also limits the amount of annual wages or self-employment income used to compute a worker's benefit, and thus sets a ceiling on the amount of a worker's initial monthly benefit.

Under current law, a small percentage of workers have earnings *at or above* the taxable earnings base. In 2010, for example, an estimated 5.7% of workers had earnings *at or above* the taxable earnings base of $106,800 that year.[25]

Supporters of raising or eliminating the taxable earnings base point out that it could reduce or eliminate Social Security's projected long-range funding shortfall. The full impact of the policy change would depend on how the proposal is structured and whether the additional taxable earnings are counted for benefit computation purposes.

Raising or eliminating the taxable earnings base for both contribution and benefit purposes would result in an increase in payroll tax revenues, as well as an increase in benefit payments to some beneficiaries. Higher benefit payments would increase program spending, however, the increase in expenditures would be more than offset by the increase in tax revenues. Some observers express concern about the potential level of initial monthly benefits that would be payable to some beneficiaries, particularly under a scenario in which all covered earnings would be taxable and counted for benefit computation purposes. If the limit on taxable earnings were raised or eliminated for contribution purposes only (i.e., if the additional taxable earnings were not counted for benefit computation purposes), the positive effect on the system's projected financial outlook would be greater. This approach, however, raises concerns of equity among some because it would break the traditional link between contributions and benefits and could potentially weaken support for the program among higher-wage workers.

Some observers maintain that the taxable earnings base should cover a steady percentage of Social Security-covered earnings. The percentage of *covered workers* with earnings below the taxable earnings base has remained relatively stable at about 94% since the 1980s. In comparison, however, the percentage of *covered earnings* subject to the payroll tax has declined over the period, from 90% in 1982 to an estimated 83% in 2011.[26] Generally, the decline in the percentage of covered earnings that are taxable is attributed in large part to relatively faster wage growth for high earners, compared with workers with wages below the taxable earnings base. The Social Security trustees project that the percentage of covered earnings subject to the payroll tax will be 82.5% in 2022.[27]

Some policy makers have proposed raising the taxable earnings base to a level that would make 90% of aggregate covered earnings subject to the payroll tax, as Congress did in 1977. This proposal has been reflected in the recommendations of recent deficit reduction commissions, including the 2010 National Commission on Fiscal Responsibility and Reform (the President's Fiscal Commission). Among the changes proposed for Social Security, the commission recommended a gradual increase in the taxable wage base such that 90% of aggregate wages in covered employment would be taxable by 2050.[28] The Social Security Administration estimates that an increase in the taxable earnings base such that 90% of earnings would be subject to the payroll tax (phased in from 2014 to 2023) would improve the system's projected long-range actuarial balance by about 28% if the additional taxable earnings are credited for benefit computation purposes, and by about 36% if the additional taxable earnings are not credited.[29]

Some critics of this approach argue that it would disproportionately affect those with earnings just above the current taxable earnings base relative to those with very high earnings. Therefore, proposals to increase the amount of wages subject to the Social Security payroll tax take different forms. For example, some proposals would (1) maintain the Social Security payroll tax on covered earnings up to the current-law taxable earnings base, and (2) make covered earnings above a second higher threshold (such as $250,000) subject to the Social Security payroll tax.[30] Still other proposals would require workers and employers each to pay an additional tax (such as 3%) on covered earnings above the current-law taxable earnings base (in addition to the 6.2% each on covered earnings up to the taxable earnings base payable under current law).[31]

Retirement Age Issue

Raising the Social Security retirement age is often considered as a way to help restore long-range solvency to the system. Some of the projected growth

Social Security Reform: Current Issues and Legislation 137

in Social Security's costs is a result of projected increases in life expectancy (and, as a result, more years spent in retirement collecting benefits). Since benefits were first paid in 1940, life expectancy at age 65 has increased from 12.7 years for men/14.7 years for women to 19.1 years for men/21.4 years for women. By 2030, life expectancy at age 65 is projected to reach 20.3 years for men and 22.5 years for women.[32]

This trend bolstered arguments for increasing the full retirement age (FRA, the age at which unreduced retirement benefits are first payable) as a way to achieve savings when the system was facing major financial problems in the early 1980s. As part of the Social Security Amendments of 1983 (P.L. 98-21), Congress raised the FRA from 65 to 67. The increase in the FRA enacted in 1983 is currently being phased-in starting with persons born in 1938, with the full two-year increase affecting persons born in 1960 or later.[33] The 1983 amendments did not raise the early retirement age (age 62). However, the benefit reduction for persons who retire at age 62 will increase from 20% (for those with an FRA of 65) to 30% (for those with an FRA of 67). Proponents of increasing the early or full retirement age view it as reasonable in light of projected increases in life expectancy. Opponents believe it would penalize workers who already get a "worse deal" from Social Security compared to current retirees, persons who work in physically demanding occupations, and racial minorities and others who have shorter life expectancies.

Cost-of-Living Adjustments

Social Security benefits are adjusted annually to reflect inflation as measured by the Bureau of Labor Statistics'(BLS's) Consumer Price Index (CPI), which measures price increases for selected goods and services.[34] The CPI has been criticized for overstating the effects of inflation, primarily because the index's market basket of goods and services was not revised regularly to reflect changes in consumer buying habits or improvements in quality.A BLS analysis in 1993 found that the annual overstatement may be as much as 0.6 percentage point. The Congressional Budget Office (CBO) estimated in 1994 that the overstatement ranged from 0.2 to 0.8 percentage point. A 1996 panel that studied the issue for the Senate Finance Committee argued that it may be 1.1 percentage points.[35] In response to its own analysis as well as outside criticisms, the BLS has since made various revisions to the

CPI. To some extent, these revisions may account for part of the slower CPI growth in recent years. However, calls for adjustments continue.[36]

In August 2002, BLS introduced a supplemental index—the chained CPI-U (C-CPI-U). The goal of the C-CPI-U is to more accurately reflect how consumers change their buying habits in response to price changes.[37] Some policy makers support using the C-CPI-U to compute the annual Social Security cost-of-living adjustment (COLA) on the basis that other CPI measures (including the CPI-W) overestimate how much money is needed to maintain a constant standard of living.[38] Although some view using a different measure of price change to adjust benefits for inflation as a necessary way to help keep Social Security and other entitlement spending under control, others view such changes as a backdoor way of reducing benefits. They maintain that the market basket of goods and services purchased by the elderly is different from that of the general population around which the CPI is constructed. It is more heavily weighted with healthcare expenditures, which rise notably faster than the overall CPI, and thus they contend that the cost of living for the elderly is higher than reflected by the CPI. For this reason, some policy makers support using the Consumer Price Index for the Elderly (CPI-E), an experimental index developed by BLS, to compute the annual Social Security COLA.[39]

Based on projections by SSA's Office of the Chief Actuary, a reduction in the Social Security COLA of 1 percentage point annually (beginning December 2014) would improve the system's projected long-range actuarial balance by about 63%. Similarly, a COLA reduction of 0.5 percentage point annually would improve the system's projected long-range actuarial balance by about 33%. Under another option, SSA projects that using a chained version of the *CPI-W* to compute the COLA would reduce the annual COLA by about 0.3 percentage point on average and improve the system's projected long-range actuarial balance by about 20%.[40]

Social Security and the Budget

By law, Social Security is considered "off budget" for many aspects of developing and enforcing annual budget goals. However, it is a federal program and its income and outgo help shape the year-to-year financial condition of the federal government. As a result, policy makers often focus on "unified" (or overall) budget totals that include Social Security. When former President William Clinton urged that the unified budget surpluses projected at

Social Security Reform: Current Issues and Legislation   139

the time be reserved until Social Security's projected long-range funding issues were resolved, and proposed using a portion of those surpluses to shore up the system, Social Security's budget treatment became a major issue. Congressional views about what to do with the surpluses were diverse, ranging from "buying down" publicly held federal debt to cutting taxes to increasing spending. There was also substantial support for setting aside a portion equal to the annual Social Security trust fund surpluses. Since that time, federal budget deficits have emerged and the Social Security trust funds have begun operating with annual cash flow deficits.

Today, some policy makers support Social Security program changes as a way to reduce federal entitlement spending and federal budget deficits. Some policy makers who support efforts to restrain the growth in major entitlement programs such as Social Security, Medicare, and Medicaid express concern that federal spending for these programs is contributing to unsustainable levels of federal budget deficits that have a negative impact on the economy. Policy makers differ as to how to restrain spending growth for these programs. With respect to Social Security, policy makers differ in particular as to how to apportion benefit reductions and tax increases between workers and retirees in the future.

On February 18, 2010, President Barack Obama established by executive order the National Commission on Fiscal Responsibility and Reform. The executive order states "the Commission shall propose recommendations that meaningfully improve the long-run fiscal outlook, including changes to address the growth of entitlement spending and the gap between the projected revenues and expenditures of the Federal Government."[41] On December 1, 2010, the President's Fiscal Commission released its final report. The recommendations proposed by the commission include Social Security program changes designed to improve benefit adequacy for certain groups while addressing long-term trust fund solvency through benefit reductions for most beneficiaries (compared with benefits scheduled under current law) and revenue increases.[42]

The proposed recommendations include changes that would increase benefits for certain beneficiaries, such as a new special minimum benefit[43] for long-term low-wage earners that would be indexed to wage growth (the benefit would be equal to 125% of the poverty level for a worker with 25 years of covered employment) and a benefit increase for older beneficiaries (i.e., a 1% increase in benefits each year from ages 82 to 86).

The proposed recommendations also include a number of benefit and revenue changes to address long-term trust fund solvency. For example, the proposal includes gradual changes to the benefit formula used to compute initial monthly benefits (making the benefit formula more progressive over time) and a gradual increase in the retirement age. Under current law, the full retirement age (FRA) is scheduled to reach age 67 for workers born in 1960 or later (i.e., it is scheduled to reach age 67 in 2027). Under the proposal, after the FRA reaches age 67, it would be further increased by one month every two years, reaching age 68 by about 2050 and age 69 by about 2075. The early eligibility age (EEA), age 62 under current law, would increase to age 63 and age 64 in step with the FRA. In conjunction with the proposed increase in the retirement age, the commission proposes a hardship exemption for those who are unable to work beyond the current EEA and may not qualify for disability benefits. The hardship exemption, which would be available for up to 20% of retirees, would allow individuals to continue to claim benefits at age 62 as the EEA and the FRA increase, with no additional actuarial reduction resulting from the increased FRA. The proposed increase in the retirement age is linked to projected increases in life expectancy. In addition, the commission recommends using a different measure of price change (the chained Consumer Price Index) to compute the Social Security COLA, on the basis that the current measure of price change used for this purpose overstates inflation.

The proposed recommendations would expand Social Security coverage by making coverage mandatory for newly hired state and local government workers after 2020. They would gradually increase the taxable wage base (the amount of covered earnings subject to the payroll tax each year) such that 90% of aggregate wages in covered employment would be taxable by 2050. The commission estimates that the taxable wage base would be about $190,000 in 2020, compared to approximately $168,000 under current law at that time.

The proposal includes other general recommendations. To provide greater flexibility in claiming benefits, the commission proposes allowing individuals to claim up to half of their benefits as early as age 62 (with the applicable actuarial reduction) and the other half at a later age. The commission directs the Social Security Administration to better inform future beneficiaries about retirement options and encourages efforts to promote greater personal savings for retirement.

Projections show that the proposed recommendations would result in lower benefits for most beneficiaries in the future compared with benefits scheduled under current law (the proposed changes would result in higher benefits for some low-wage earners).[44] In addition, projections show that the proposed recommendations would restore long-range trust fund solvency (i.e.,

Social Security Reform: Current Issues and Legislation

the proposed changes would close 112% of the system's projected average 75-year funding gap).[45]

On December 3, 2010, a majority of commission members expressed support for the recommendations in the final report (11 out of 18 members), three short of the super-majority needed to require congressional action on the recommendations.

INITIATIVES FOR CHANGE

The 1994-1996 Social Security Advisory Council presented three different approaches to restore long-range solvency to the system, none of which was endorsed by a majority of council members. The first (the "maintain benefits" plan) would maintain the system's current benefit structure by increasing revenues (including an eventual increase in the payroll tax) and making minor benefit reductions. It was also suggested that a portion of the Social Security trust funds be invested in stocks. The second (the "individual account" plan) addressed the problem mostly with benefit reductions, and would require workers to make an extra 1.6% of pay contribution to individual accounts. The third (the "personal security account" plan) proposed a major redesign of the system that would gradually replace the current earnings-related retirement benefit with a flat-rate benefit based on length of service and establish individual accounts funded by redirecting 5 percentage points of the current payroll tax. It would cover transition costs with an increase in payroll taxes of 1.52% of pay and government borrowing. The conceptual approaches incorporated in the three plans are reflected in many of the reform bills introduced in recent years.

During his last three years in office, former President William Clinton repeatedly called for using Social Security's share of budget surpluses projected at the time to reduce publicly held federal debt and crediting the trust funds for the reduction.[46] In the 1999 State of the Union address, he proposed crediting $2.8 trillion of some $4.9 trillion in budget surpluses projected for the next 15 years to the trust funds—nearly $0.6 trillion was to be invested in stocks, the rest in federal securities. The plan was estimated to keep the system solvent until 2059. Concerns were raised that the plan would be crediting the Social Security trust funds twice for its surpluses, and that the plan would lead to government ownership of private companies. Former President William Clinton further proposed that $0.5 trillion of the budget surpluses be used to create new Universal Savings Accounts—401(k)-type accounts intended to supplement Social Security benefits. In June 1999, he revised the plan by calling for general fund infusions to the trust funds equal to the interest savings achieved by using Social Security's share of the budget surpluses to reduce federal debt. The infusions were to be invested in stocks until the stock portion of the trust funds' holdings reached 15%. In October 1999, former President William Clinton revised the plan again by dropping the stock investment idea and calling for all the infusions to be invested in federal bonds. Former President William Clinton's last plan, offered in January 2000, was similar but again called for investing up to 15% of the trust funds in stocks.

During his first term, former President George W. Bush appointed a commission to make recommendations to reform Social Security. As principles for reform, he stated that any reform plan must preserve the benefits of current retirees and older workers, return Social Security to a firm financial footing, and allow younger workers to invest in individual savings accounts. The commission's final report, which was issued on December 21, 2001, included three reform options. Each option would allow workers to participate in individual accounts on a voluntary basis and reduce their future Social Security benefit by the projected value of the account based on an assumed (rather than the actual) rate of return.

The first option would allow workers to redirect 2% of taxable earnings to individual accounts and would make no other changes. The second option would allow workers to redirect 4% of taxable earnings, up to an annual limit of $1,000, to individual accounts; reduce initial benefits for future retirees by indexing the growth of initial benefits to prices rather than wages; and increase benefits for lower-wage workers and widow(er)s. The third option would allow workers to contribute an additional 1% of taxable earnings to individual accounts and receive a government match of 2.5% of taxable earnings, up to an annual limit of $1,000; reduce initial benefits for future retirees by slowing the growth of initial benefits to reflect projected increases in life expectancy, and, for higher-wage workers, by modifying the benefit formula; and increase benefits for lower-wage workers and widow(er)s.

During his second term, former President George W. Bush continued efforts to build support for Social Security reform. Although the former President did not present a detailed plan for reform, he put forth guidelines for Congress to consider in the development of legislation to create individual accounts within a program that he described as in need of "wise and effective reform." During the 2005 State of the Union address, former President George W. Bush offered the following guidelines for reform: (1) workers born before

Social Security Reform: Current Issues and Legislation 143

1950 (aged 55 or older in 2005) would not be affected by individual accounts or other components of reform; (2) participation in individual accounts would be voluntary; (3) eligible workers would be allowed to redirect up to 4% of covered earnings to an individual account, initially up to $1,000 per year; (4) accounts would be administered by a centralized government entity; and (5) workers would be required to annuitize the portion of the account balance needed to provide at least a poverty-level stream of life-long income, with any remaining balance available as a lump sum.

In addition to restating support for individual accounts as part of the creation of an "ownership society," former President George W. Bush acknowledged that other changes would be needed to address the system's projected long-range funding shortfall. He cited potential program changes that would be on the table for consideration, including (1) raising the full retirement age; (2) reducing benefits for wealthy beneficiaries; and (3) modifying the benefit formula. At the time, the only approach ruled out by former President George W. Bush was an increase in the payroll tax rate.

On April 28, 2005, during a television news conference, former President George W. Bush proposed a change in the Social Security benefit formula in which future "benefits for low-income workers [would] grow faster than benefits for people who are better off." Although details of the proposal were not released, a White House press statement indicated that the President was referring to a proposal similar to one put forth by Robert Pozen, a member of the 2001 *President's Commission to Strengthen Social Security* appointed by former President George W. Bush. Mr. Pozen's proposal, known as "progressive indexing," would restrain the growth of initial benefits for future retirees by using a combination of wage indexing and price indexing mechanisms in the benefit formula (rather than wage indexing only) to apply differing degrees of benefit reduction based on the worker's level of earnings.[47] Under progressive indexing, lower-wage workers would receive a benefit that is indexed closer to wage growth (as under current law) and higher-wage workers would receive a benefit that is indexed closer to price growth (or inflation). Based on current wage and price growth projections, a shift from wage indexing toward price indexing would result in lower initial benefits for many future retirees compared to current law.[48]

As the first session of the 109th Congress came to a close at the end of 2005, the reform debate focused on legislation introduced by Senator DeMint (S. 1302) that would have established voluntary individual accounts funded with surplus Social Security tax revenues and reduced Social Security benefits to reflect account assets (S. 1302 is described in the following section of the report). On November 15, 2005, Senator Santorum made unanimous consent requests to discharge S. 1302 and a second measure (S. 1750, 109th Congress) from the Senate Finance Committee and bring those measures to the Senate floor for consideration. S. 1750, introduced by Senator Santorum, would have provided for the issuance of Social Security "benefit guarantee certificates" to persons born before 1950 for the stated purpose of "guaranteeing their right to receive Social Security benefits ... in full with an accurate annual cost-of-living adjustment." The unanimous consent requests provided for 10 hours of debate on each measure followed by a vote on passage, with no amendments. Objections raised against the unanimous consent requests prevented further action on the measures.[49]

During the 2006 State of the Union address, former President George W. Bush expressed concern regarding the level of federal spending for entitlement programs, citing projections that Social Security, Medicare, and Medicaid would account for almost 60% of the federal budget by 2030. The former President called for the creation of a commission that would include Members of Congress from both parties to "examine the full impact of baby boom retirements on Social Security, Medicare, and Medicaid." In addition, former President George W. Bush included in his *Fiscal Year 2007 Budget* a proposal for voluntary individual accounts funded with a portion of current payroll taxes similar to the one he outlined in the 2005 State of the Union address. The *Fiscal Year 2007 Budget* also restated the former President's support for a change in the Social Security benefit formula known as "progressive indexing" to restrain the growth of initial benefits for future retirees as a cost-saving measure.

Immediately following the November 2006 congressional elections, in which Democrats gained a majority in both the House and the Senate, former President George W. Bush and Administration officials publicly expressed interest in resuming discussions with congressional leaders on the issue of Social Security reform. In the *Fiscal Year 2009 Budget*, former President George W. Bush restated support for voluntary individual accounts funded with a portion of current payroll taxes. Under his proposal, starting in 2013, individual accounts would be funded with 4% of taxable earnings, up to a limit of $1,400 (the contribution limit would increase by $100 more than average wage growth each year through 2018). The former President also restated support for "progressive indexing" of initial Social Security benefits for future retirees.

In the 2010 State of the Union address, President Barack Obama expressed concern regarding the federal budget outlook, including the

Social Security Reform: Current Issues and Legislation 145

projected growth in spending for Medicare, Medicaid, and Social Security, and called for the formation of a bipartisan fiscal commission. As discussed above, the National Commission on Fiscal Responsibility and Reform established by President Barack Obama in February 2010 released its final report on December 1, 2010, which includes a number of proposed changes to the Social Security program. On December 3, 2010, a majority of commission members expressed support for the recommendations (11 out of 18 members), three short of the super-majority needed to require congressional action on the recommendations.

In the *Fiscal Year 2012 President's Budget*, released February 14, 2011, President Barack Obama expressed support for bipartisan efforts "to strengthen Social Security for the future" and outlined six principles for reform. The President's budget states

- "Any reform should strengthen Social Security for future generations and restore long-term solvency.
- The Administration will oppose any measures that privatize or weaken the Social Security system.
- While all measures to strengthen solvency should be on the table, the Administration will not accept an approach that slashes benefits for future generations.
- No current beneficiaries should see their basic benefits reduced.
- Reform should strengthen retirement security for the most vulnerable, including low-income seniors.
- Reform should maintain robust disability and survivors' benefits."[50]

On April 13, 2011, President Barack Obama put forth a deficit reduction framework that includes references to Social Security reform. The President's document states

The President does not believe that Social Security is a driver of our near-term deficit problems or is currently in crisis. But he supports bipartisan efforts to strengthen Social Security for the long haul, because its long-term challenges are better addressed sooner than later to ensure that it remains the rock-solid benefit for older Americans that it has been for past generations. The President in the State of the Union laid out his principles for Social Security reform which he believes should form the basis for bipartisan negotiations that could proceed in parallel to deficit negotiations:

- Strengthen retirement security for the low-income and vulnerable; maintain robust disability and survivors' benefits.
- No privatization or weakening of the Social Security system; reform must strengthen Social Security and restore long-term solvency.
- No current beneficiary should see the basic benefit reduced; nor will we accept an approach that slashes benefits for future generations.[51]

In the *Fiscal Year 2013 President's Budget*, released February 13, 2012, President Barack Obama stated that he is "strongly opposed to privatizing Social Security and looks forward to working on a bipartisan basis to preserve it for future generations."[52]

In the *Fiscal Year 2014 President's Budget*, released April 10, 2013, President Barack Obama proposed using the chained Consumer Price Index to compute the annual Social Security COLA. To offset this proposal, which is projected to result in lower annual COLAs compared with current law, the President also proposed an increase in Social Security benefits for older beneficiaries.[53]

LEGISLATION INTRODUCED IN THE 113TH CONGRESS

A number of Social Security reform bills have been introduced in the 113th Congress; none have received congressional action. This section provides examples of current legislation, specifically, bills that have been scored by the Social Security Administration's Office of the Chief Actuary.[54]

S. 500. Senator Bernard Sanders introduced S. 500 (Keeping Our Social Security Promises Act) on March 7, 2013. In addition to the 12.4% Social Security payroll tax on earnings in covered employment up to the taxable wage base under current law ($117,000 in 2014), the measure would apply the 12.4% Social Security payroll tax to covered earnings in excess of $250,000 beginning in calendar year 2014. The additional taxable earnings (earnings above the current-law taxable wage base) would not be counted for benefit computation purposes. SSA estimates that the measure would extend trust fund solvency for an additional 28 years (under the intermediate assumptions of the 2012 trustees report).[55]

S. 567. Senator Tom Harkin introduced S. 567 (Strengthening Social Security Act of 2013) on March 14, 2013.

The measure would make all earnings in covered employment subject to the Social Security payroll tax, fully effective in 2018, and credit the additional taxable earnings using a modified benefit computation. In addition, it would increase the first bend point in the current-law benefit formula for those who become newly eligible for benefits beginning in 2019, resulting in a higher initial monthly benefit. It would use the Consumer Price Index for the Elderly (CPI-E) to compute the annual Social Security COLA, effective December 2014. SSA estimates that using the CPI-E would increase the annual COLA by about 0.2 percentage points, on average.

Overall, SSA estimates that the measure would extend trust fund solvency for an additional 16 years (under the intermediate assumptions of the 2012 trustees report).[56]

H.R. 1374. Representative Gwen Moore introduced H.R. 1374 (Social Security Enhancement and Protection Act of 2013) on March 21, 2013. The measure would (1) increase the special minimum benefit for workers who become newly eligible for retirement or disability benefits or die in 2015 or later; (2) provide a benefit increase after 16 years of initial benefit eligibility; (3) extend benefit eligibility for the child of a disabled or deceased worker until age 22 if the child is in high school, college, or vocational school; (4) make all covered earnings subject to the Social Security payroll tax, fully effective in 2024, and modify the benefit formula; and (5) increase the Social Security payroll tax rate to 13.0%, fully effective in 2020. SSA estimates that the measure would extend trust fund solvency for an additional 35 years (under the intermediate assumptions of the 2012 trustees report).[57]

APPENDIX. SELECTED LEGISLATION, 109TH-112TH CONGRESSES

During the past several Congresses, many Social Security reform bills have been introduced. The legislation reflects a range of approaches to reform, from traditional program changes to the creation of individual accounts within the Social Security system.

This section provides summary information on selected Social Security reform legislation introduced in recent years.[58]

Legislation Introduced in the 109th Congress

In the 109th Congress, 10 Social Security reform measures were introduced: H.R. 440 (Kolbe and Boyd), H.R. 530 (Johnson), H.R. 750 (Shaw), H.R. 1776 (Ryan), H.R. 2472 (Wexler), H.R. 3304 (McCrery), S. 540 (Hagel), S. 857 (Sununu), S. 1302 (DeMint), and S. 2427 (Bennett). All but two of the measures (H.R. 2472 and S. 2427) would have established individual accounts to supplement or replace traditional Social Security benefits, among other changes. This section provides a summary of Social Security reform legislation introduced in the 109th Congress, with the exception of H.R. 530, H.R. 750, S. 540, and H.R. 2472. These measures, which were re-introduced in the 110th Congress, are included in the section that follows ("Legislation Introduced in the 110th Congress"). Despite intense debate on the issue of Social Security reform in the 109th Congress, there was no congressional action on Social Security reform legislation.

H.R. 440. Representatives Jim Kolbe and Allen Boyd introduced H.R. 440 (Bipartisan Retirement Security Act of 2005) on February 1, 2005. For workers under the age of 55, the measure would have redirected 3% of the first $10,000 of covered earnings (indexed to wage growth) and 2% of remaining covered earnings to mandatory individual accounts. Workers would have been allowed to make additional contributions of up to $5,000 annually (indexed to inflation), and lower-wage workers would have been eligible for an additional credit of up to $600 toward their account.

With respect to traditional Social Security benefits, the measure would have made a number of benefit computation changes, including several adjustments to the "replacement factors" used in the benefit formula. It would have constrained the growth of initial monthly benefits for future retirees by indexing initial benefits to increases in life expectancy, a provision known as "longevity indexing" of benefits. The measure would have modified the calculation of the worker's "average indexed monthly earnings" (AIME) for benefit computation purposes. In the future, the worker's AIME would have been based on the worker's average career earnings— counting all years of earnings divided by a 40-year computation period (rather than the worker's average career earnings, counting the 35 years of highest earnings divided by a 35-year computation period).

In addition, the measure would have accelerated the increase in the full retirement age from 65 to 67 scheduled under current law, so that it would have reached age 67 for persons born in 1956 or later (four years earlier than under current law). It would have modified the early retirement reduction factors and delayed retirement credits; set widow(er)s' benefits equal to 75% of the couple's combined pre-death benefit (rather than 50%-67%); limited benefits for aged spouses of higher earners; provided a minimum benefit tied to the poverty level for workers who meet specified coverage requirements; and reduced cost-of-living adjustments.

With respect to tax changes, the measure would have increased the taxable wage base gradually so that 87% of covered earnings would be taxable. It would have credited all revenues from the taxation of Social Security benefits to the Social Security trust funds (instead of crediting part to the Medicare Hospital Insurance trust fund).

H.R. 440 would have established a central authority to administer the accounts and provided initial investment options similar to those available under the Thrift Savings Plan for federal employees. Once the account balance reached $7,500 (indexed to inflation), the worker would have been allowed to choose among a broader range of centrally managed investment options. The account would have become available at retirement, or earlier if the account balance were sufficient to provide a payment at least equal to 185% of the poverty level. The worker would have been required to annuitize the portion of the account balance needed to provide a combined monthly payment (traditional benefit plus annuity) at least equal to 185% of the poverty level. Any remaining balance could have been taken as a lump sum.

H.R. 3304. Representative Jim McCrery introduced H.R. 3304 (Growing Real Ownership for Workers Act of 2005) on July 14, 2005. The measure, which is similar to S. 1302, would have established voluntary individual accounts for workers born after 1949 (workers would have been enrolled automatically in the individual account system and given the option to disenroll). Individual accounts would have been funded with general revenues in amounts equal to surplus Social Security tax revenues projected at the time from 2006 to 2016.

H.R. 3304 would have established a central authority to administer the accounts. Initially, funds would have been invested in long-term Treasury bonds. Beginning in 2009, additional investment options may have been made available. The account would have become available at retirement, or in the event of the worker's death. At retirement, the worker would have been required to annuitize the portion of the account balance needed to provide a combined monthly payment (traditional benefit plus annuity) at least equal to the poverty level. Any remaining balance could have been taken as a lump sum. For account participants, traditional Social Security benefits would have been offset by an amount equal to the annuity value of a hypothetical (or "shadow") account assumed to have earned, on average, a 2.7% real rate of return. (The assumed rate of return for the hypothetical account was based on the projected ultimate real rate of return for the Social Security trust funds (3% on average) minus 0.3 percentage point to reflect administrative expenses.) The measure would have made no other changes to traditional Social Security benefits.

S. 857/H.R. 1776. Senator John Sununu introduced S. 857 (Social Security Personal Savings Guarantee and Prosperity Act of 2005) on April 20, 2005. Representative Paul Ryan introduced a companion measure (H.R. 1776) on April 21, 2005. The measures would have allowed workers under the age of 55 to redirect a portion of payroll taxes to voluntary individual accounts (workers would have been enrolled automatically in the individual account system and given the option to disenroll). From 2006 to 2015, workers would have been allowed to redirect 5% of covered earnings up to a base amount ($10,000 in 2006, indexed to wage growth thereafter) and 2.5% of remaining covered earnings to individual accounts. Beginning in 2016, workers would have been allowed to redirect 10% of covered earnings up to the base amount and 5% of remaining covered earnings to the accounts. Workers participating in individual accounts would have been issued a "benefit credit certificate" (or recognition bond) to reflect the value of benefits accrued under the traditional system. The recognition bond would have been redeemable at retirement, though the value of accrued benefits would have been reduced to reflect the payroll taxes redirected to the worker's account. The measures would have provided account participants a combined monthly payment (traditional benefit plus annuity) at least equal to benefits scheduled under current law. Workers choosing not to participate in individual accounts would have received traditional Social Security benefits.

The measures would have provided 6 indexed investment accounts, including a default "lifecycle investment account" with an expected average investment mix of 65% equities/35% fixed income instruments. Once the worker's account balance reached $25,000 (indexed to inflation), additional investment options would have become available. At retirement, the worker would have been required to annuitize the portion of the account balance needed to provide a combined monthly payment (traditional benefit plus inflation-indexed annuity) at least equal to benefits scheduled under current law. Any excess balance could have been withdrawn in a manner chosen by

Social Security Reform: Current Issues and Legislation   151

the worker. Pre-retirement distribution would have been allowed if the account balance were sufficient to provide an annuity at least equal to a required minimum payment. The measures also included several financing provisions that would have constrained future growth rates for federal spending and dedicated the savings to Social Security; "reserved" annual Social Security cash flow surpluses for Social Security purposes; and dedicated a portion of projected corporate tax revenue increases to Social Security.

S. 1302. Senator Jim DeMint introduced S. 1302 (Stop the Raid on Social Security Act of 2005) on June 23, 2005. The measure would have established voluntary individual accounts for workers born after 1949 (workers would have been enrolled automatically in the individual account system and given the option to disenroll). Individual accounts would have been funded with surplus Social Security tax revenues projected at the time from 2006 to 2016. Given the redirection of surplus Social Security tax revenues to individual accounts, the measure would have provided for general revenue transfers to the trust funds in amounts needed to maintain trust fund solvency based on current-law projections.

S. 1302 would have established a central authority to administer the accounts. Initially, funds would have been invested in long-term Treasury bonds. Beginning in 2008, additional investment options may have been made available. The account would have become available at retirement, or in the event of the worker's death. At retirement, the worker would have been required to annuitize the portion of the account balance needed to provide a combined monthly payment (traditional benefit plus annuity) at least equal to the poverty level. Any remaining balance could have been taken as a lump sum. For account participants, traditional Social Security benefits would have been offset by an amount equal to the annuity value of a hypothetical (or "shadow") account assumed to have earned, on average, a 2.7% real rate of return. (The assumed rate of return for the hypothetical account was based on the projected ultimate real rate of return for the Social Security trust funds (3% on average) minus 0.3 percentage point to reflect administrative expenses.) The measure would have made no other changes to traditional Social Security benefits.

S. 2427. Senator Robert Bennett introduced S. 2427 (Sustainable Solvency First for Social Security Act of 2006) on March 16, 2006. The measure would have modified the benefit formula to provide "progressive indexing" of initial Social Security benefits for future retirees. Progressive indexing applies a combination of wage indexing and price indexing to the benefit formula that, under current projections, would result in lower benefits for workers with earnings above a certain level (with larger reductions for relatively higher earners) compared to current law. The measure would have further constrained the growth of initial Social Security benefits for future retirees by indexing initial benefits to increases in life expectancy, a provision known as "longevity indexing" of benefits. It would have accelerated the increase in the full retirement age (from 65 to 67) being phased-in under current law so that the full retirement age would have reached 67 for persons born in 1955 or later (five years earlier than under current law). The measure would have provided general revenue transfers to the Social Security trust funds as needed to maintain adequate trust fund balances.

Legislation Introduced in the 110th Congress

During the 110th Congress, six Social Security reform bills were introduced: H.R. 1090 (Lewis), H.R. 2002 (Johnson), H.R. 4181 (Flake), S. 2765 (Hagel), H.R. 5779 (Wexler), and H.R. 6110 (Ryan). H.R. 1090 (which is similar to H.R. 750 in the 109th Congress[59]) would have established voluntary individual accounts funded with general revenues, among other changes. H.R. 2002 (which is similar to H.R. 530 in the 109th Congress), H.R. 4181, S. 2765 (which is similar to S. 540 in the 109th Congress) and H.R. 6110 would have established individual accounts funded with a redirection of current payroll taxes, among other changes. H.R. 5779 (which is similar to H.R. 2472 in the 109th Congress) would have increased Social Security revenues by requiring workers and employers each to contribute 3% of earnings above the Social Security taxable wage base (in addition to payroll tax contributions under current law). This section provides a summary of Social Security reform legislation introduced in the 110th Congress, with the exception of H.R. 4181, H.R. 5779 and H.R. 6110. These measures were re-introduced in the 111th Congress and are included in the next section (see H.R. 107, H.R. 1863, and H.R. 4529 in "Legislation Introduced in the 111th Congress"). There was no congressional action on these measures during the 110th Congress.

H.R. 1090. Representative Ron Lewis introduced H.R. 1090 (Social Security Guarantee PlusAct of 2007) on February 15, 2007. The measure would have allowed workers aged 18 and older (who have been assigned a

Social Security Number) to participate in voluntary individual accounts funded with general revenues. Account contributions would have been equal to 4% of taxable earnings, up to a limit of $1,000 (the limit would have been indexed to wage growth).

With respect to traditional Social Security benefits, the measure would have provided up to five years of earnings credits for workers who stay at home to care for a child under age seven and eliminated the earnings test for beneficiaries below the full retirement age. In addition, it would have set widow(er)'s benefits equal to 75% of the couple's combined pre-death benefit (compared to 50%-67% under current law); allowed widow(er)s to qualify for benefits based on a disability regardless of age and the time frame in which the disability occurred; and lowered the Social Security spousal/widow(er)'s benefit reduction under the Government Pension Offset from two-thirds to one-third of the individual's pension from noncovered employment.

Under H.R. 1090, accounts would have been administered by private financial institutions selected by the government. The measure would have provided three initial investment options with specified allocations in equities and corporate bonds (60/40, 65/35, 70/30). The account would have become available upon the worker's entitlement to retirement or disability benefits, or upon the worker's death. Upon benefit entitlement, the worker would have received a lump sum equal to 5% of the account balance. The remaining balance would have been used to finance all or part of the worker's benefit. The account balance would have been withdrawn gradually and transferred to the trust funds for the payment of monthly benefits. In addition to the 5% lump sum, the measure would have provided a monthly payment equal to the higher of a benefit scheduled under current law and an annuity based on 95% of the account balance.

H.R. 2002. Representative Sam Johnson introduced H.R. 2002 (Individual Social Security Investment Program Act of 2007) on April 23, 2007. The measure would have established individual accounts funded with 6.2 percentage points of the current Social Security payroll tax. Participation in the individual account system would have been voluntary for workers aged 22 to 54 (in 2007) and mandatory for younger individuals. Workers participating in the individual account system would no longer have accrued benefits under the current system and would have been issued a marketable "recognition bond" equal to the value of benefits already accrued. The measure would have provided workers participating in the individual account system a minimum benefit equal to a specified percentage of the poverty level, up to 100% for workers who have at least 35 years of earnings.

Workers choosing not to participate in the individual account system would have remained in the current system, however, initial monthly benefits would have been lower than those scheduled under current law. The measure would have constrained the growth of initial monthly benefits for future retirees by indexing initial benefits to price growth (rather than wage growth), a provision known as "price indexing" of benefits.

H.R. 2002 would have established a central authority to administer the accounts and provided at least three initial investment options with specified allocations in equities and fixed income instruments (government bonds and corporate bonds), including a default 60/40 investment mix. Once the account balance reached $10,000 (indexed to inflation), the worker would have been allowed to transfer the balance to a private financial institution. The account would have become available at retirement (i.e., at the Social Security full retirement age), or earlier if the account balance were sufficient to provide an annuity at least equal to 100% of the poverty level. In the case of pre-retirement account distribution, the worker would have received an annual rebate of future payroll tax contributions (the employer share of the payroll tax would not have been subject to rebate). The worker would have been required to annuitize the portion of the account balance needed to provide an annuity at least equal to 100% of the poverty level. Any remaining balance could have been taken as a lump sum. At retirement, if the account balance were not sufficient to provide the prescribed minimum payment, a supplemental payment would have been made to the account from general revenues.

S. 2765. Senator Chuck Hagel introduced S. 2765 (Saving Social Security Act of 2008) on March 13, 2008. The measure would have allowed workers born in 1963 or later (workers aged 45 or younger in 2008) to redirect 4 percentage points of the current Social Security payroll tax to an individual account (a SAFE account). Eligible workers would have been enrolled automatically in the individual account system and allowed to waive their eligibility for a SAFE account.

With respect to traditional Social Security benefits, the measure would have constrained the growth of initial benefits for future retirees by indexing initial benefits to increases in life expectancy, a provision known as "longevity indexing" of benefits. In addition, the measure would have increased the full retirement age from 67 to 68 for persons born in 1963 or later and increased the early retirement reduction factors. For workers participating in the individual account system, traditional Social Security benefits would have been offset by an amount equal to the annuity value of a hypothetical (or "shadow") account assumed to earn a 3% real rate of return. The measure would have provided a minimum "primary insurance amount" (basic benefit amount before any adjustments for early or delayed retirement) up to 135% of the poverty level for workers with 35 years of Social Security-covered employment (lower percentages would have applied to workers with fewer years of coverage).

The bill would have established a central authority to administer the individual accounts and provided initial investment options such as those offered by the Thrift Savings Plan for federal employees. The individual account would have become available at retirement, or in the event of the worker's death. Upon entitlement to benefits, the worker would have been required to annuitize the portion of the account balance needed to provide a combined monthly payment (traditional benefit plus annuity) at least equal to 135% of the poverty level. Any remaining balance could have been withdrawn in a manner chosen by the worker.

Legislation Introduced in the 111th Congress

During the 111th Congress, four Social Security reform bills were introduced: H.R. 107 (Flake), S. 426 (Bennett), H.R. 1863 (Wexler), and H.R. 4529 (Ryan). There was no congressional action on these measures during the 111th Congress.

H.R. 107. Representative Jeff Flake introduced H.R. 107 (Securing Medicare and Retirement for Tomorrow Act of 2009) on January 6, 2009.[60] Among other provisions, the measure would have established individual accounts funded with 6.2 percentage points of the current Social Security payroll tax. Participation in the individual account system would have been mandatory for workers below the Social Security full retirement age. At retirement, workers would have been allowed to choose between a Social Security retirement benefit (Part A retirement benefit payable to workers and spouses) and a retirement distribution from the individual account (Part B benefit). Part A retirement benefits would have been phased-out over time. Individuals reaching retirement age after a period of 42 calendar years following enactment of the bill would not have had the option of choosing Part A retirement benefits.[61]

The worker's individual account would have been maintained by the employer and contributions would have been invested in a qualified Social Security mutual fund. Workers would have designated an investment fund from among five qualified Social Security mutual funds selected by the employer.

H.R. 107 would have established a Social Security Escrow Fund within the U.S. Treasury. The fund would have included securities held by the Social Security trust funds, 6.2 percentage points of the current Social Security payroll tax, Medicare Hospital Insurance (HI) payroll taxes, and amounts appropriated for the Supplemental Security Income (SSI) program, among other funding sources.[62] Amounts held in the Social Security Escrow Fund would have been available for the payment of various types of Social Security benefits—including Part A retirement benefits, benefits payable to a worker's family members (such as children and surviving spouses), disability benefits, and lump-sum death benefits—as well as for the payment of SSI benefits. In addition, transfers would have been made from the fund to the Medicare HI trust fund in the amount of Medicare Part A benefits.

The measure would have established the Personal Accounts Management and Review Board as an independent agency within the executive branch of the government. Among other duties, the board would have operated the Social Security Escrow Fund and designated and regulated qualified Social Security mutual funds. The Secretary of the Treasury would have served as managing trustee of the Social Security Escrow Fund.

S. 426. Senator Robert Bennett introduced S. 426 (Social Security Solvency Act of 2009) on February 12, 2009.[63] The measure would have modified the benefit formula to provide "progressive indexing" of initial Social Security benefits for future retirees. Progressive indexing applies a combination of wage indexing and price indexing to the benefit formula that, under current projections, would result in lower benefits for workers with earnings above a certain level (with larger reductions for relatively higher earners) compared to current law. The measure would have further constrained the growth of initial benefits for future retirees by indexing initial benefits to increases in life expectancy, a provision known as "longevity indexing" of benefits. In addition, it would have accelerated the increase in the full retirement age (from 65 to 67) being phased-in under current law so that the full retirement age would have reached 67 for persons born in 1955 or later (five years earlier than under current law). The measure would have provided

Social Security Reform: Current Issues and Legislation   157

general revenue transfers to the Social Security trust funds as needed to maintain adequate trust fund balances.

H.R. 1863. Representative Robert Wexler introduced H.R. 1863 (Social Security Forever Act of 2009) on April 1, 2009.[64] The measure would have increased Social Security revenues by requiring workers and employers each to contribute 3% of covered earnings above the Social Security taxable wage base, in addition to the payroll tax contributions payable under current law.

Under current law, workers and employers each contribute 6.2% of covered earnings up to the taxable wage base. (The taxable wage base increases each year according to average wage growth if a Social Security COLA is payable.) Earnings up to the taxable wage base (earnings on which payroll tax contributions are paid) are credited for benefit computation purposes.

Under the measure, workers and employers each would have been required to contribute 3% of earnings *above* the taxable wage base, in addition to the 6.2% of earnings *up to* the taxable wage base payable under current law. Earnings above the taxable wage base taxed at the 3% rate would not have been credited for benefit computation purposes.

H.R. 4529. Representative Paul Ryan introduced H.R. 4529 (Roadmap for America's Future Act of 2010) on January 27, 2010, to provide for the reform of health care, the Social Security system, the tax code for individuals and business, job training, and the budget process.[65] Title IV of the bill (Social Security Personal Savings Guarantee and Prosperity Act of 2010) would have allowed workers aged 55 or younger in 2012 to redirect a portion of their payroll tax contributions to voluntary individual accounts. From 2012 to 2021, workers would have been allowed to redirect 2% of taxable earnings up to a base amount ($10,000 in 2012, indexed to average wage growth thereafter) and 1% of remaining taxable earnings to an individual account. The amount of Social Security contributions to be redirected to an individual account would have increased over time. From 2022 to 2031, workers would have been allowed to redirect 4% of taxable earnings up to the base amount and 2% of remaining taxable earnings. From 2032 to 2041, workers would have been allowed to redirect 6% of taxable earnings up to the base amount and 3% of remaining taxable earnings. For calendar years after 2041, workers would have been allowed to redirect 8% of taxable earnings up to the base amount and 4% of remaining taxable earnings to an individual account.

Workers choosing to participate in the individual account system would have been issued a "benefit credit certificate" to reflect the value of benefits accrued under the traditional system. The benefit credit certificate would have been redeemable at retirement and the value of accrued benefits would have been reduced to reflect the payroll taxes redirected to the worker's individual account. The measure would have provided a guarantee by the government that the value of a participant's individual account would be at least equal to the sum of his or her contributions to the account, adjusted for inflation. Workers choosing not to participate in the individual account system would have received traditional benefits (subject to changes to the system).

The measure would have provided six indexed investment accounts, including a default "lifecycle investment account." Once the worker's account balance reached a specified threshold ($25,000 in 2012, indexed to inflation thereafter), additional investment options would have become available. The account would have become available at retirement, or earlier if the account balance were sufficient to provide an annuity at least equal to 150% of the poverty line.

At retirement, the worker would have been required to annuitize the portion of the account balance needed to provide a monthly payment at least equal to 150% of the poverty line, and any excess balance could have been withdrawn in a manner chosen by the worker. Any funds remaining in the account at the time of the individual's death would have been payable to designated beneficiaries or to the individual's estate.

Among other changes, the measure would have modified the Social Security benefit formula to provide "progressive price indexing" of initial monthly benefits for future retirees (the change would have applied to workers aged 55 or younger in 2011).

Progressive price indexing applies a combination of wage indexing and price indexing to the benefit formula that is projected to result in lower initial monthly benefits for workers with earnings above a certain level (with larger benefit reductions for relatively higher earners) compared to current law. In addition, the measure would have accelerated the increase in the full retirement age (FRA) scheduled under current law, so that the FRA would have reached 67 for persons born in 1959 (one year earlier than under current law). It would have further increased the FRA for persons born in later years to reflect projected increases in life expectancy.[66]

Legislation Introduced in the 112th Congress

During the 112th Congress, several Social Security reform measures were introduced, including H.R. 539 (Deutch), H.R. 797 (DeFazio), S. 804 (Graham, Paul, and Lee), S. 1213 (Hutchison), H.R. 2889 (McCotter), S. 1558 (Sanders), and S. 3533 (Hutchison).[67] There was no congressional action on these measures during the 112th Congress.

H.R. 539. Representative Theodore Deutch introduced H.R. 539, Preserving Our Promise to Seniors Act, on February 8, 2011. Among other provisions, the measure would have gradually eliminated the taxable wage base, making all covered earnings subject to the Social Security payroll tax (12.4%) in 2018 and later. The additional taxable earnings would have been counted for benefit computation purposes using a modified benefit formula. The measure would have based the Social Security COLA on the Consumer Price Index for the Elderly (CPI-E) and provided a supplemental payment to Social Security and other beneficiaries in years for which no COLA is payable. It would have created a point of order against legislation to "privatize" Social Security or reduce Social Security benefits.

H.R. 797. Representative Peter DeFazio introduced H.R. 797, the No Loopholes in Social Security Taxes Act, on February 18, 2011. In addition to the 12.4% Social Security payroll tax on earnings in covered employment up to the taxable wage base under current law, the measure would have applied the 12.4% Social Security payroll tax to earnings in covered employment in excess of $250,000 beginning in calendar year 2012. The additional taxable earnings (earnings above the taxable wage base under current law) would not have been counted for benefit computation purposes.[68]

S. 804. Senators Lindsey Graham, Rand Paul, and Mike Lee introduced S. 804, Social Security Solvency and Sustainability Act, on April 13, 2011. The measure would have increased the full retirement age (FRA) by three months each year, beginning with persons who attain age 62 in 2017, until the FRA reaches age 70. After the FRA reaches age 70 (for persons who attain age 62 in 2032), the FRA would have been increased further by about one month every two years to maintain a constant ratio of expected retirement years to potential working years. In addition, the earliest eligibility age (EEA) would have been increased from age 62 to age 64. The EEA would have been increased by three months each year, beginning with persons who attain age

62 in 2021. The EEA would have reached age 64 for persons who attain age 62 in 2028 or later. The measure would have modified the Social Security benefit formula to provide "progressive price indexing" of initial monthly benefits for future retirees. Progressive price indexing applies a combination of wage indexing and price indexing to the benefit formula that is projected to result in lower initial monthly benefits for workers with earnings above a certain level compared with current law (with larger benefit reductions for relatively higher earners).[69]

S. 1213. Senator Kay Bailey Hutchison introduced S. 1213, Defend and Save Social Security Act, on June 16, 2011. The measure would have increased the full retirement age by three months each year, beginning with persons who attain age 62 in 2016, until the FRA reaches age 69 for persons who attain age 62 in 2027 or later. The earliest eligibility age would have been increased from age 62 to age 64. The EEA would have been increased by three months each year, beginning with persons who attain age 62 in 2016, until the EEA reaches age 64 for persons who attain age 62 in 2023 or later. Under the measure, the annual Social Security COLA would have been computed as under current law and reduced by 1 percentage point (but not to less than zero).[70] (See related measure S. 3533 described below.)

H.R. 2889. Representative Thaddeus McCotter introduced H.R. 2889, a bill to reform Social Security by establishing a Personal Social Security Savings Program, on September 12, 2011. Among other provisions, the measure would have established a system of voluntary personal accounts for workers under the age of 50 in 2012 (persons born in 1962 or earlier). The accounts would have been funded with general revenues in an amount equal to (1) 5% of earnings subject to the Social Security payroll tax, up to $10,000 in 2012, plus (2) 2.5% of taxable earnings above that amount. For years after 2012, the $10,000 threshold would have been indexed to average wage growth.

The personal account system would have been administered by a central authority similar to the Thrift Savings Plan for federal employees. Withdrawals from the accounts would have been allowed when a participant attains the earliest eligibility age for retirement benefits (age 62 for retired workers) or when a disabled worker beneficiary attains the full retirement age. Traditional Social Security benefits (retirement and aged survivor benefits) would have been reduced by up to 50% for those who participate in the personal account system. Under the proposal, account participants would have

Social Security Reform: Current Issues and Legislation 161

been guaranteed a combined monthly payment (i.e., a reduced Social Security benefit plus an annuity based on the personal account) at least equal to the Social Security benefit that would be payable had the beneficiary not participated in the personal account system. The cost of the benefit guarantee would have been funded with general revenues.

The proposal would have provided authority for the Social Security trust funds to borrow from the general fund of the Treasury if needed to pay benefits on time should the trust funds become exhausted. In addition, the proposal would have provided for excess Social Security trust fund income (i.e., income above what is needed to maintain a level of assets equal to annual program costs) to be redirected to the general fund of the Treasury to help finance personal account contributions and the cost of the benefit guarantee.[71]

S. 1558. Senator Bernard Sanders introduced S. 1558 on September 14, 2011. The measure, which is similar to H.R. 797 described above, would have applied the 12.4% Social Security payroll tax to earnings in covered employment in excess of $250,000 beginning in 2012. Earnings in covered employment up to the taxable wage base under current law would have continued to be subject to the 12.4% payroll tax. The additional taxable earnings (earnings above the taxable wage base under current law) would not have been counted for benefit computation purposes.[72]

S. 3533. Senator Kay Bailey Hutchison introduced S. 3533, Defend and Save Social Security Act of 2012, on September 12, 2012. The measure would have increased the full retirement age by three months each year, beginning with persons who attain age 62 in 2016, until the FRA reaches age 70 for persons who attain age 62 in 2031 or later. The earliest eligibility age would have been increased from age 62 to age 64. The EEA would have been increased by three months each year, beginning with persons who attain age 62 in 2016, until the EEA reaches age 64 for persons who attain age 62 in 2023 or later. Under the measure, the annual Social Security COLA would have been computed as under current law and reduced by 1 percentage point (but not to less than zero).[73] (See related measure S. 1213 described above.)

End Notes

[1] The Social Security Board of Trustees is composed of three officers of the President's Cabinet (the Secretary of the Treasury, the Secretary of Labor, and the Secretary of Health and Human Services), the Commissioner of Social Security, and two public representatives who

162   Dawn Nuschler

are appointed by the President and subject to confirmation by the Senate. The trustees report annually on the financial status of the trust funds based on three sets of assumptions (low cost, intermediate, and high cost) given the uncertainty surrounding projections for a 75-year period. The projections discussed in this CRS report are the intermediate (or "best estimate") projections from the 2013 trustees report (see The 2013 Annual Report of the Board of Trustees of the Federal Old-Age and Survivors Insurance and Federal Disability Insurance Trust Funds, May 31, 2013, available at http://www.socialsecurity.gov/OACT/ TR/2013/).

[2] For more information, see CRS Report R42035, *Social Security Primer*, by Dawn Nuschler.

[3] Social Security Administration (SSA), *Monthly Statistical Snapshot, November 2013*, Table 2. The latest edition of the *Monthly Statistical Snapshot* is at http://www.socialsecurity.gov/ policy/docs/quickfacts/stat_snapshot/index.html.

[4] SSA, *2014 Social Security/SSI/Medicare Information*, January 7, 2014, p. 1, http://www.socialsecurity.gov/ legislation/2014factsheet.pdf.

[5] OASDI is the formal name for Social Security. There are two separate trust funds: the Old-Age and Survivors Insurance (OASI) trust fund and the Disability Insurance (DI) trust fund. This report refers to the two trust funds on a combined basis as the Social Security trust funds.

[6] SSA, Trust Fund FAQs, http://www.ssa.gov/OACT/ProgData/fundFAQ.html.

[7] SSA, Trust Fund Data, http://www.ssa.gov/OACT/STATS/table4a3.html.

[8] **Table 1** includes data through 2009, the last year in which the trust funds operated with an annual cash flow surplus.

[9] On a combined basis, the assets of the OASDI (Social Security) trust funds are projected to be exhausted in 2033. Separately, the OASI trust fund is projected to be exhausted in 2035, and the DI trust fund is projected to be exhausted in 2016. The trustees note "the DI Trust Fund reserves become depleted in 2016, at which time continuing income to the DI Trust Fund would be sufficient to pay 80 percent of DI benefits. Therefore, legislative action is needed as soon as possible to address the DI program's financial imbalance. In the absence of a long-term solution, lawmakers could choose to reallocate a portion of the payroll tax rate between OASI and DI, as they did in 1994." (2013 trustees report, p. 4.) For more information, see CRS Report R43318, *Social Security Disability Insurance (DI) Trust Fund: Background and Solvency Issues*, by William R. Morton.

[10] The Congressional Budget Office (CBO) projects that the Social Security trust funds will be exhausted in calendar year 2031 under its extended baseline. On a separate basis, CBO projects that the OASI trust fund will be exhausted in calendar year 2033, and the DI trust fund will be exhausted in fiscal year 2017. For more information, see *The 2013 Long-Term Projections for Social Security: Additional Information*, December 2013, p. 2, http://www.cbo.gov/sites/ default/files/cbofiles/attachments/44972-SocialSecurity.pdf. For CBO's near-term baseline estimates, see *Combined Old-Age, Survivors, and Disability Insurance Trust Funds - May 2013 Baseline*, http://www.cbo.gov/sites/default/files/ cbofiles/attachments/44208_Old%20AgeSurvivorsDisabilityInsuranceTrustFunds.pdf. In the CBO table, the line labeled "Primary Surplus/Deficit" shows annual cash flows (excluding interest paid to the trust funds); the line labeled "Surplus/Deficit" shows annual totals including interest paid to the trust funds.

[11] 2013 trustees report, intermediate assumptions, table V.A2.

[12] 2013 trustees report, intermediate assumptions, table IV.B2.

[13] Program costs and income are evaluated as a percentage of taxable payroll because Social Security payroll taxes are the primary source of funding for the program.

[14] Under current law, employers and employees each contribute 6.2% of covered earnings up to the taxable wage base ($113,700 in 2013). Self-employed workers contribute 12.4% of net self-employment income up to the taxable wage base. A temporary reduction was in the payroll tax rate for workers in 2011 and 2012. P.L. 111-312 (the Tax Relief, Unemployment Insurance Reauthorization, and Job Creation Act of 2010, signed by President Barack Obama on December 17, 2010) provided a temporary 2 percentage point reduction in the

Social Security Reform: Current Issues and Legislation   163

payroll tax rate for employees and the self-employed in 2011, making the Social Security payroll tax 4.2% for employees and 10.4% for the self-employed. P.L. 111-312 did not change the employer's share of the Social Security payroll tax (6.2%) or the taxable wage base ($106,800 in 2011). P.L. 111-312 provided general revenue transfers to the Social Security trust funds in amounts needed to protect the trust funds from the loss of payroll tax revenues. Similarly, P.L. 112-78 (the Temporary Payroll Tax Cut Continuation Act of 2011, signed by President Barack Obama on December 23, 2011) extended the payroll tax reduction for workers through February 2012. P.L. 112-96 (the Middle Class Tax Relief and Job Creation Act of 2012, signed by President Obama on February 22, 2012) further extended the payroll tax reduction for workers through December 2012. For more information, see CRS Report R41648, *Social Security: Temporary Payroll Tax Reduction*, by Dawn Nuschler.

[15] For more information on the taxation of Social Security benefits, see CRS Report RL32552, *Social Security: Calculation and History of Taxing Benefits*, by Christine Scott.

[16] Polling results are from PollingReport.com at http://www.pollingreport.com/social.htm (see ABC News/Washington Post Poll, February 19-22, 2009).

[17] For more information on Social Security trust fund operations, see CRS Report RL33028, *Social Security: The Trust Fund*, by Dawn Nuschler and Gary Sidor.

[18] Polling results are from PollingReport.com at http://www.pollingreport.com/social.htm (see CNN/Opinion Research Corporation Poll, August 6-10, 2010).

[19] For more information on Social Security Statements, go to http://www.ssa.gov/mystatement/.

[20] *Report of the 1994-1996 Advisory Council on Social Security, Volume 1: Findings and Recommendations*, Washington, DC, January 1997.

[21] For more information on the pension system in Chile, see CRS Report R42449, *Chile's Pension System: Background in Brief*.

[22] *Strengthening Social Security and Creating Personal Wealth for All Americans*, Final Report of the President's Commission to Strengthen Social Security, December 21, 2001.

[23] For examples of arguments in support of individual accounts, see *Strengthening Social Security and Creating Personal Wealth for All Americans*, Final Report of the President's Commission to Strengthen Social Security, December 21, 2001, and a variety of sources available from the Cato Institute at http://www.socialsecurity.org/.

[24] Under current law, employers and employees each contribute 6.2% of an employee's covered earnings up to the annual taxable limit, and self-employed workers contribute 12.4% of net self-employment income up to the annual taxable limit. Some workers (approximately 6%) are not covered under the Social Security program and therefore do not pay Social Security payroll taxes.

[25] Social Security Administration, *Annual Statistical Supplement, 2012*, Table 4.B4, available at http://www.socialsecurity.gov/policy/docs/statcomps/supplement/2012/4b.pdf.

[26] Social Security Administration, *Annual Statistical Supplement, 2012*, Table 4.B4 and Table 4.B1, available at http://www.socialsecurity.gov/policy/docs/statcomps/supplement/2012/4b.pdf. The Social Security Amendments of 1977 (P.L. 95-216) increased the taxable earnings base to a level that made 90% of aggregate earnings in covered employment taxable by 1982, as a revenue raising measure.

[27] 2013 trustees report, intermediate assumptions, p. 138.

[28] More information on the Social Security recommendations of the President's Fiscal Commission is provided in a later section of this report.

[29] Social Security Administration, Office of the Chief Actuary, *Provisions Affecting Payroll Tax Rates*, available at http://www.ssa.gov/OACT/solvency/provisions/payrolltax.html (see options E3.1 and E3.2, respectively). Estimates are based on the intermediate assumptions of the 2013 trustees report.

[30] For example, see H.R. 797 and S. 1558 introduced in the 112th Congress (described in the **Appendix** to this report).

[31] For example, see H.R. 1863 introduced in the 111th Congress (described in the **Appendix** to this report).

[32] 2013 trustees report, intermediate assumptions, table V.A4 (cohort life expectancy).

[33] For more information, see CRS Report R41962, *Fact Sheet: The Social Security Retirement Age*.

[34] Under current law, the CPI measure used to adjust Social Security benefits is the Consumer Price Index for Urban Wage Earners and Clerical Workers (CPI-W).

[35] *Toward a More Accurate Measure of the Cost of Living*, Final Report to the Senate Finance Committee from the Advisory Commission to Study the Consumer Price Index, December 4, 1996.

[36] For more information, see CRS Report RL30074, *The Consumer Price Index: A Brief Overview*, by Brian W. Cashell, and CRS Report RL34168, *Automatic Cost of Living Adjustments: Some Economic and Practical Considerations*, by Brian W. Cashell.

[37] For more information, see CRS Report RL32293, *The Chained Consumer Price Index: What Is It and Would It Be Appropriate for Cost-of-Living Adjustments?*, by Julie M. Whittaker, and CRS Report R43347, *Budgetary and Distributional Effects of Adopting the Chained CPI*, by Donald J. Marples.

[38] For more information, see CRS Report R43363, *Alternative Inflation Measures for the Social Security Cost-of-Living Adjustment (COLA)*, by Noah P. Meyerson.

[39] For information on the CPI-E, see CRS Report RS20060, *A Separate Consumer Price Index for the Elderly?*, by Linda Levine. For information on the projected effects of using the C-CPI-U and the CPI-E to compute the annual Social Security COLA, see Social Security Administration, Office of the Chief Actuary, Memo to the Honorable Xavier Becerra, June 21, 2011, available at http://ssa.gov/OACT/solvency/index.html.

[40] Social Security Administration, Office of the Chief Actuary, *Provisions Affecting Cost of Living Adjustment*, available at http://www.ssa.gov/OACT/solvency/provisions/cola.html (see options A1, A2 and A3, respectively). Estimates are based on the intermediate assumptions of the 2013 trustees report.

[41] Executive Order–National Commission on Fiscal Responsibility and Reform, February 18, 2010, available at http://www.whitehouse.gov/the-press-office/executive-order-national-commission-fiscal-responsibility-and-reform.

[42] *The Moment of Truth: Report of the National Commission on Fiscal Responsibility and Reform*, December 1, 2010, http://www.fiscalcommission.gov/sites/fiscalcommission.gov/files/documents/TheMomentofTruth12_1_2010.pdf (hereinafter cited as Report of the President's Fiscal Commission).

[43] For more information, see CRS Report R41518, *Social Security: The Minimum Benefit Provision*.

[44] Report of the President's Fiscal Commission, p. 55.

[45] Report of the President's Fiscal Commission, p. 54.

[46] For more information, see U.S. Congress, House Committee on Ways and Means, *The President's Social Security Framework*, hearing, 106th Cong., 1st sess., February 23, 1999, Serial 106-32 (Washington: GPO, 2000).

[47] For more information, see *Testimony on Progressive Indexing* before the Senate Finance Committee, April 26, 2005, by Robert C. Pozen.

[48] Under the trustees' 2013 intermediate projections, wages are projected to increase at an average annual rate of 3.93% over the long run, compared with a 2.80% growth rate for prices.

[49] For more information on S. 1750, see CRS Report RL32822, *Social Security Reform: Legal Analysis of Social Security Benefit Entitlement Issues*, by Kathleen S. Swendiman and Thomas J. Nicola.

[50] *Budget of the United States Government, Fiscal Year 2012*, available at http://www.gpo.gov/fdsys/pkg/BUDGET-2012-BUD/pdf/BUDGET-2012-BUD.pdf, pp. 26-27. For additional information on Social Security-related proposals, see section titled "Social Security Administration," pp. 163-165.

Social Security Reform: Current Issues and Legislation 165

[51] *The President's Framework for Shared Prosperity and Shared Fiscal Responsibility*, at http://www.whitehouse.gov/ the-press-office/2011/04/13/fact-sheet-presidents-framework-shared-prosperity-and-shared-fiscal-resp.

[52] *Budget of the United States Government, Fiscal Year 2013*, at http://www.whitehouse.gov/ sites/default/files/omb/budget/fy2013/assets/budget.pdf, p. 195.

[53] *Budget of the United States Government, Fiscal Year 2014*, at http://www.whitehouse.gov/ sites/default/files/omb/ budget/fy2014/assets/budget.pdf, p. 46; and Office of Management and Budget, *Chained CPI Protections*, at http://www.whitehouse.gov/omb/budget/ factsheet/chained-cpi-protections.

[54] Information on proposals scored by SSA is available at http://www.socialsecurity.gov/ OACT/solvency/index.html.

[55] Social Security Administration, Office of the Chief Actuary, Memo to the Honorable Bernie Sanders, March 19, 2013, available at http://www.ssa.gov/OACT/solvency/index.html.

[56] Social Security Administration, Office of the Chief Actuary, Memo to the Honorable Tom Harkin, March 18, 2013, available at http://www.ssa.gov/OACT/solvency/index.html.

[57] Social Security Administration, Office of the Chief Actuary, Memo to the Honorable Gwen Moore, March 29, 2013, available at http://www.ssa.gov/OACT/solvency/index.html.

[58] More detailed descriptions and estimates of the financial effects of many of these proposals are available from the Social Security Administration, Office of the Chief Actuary, at http://www.ssa.gov/OACT/solvency/index.html. A complete listing of Social Security legislation is available through the Legislative Information System (LIS).

[59] In the 109th Congress, H.R. 750 was introduced by Representative Shaw.

[60] H.R. 107 is similar to H.R. 4181 introduced by Representative Flake in the 110th Congress.

[61] The measure also would have made changes to the Medicare program in connection with the establishment of Social Security individual accounts.

[62] If an individual had elected to receive Part A retirement benefits (in lieu of Part B benefits), the qualified Social Security mutual fund in which the individual's account contributions were invested would have been required to transfer the amount of the individual's Part B benefits to the Social Security Escrow Fund.

[63] S. 426 is similar to S. 2427 introduced by Senator Bennett in the 109th Congress.

[64] Former Representative Robert Wexler retired from Congress in January 2010.

[65] H.R. 4529 is similar to H.R. 6110 introduced by Representative Ryan in the 110th Congress and includes provisions similar to H.R. 1776 introduced by Representative Ryan in the 109th Congress.

[66] For more information, see Congressional Budget Office, *An Analysis of the Roadmap for America's Future Act of 2010*, January 27, 2010, available at http://www.cbo.gov/ftpdocs/ 108xx/doc10851/01-27-Ryan-Roadmap-Letter.pdf.

[67] Generally, the Social Security reform bills included here are those that have been scored by the Social Security Administration's Office of the Chief Actuary as restoring long-range solvency to the Social Security trust funds.

[68] Social Security Administration, Office of the Chief Actuary, Memo to the Honorable Peter DeFazio on H.R. 797, March 3, 2011, available at http://www.ssa.gov/OACT/solvency/ index.html.

[69] Social Security Administration, Office of the Chief Actuary, Memo to Senator Graham, Senator Paul and Senator Lee on S. 804, April 13, 2011, available at http://www.ssa.gov/ OACT/solvency/index.html.

[70] Social Security Administration, Office of the Chief Actuary, Memo to the Honorable Kay Bailey Hutchison, June 9, 2011, available at http://www.ssa.gov/OACT/solvency/index. html.

[71] Social Security Administration, Office of the Chief Actuary, Memo to the Honorable Thaddeus McCotter, September 12, 2011, available at http://www.ssa.gov/OACT/solvency/index. html.

[72] Social Security Administration, Office of the Chief Actuary, Memo to the Honorable Bernard Sanders, September 7, 2011, available at http://www.ssa.gov/OACT/solvency/index.html.

[73] Social Security Administration, Office of the Chief Actuary, Memo to the Honorable Kay Bailey Hutchison, September 12, 2012, available at http://www.ssa.gov/OACT/solvency/index.html.

INDEX

#

401(k)s, viii, 115, 117, 128

A

abuse, 94
access, 65, 66
accountability, 63, 72, 95
actuarial methods, 127
ADA, 104
adjustment, 4, 45, 46, 47, 135, 138, 144
administrative costs, viii, 95, 116, 130
adults, 131
agencies, 24, 25, 67, 69, 95
aging population, 129
aging society, 127
alcoholics, 88
alcoholism, 91
annual rate, 164
appropriations, 4
architects, 25, 27
assessment, 95
assets, 118, 119, 122, 130, 131, 143, 161, 162, 165
authority, 56, 67, 95, 149, 151, 154, 155, 160, 161
average earnings, 23, 56, 58
aviation industry, 98

B

base, 19, 20, 22, 25, 29, 35, 36, 40, 43, 44, 45, 46, 49, 51, 53, 54, 56, 85, 129, 135, 136, 140, 146, 149, 150, 152, 157, 159, 161, 162, 163
beneficiaries, 118, 120, 124, 127, 129, 131, 132, 134, 135, 139, 140, 143, 145, 146, 153, 158, 159
blindness, 38, 41
bonds, 13, 119, 128, 134, 142, 149, 151, 153, 154
breakdown, 4, 107
Budget Committee, 62, 63, 76, 77, 83
budget deficit, viii, 75, 83, 84, 115, 117, 131, 134, 139
budget resolution, 75, 76, 77, 79
budget surplus, 133, 138, 141
Bureau of Labor Statistics, 137
bureaucracy, 6
businesses, 6, 79

C

Cabinet, 89, 161
candidates, 91
capital markets, 129, 134
cash, viii, 14, 37, 79, 116, 118, 119, 121, 128, 131, 139, 151, 162

168 Index

cash flow, viii, 116, 118, 119, 121, 128, 131, 139, 151, 162
C-C, 138, 164
Census, 12
certificate, 150, 158
challenges, 145
chaos, 73, 74
childcare, 89
children, 6, 19, 79, 81, 82, 95, 118, 156
Chile, 133, 163
citizens, 14, 25
civil service, 39, 70, 71, 76
classes, 60
Clinton Administration, 88
CNN, 163
combined effect, 72
commerce, 2, 5
commercial, 12
compensation, 6, 24, 77, 81, 82
competition, 6
competitive advantage, 13
compliance, 72
compulsion, 8
computation, 25, 52, 109, 135, 136, 146, 147, 148, 157, 159, 161
computing, 23, 81
confinement, 96
congressional budget, 76, 88
Congressional Budget Office, 137, 162, 165
consensus, 73, 127
consent, 10, 17, 18, 34, 59, 61, 68, 90, 92, 93, 97, 98, 100, 144
construction, 99
consumer price index (CPI), 45, 46, 47, 49, 137, 138, 140, 146, 147, 159, 164, 165
consumers, 138
controversial, 17, 20, 28, 45, 47, 63
conviction, 96
cost, 7, 12, 31, 40, 44, 47, 49, 53, 58, 62, 66, 69, 94, 121, 124, 128, 129, 130, 131, 135, 138, 144, 149, 161, 162
cost of living, 7, 44, 47, 138
Court of Appeals, 112
covering, 5, 27, 36, 52
crimes, 61

CT, 38

D

debts, 8
decoupling, 52, 54
defects, 13
deficit, viii, 51, 54, 69, 75, 76, 78, 79, 83, 84, 93, 115, 116, 117, 118, 119, 121, 127, 130, 131, 136, 145
Democrat, 4
demographic change, 128
demographics, viii, 116
Department of Health and Human Services, 65, 67, 72
depression, 128
dignity, 132
directors, 25, 27
discrimination, 55
disposable income, 97
distribution, 151, 154, 155
diversity, 128
doctors, 19, 23, 26, 27, 36, 58
drug addict, 88, 91
drug addiction, 91

E

early retirement, 70, 137, 149, 154
economic development, 6
economic growth, 133, 134
economic power, 134
educational institutions, 13
EEA, 140, 159, 160, 161
election, 24, 91
emergency, 8, 66, 68
employee compensation, 125
employees, 5, 8, 9, 10, 11, 13, 14, 16, 17, 18, 19, 25, 26, 27, 29, 39, 40, 43, 52, 54, 56, 69, 70, 71, 83, 89, 98, 100, 107, 124, 149, 155, 160, 162, 163
employers, 5, 7, 9, 10, 11, 13, 14, 18, 25, 29, 38, 40, 43, 54, 56, 98, 118, 124, 131, 136, 152, 157, 162, 163

Index 169

employment, 9, 11, 48, 50, 69, 80, 96, 135, 136, 139, 140, 146, 147, 153, 155, 159, 161, 163
enforcement, 96
enrollment, 88
equities, 133, 150, 153, 154
equity, viii, 116, 117, 129, 134, 135
erosion, 29
evidence, 68, 74, 132
examinations, 23
exclusion, 82
executive branch, 156
Executive Order, 164
expenditures, 16, 52, 62, 69, 84, 118, 119, 122, 123, 124, 130, 131, 135, 138, 139

F

fairness, 129
families, 132
family members, 118, 156
farmers, 7, 25, 27
fear, 15
federal assistance, 18
federal courts, 72
federal debt limit, viii, 115
federal funds, 31
federal government, viii, 5, 7, 30, 56, 116, 117, 118, 119, 122, 131, 138, 139
federal law, 72
federal regulations, 17
felon, 96
fertility, 123
fertility rate, 123
financial, viii, ix, 5, 7, 8, 12, 51, 70, 71, 85, 88, 93, 116, 117, 122, 126, 127, 131, 132, 133, 134, 135, 137, 138, 142, 153, 154, 162, 165
financial condition, 138
financial institutions, 153
financial markets, 133
financial outlook, viii, ix, 85, 116, 117, 126, 133, 135
financial resources, 131
financial soundness, 5

financial stability, viii, 116, 117
fiscal deficit, 85
fiscal policy, 88
flexibility, 140
floor amendments, vii, 1, 20, 28, 39, 41, 42
force, 84
Ford, 52
formation, 9, 145
formula, 25, 51, 52, 59, 75, 80, 124, 140, 142, 143, 144, 147, 148, 151, 156, 158, 159, 160
fraud, 94
freezing, 76
fund transfers, 112
funding, 4, 31, 55, 57, 77, 117, 123, 125, 127, 129, 130, 134, 135, 139, 141, 143, 156, 162
funds, viii, 5, 15, 31, 37, 53, 59, 65, 69, 75, 91, 94, 95, 116, 117, 118, 119, 121, 131, 133, 139, 141, 149, 151, 156, 158, 161, 162, 163

G

Gross Domestic Product (GDP), 124, 125, 126, 131
General Accounting Office, 96
general election, 41
goal-setting, 76
goods and services, 12, 137, 138
government securities, 118, 119, 122, 131
government spending, 128
grants, 6, 21, 22, 32
growth, 4, 89, 90, 124, 127, 129, 135, 136, 138, 139, 142, 143, 144, 145, 148, 150, 151, 152, 153, 154, 156, 157, 160, 164
growth rate, 151, 164
guidelines, 62, 142

H

hazards, 17
health, 6, 20, 21, 30, 31, 32, 36, 37, 39, 57, 99, 100, 105, 157

Health and Human Services (HHS), 88, 161
health care, 30, 32, 157
health insurance, 20, 21, 30, 31, 36, 39, 57, 105
health services, 6
high school, 62, 147
history, 104
hospitalization, 36, 37
House of Representatives, 12, 111

I

ID, 46, 55
ideology, 16
impairments, 60, 72
improvements, 13, 137
income tax, 39, 69, 78, 85, 108, 118, 120, 124
independence, 88, 105
indexing, 124, 142, 143, 144, 148, 151, 154, 156, 158, 160
individuals, 44, 60, 67, 68, 70, 74, 80, 91, 93, 94, 96, 132, 140, 153, 157
industry(s), 2, 4, 5, 6, 7
inflation, 4, 29, 49, 51, 55, 59, 76, 78, 95, 134, 137, 138, 140, 143, 148, 149, 150, 154, 158
ingredients, 74
injury, 7
inmates, 66
institutions, 23
integrity, 34
interest groups, 127
interest rates, 75
investment(s), viii, 9, 115, 117, 118, 128, 130, 133, 134, 142, 149, 150, 151, 153, 154, 155, 156, 158
IRAs, viii, 115, 117, 128
issues, vii, 1, 17, 56, 70, 117, 118, 127, 129, 139

J

job training, 157

jurisdiction, 31

L

labor market, 33
law enforcement, 96
laws, 18
lawyers, 19, 27
lead, 5, 23, 58, 88, 141
leadership, 63, 76, 84, 88
legislation, vii, viii, 1, 16, 24, 31, 49, 57, 62, 68, 73, 74, 88, 94, 97, 100, 102, 103, 109, 111, 112, 115, 117, 134, 142, 143, 146, 147, 148, 152, 159, 162, 165
legislative action, vii, 1, 162
liberalization, 12
life expectancy, 123, 137, 140, 142, 148, 152, 154, 156, 158, 164
lifetime, 93, 94
light, 137
loans, 53, 56
local government, 19, 25, 26, 38, 52, 83, 95, 96, 140
longevity, 148, 152, 154, 156

M

majority, 6, 23, 69, 83, 84, 101, 128, 131, 141, 144, 145
marriage, 83
masking, 84
matter, 9, 78, 103, 129
media, 89
Medicaid, 37, 44, 92, 128, 139, 144, 145
medical, 4, 26, 27, 30, 31, 32, 36, 37, 72, 74
medical assistance, 30, 31, 37
medical care, 31, 32, 36
medical reason, 72
Medicare, 4, 36, 37, 38, 39, 44, 47, 48, 57, 67, 70, 83, 85, 87, 92, 109, 112, 128, 139, 144, 145, 149, 155, 156, 162, 165
medicine, 23, 24
mental impairment, 72, 73
military, 20, 23, 76, 79, 103

Index 171

Missouri, 105
misuse, 95
modifications, 44, 63, 74
momentum, 33, 94
moratorium, 73

N

national debt, 75
national policy, 17
needy, 6, 21, 22, 32, 37, 47, 48, 78
New Deal, 5
noncitizens, 95
non-citizens, 13
nonprofit organizations, 19, 52
nurses, 13
nursing, 31, 37
nursing home, 31, 37

O

Obama, 139, 144, 145, 146, 162
obstacles, 85
Office of Management and Budget, 52, 165
officials, 96, 144
OH, 7, 21, 58, 63
oil, 66, 99
old age, 5, 7, 17
operations, 163
opinion polls, viii, 116
ownership, 117, 128, 134, 141, 143

P

pain, 72
parallel, 145
parental support, 6
parents, 27, 29, 62, 132
parole, 96
participants, 130, 134, 150, 151, 160
penalties, 94
pension plans, 4, 10, 19, 25, 39
permit, 24, 28, 32, 37, 38, 133
personal accounts, 160

personal savings, viii, 115, 117, 140
Philadelphia, 9
pipeline, 99
playing, 21
policy, vii, viii, 20, 88, 115, 116, 117, 127, 128, 131, 135, 136, 138, 139, 162, 163
policy choice, 88
policy makers, vii, viii, 115, 116, 117, 127, 128, 131, 136, 138, 139
political party, 4
polling, 132
poor performance, 134
population, 138
poverty, 65, 109, 132, 139, 143, 149, 151, 154, 155, 158
poverty line, 158
precedents, 16
premature death, 17
present value, 130
President Clinton, 85, 88, 89, 91, 92, 93
President Obama, 97, 99, 100, 163
price changes, 138
price index, 38, 143, 152, 154, 156, 158, 160
principles, 85, 142, 145
prisoners, 59, 60, 61, 65
private investment, 128
privatization, 146
professionals, 26, 27, 55
profit, 17, 66
project, viii, 96, 116, 119, 122, 123, 124, 136
prosperity, 12, 165
protection, 5, 17, 20, 47, 130, 134
public assistance, 18, 20, 21, 22, 24, 29, 30, 31, 32, 37, 47
public awareness, 89
public debt, 16, 45
public opinion, 126, 131
public pension, 62
public safety, 100
public support, ix, 116, 127, 129
Puerto Rico, 19, 21
purchasing power, 4, 12

Q

qualifications, 72
quotas, 44

R

racial minorities, 137
rate of return, 133, 142, 150, 151, 155
real terms, 131
recession, 51
recognition, 150, 153
recommendations, 10, 11, 20, 34, 47, 52, 57, 62, 63, 69, 70, 136, 139, 140, 141, 142, 145, 163
reconciliation, 62, 64, 65, 79, 84, 85, 87, 111
recovery, 8
reform(s), i, iii, v, vii, viii, ix, 2, 3, 42, 43, 69, 71, 88, 89, 110, 115, 116, 117, 127, 128, 133, 136, 139, 141, 142, 143, 144, 145, 146, 147, 148, 152, 155, 157, 159, 160, 164, 165
regulations, 16, 72
rehabilitation, 60, 92
rehabilitation program, 60
rejection, 21
relief, 14, 72, 98
rendition, 17
replacement rate, 51
requirements, 19, 31, 34, 35, 62, 91, 149
reserves, 4, 9, 15, 53, 59, 162
resolution, 14, 17, 20, 65, 78, 86
resources, 31, 37, 129, 131
response, 98, 137, 138
restrictions, 94
restructuring, 117
retail, 38
retirement age, 9, 28, 33, 50, 55, 69, 70, 71, 91, 93, 94, 127, 129, 132, 136, 137, 140, 143, 148, 152, 153, 154, 155, 156, 158, 159, 160, 161
retirement pension, 39

revenue, 15, 53, 56, 82, 86, 88, 98, 99, 112, 139, 151, 152, 157, 163
rights, 18, 20, 23
risk(s), ix, 104, 116, 127, 130, 134
rubber, 63
rules, 17, 23, 26, 28, 46, 57, 59, 83, 85, 98, 109

S

sanctions, 88
savings, viii, ix, 13, 66, 76, 78, 85, 91, 93, 115, 116, 117, 126, 128, 129, 130, 133, 134, 137, 140, 142, 151
savings account, 129, 142
school, 11, 34, 36, 62, 147
Secretary of the Treasury, 156, 161
security(s), viii, 10, 16, 17, 21, 75, 116, 118, 119, 121, 131, 134, 141, 145, 146, 156
self-employed, 18, 19, 25, 26, 27, 29, 33, 60, 69, 97, 98, 99, 100, 163
self-employment, 36, 135, 162, 163
services, 6, 31, 32, 36, 62, 92, 95, 104, 137
shape, 138
shortfall, 117, 123, 125, 129, 130, 134, 135, 143
showing, viii, 116
social insurance system, viii, 6, 115, 117, 118
social programs, 88
Social Security Administration (SSA), 17, 72, 74, 81, 82, 88, 89, 95, 96, 102, 104, 105, 106, 107, 108, 109, 110, 112, 120, 132, 136, 138, 140, 146, 147, 162, 163, 164, 165, 166
Social Security Disability Insurance, 162
social welfare, 128
society, 123, 128, 143
solution, 13, 69, 162
specter, 129
spending, viii, 5, 62, 83, 116, 119, 122, 124, 128, 129, 134, 135, 138, 139, 144, 145, 151
SS, 99

Index 173

SSI, 47, 48, 49, 51, 57, 72, 88, 91, 94, 95, 96, 156, 162
stability, 59
standard of living, 138
state(s), 5, 6, 8, 18, 19, 21, 22, 24, 25, 26, 29, 31, 32, 37, 38, 52, 56, 62, 66, 69, 72, 73, 83, 95, 96, 139, 140, 145
State of the Union address, 141, 142, 144
stock, 128, 142
structure, ix, 116, 117, 127, 141
subsistence, 21
Supreme Court, 17, 111
surplus, viii, 116, 118, 119, 121, 128, 134, 143, 149, 151, 162
survivors, 4, 11, 14, 21, 27, 29, 102, 109, 118, 129, 134, 145, 146
sustainability, 133

T

tariff, 54
tax cuts, 99
tax increase, 14, 15, 16, 28, 41, 49, 52, 56, 66, 69, 83, 127, 139
tax rates, 16, 33, 43, 51, 56, 59, 69, 85, 98, 100, 107, 126, 132
taxation, 7, 68, 85, 87, 111, 124, 127, 149, 163
teachers, 21
technical change, 69
tellers, 7, 101
terminally ill, 58
time frame, 153
Title I, 5, 6, 7, 8, 32, 37, 75, 157
Title II, 5, 6, 7, 75
Title IV, 37, 157
Title V, 5, 6, 7, 8
training, 79
transactions, 7
Treasury, viii, 13, 16, 52, 75, 116, 118, 149, 151, 161
treatment, 52, 61, 75, 85, 88, 139
tuition, 56

U

U.S. Treasury, 98, 118, 156
unemployment insurance, 8, 17, 22, 99, 100
uniform, 9, 72, 75
United, 14, 16, 21, 95, 96, 103, 112, 130, 164, 165
United States, 14, 16, 21, 95, 96, 103, 112, 130, 164, 165

V

vessels, 13
veto, 15, 17, 18, 19, 45
Vice President, 111, 112
Vietnam, 39
vocational rehabilitation, 24, 57, 62
voting, 101, 102, 103, 104, 105, 106, 107, 108, 109, 110, 111, 112, 113
vouchers, 92

W

wages, 5, 11, 17, 23, 47, 52, 81, 82, 83, 89, 90, 97, 124, 125, 135, 136, 140, 142, 164
war, 16
Washington, 101, 102, 103, 105, 109, 163, 164
wealth, 8, 128
welfare, 5, 6, 8, 17, 28, 39, 44, 45, 47, 48, 53, 56, 85, 100
welfare reform, 45, 47
White House, 143
Wisconsin, 101
witnesses, 20
World War I, 123

Y

yield, 76, 128